FRIEDRICH SCHLEIERMACHER ON CREEDS, CONFESSIONS AND CHURCH UNION

THAT THEY MAY BE ONE

FRIEDRICH SCHLEIERMACHER ON CREEDS, CONFESSIONS AND CHURCH UNION
THAT THEY MAY BE ONE

Friedrich Schleiermacher

Translated, with an Introduction and Notes by
Iain G. Nicol

Schleiermacher Studies and Translations
Volume 24

The Edwin Mellen Press
Lewiston•Queenston•Lampeter

Library of Congress Cataloging-in-Publication Data

Schleiermacher, Friedrich.
   Friedrich Schleiermacher on creeds, confessions and church union : that they may be one / translated, with an introduction and notes by Iain G. Nicol.
        p.   cm. -- (Schleiermacher studies and translations ; v. 24)
   Includes bibliographical references and index.
   ISBN 0-7734-6464-6

This is volume 24 in the continuing series
Schleiermacher Studies and Translations
Volume 24 ISBN 0-7734-6464-6
SST Series ISBN 0-88946-362-X

A CIP catalog record for this book is available from the British Library.

Copyright © 2004 Iain G. Nicol

The Edwin Mellen Press
Box 450
Lewiston, New York
USA 14092-0450

The Edwin Mellen Press
Box 67
Queenston, Ontario
CANADA L0S 1L0

The Edwin Mellen Press, Ltd.
Lampeter, Ceredigion, Wales
UNITED KINGDOM SA48 8LT

Printed in the United States of America

Many thanks to Walter de Gruyter publishing company for their permission to translate the following:

- Friedrich Daniel Ernst Schleiermacher, *Oratio in sollemnibus ecclesiae per Lutherum emendatae saecularibus tertiis in Universitate litterarum Berolinensi die III. Novembris A. MDCCCXVII habita* (1817), *Theologisch-dogmatische Abhandlungen und Gelegenheitsschriften*, hrsg. Hans-Friedrich Traulsen unter Mitwirkung von Martin Ohst, *Kritische Gesamtausgabe* I/10, hrsg. Hans-Joachim Birkner et al. (Berlin/New York: Walter de Gruyter, 1990), pp. 1-15.

- Friedrich Daniel Ernst Schleiermacher, *An Herrn Oberhofprediger D. Ammon über seine Prüfung der Harmsischen Sätze* (1818), *Theologisch-dogmatische Abhandlungen und Gelegenheitsschriften*, hrsg. Hans-Friedrich Traulsen unter Mitwirkung von Martin Ohst, *Kritische Gesamtausgabe* I/10, hrsg. Hans-Joachim Birkner et al. (Berlin/New York: Walter de Gruyter, 1990), pp. 17-92

- Friedrich Daniel Ernst Schleiermacher, *Zugabe zu meinem Schreiben an Herrn Ammon* (1818), *Theologisch-dogmatische Abhandlungen und Gelegenheitsschriften*, hrsg. Hans-Friedrich Traulsen unter Mitwirkung von Martin Ohst, *Kritische Gesamtausgabe* I/10, hrsg. Hans-Joachim Birkner et al. (Berlin/New York: Walter de Gruyter, 1990), pp. 93-116.

- Friedrich Daniel Ernst Schleiermacher, *Über den eigentümlichen Wert und das bindende Ansehen symbolischer Bücher* (1819), *Theologisch-dogmatische Abhandlungen und Gelegenheitsschriften*, hrsg. Hans-Friedrich Traulsen unter Mitwirkung von Martin Ohst, *Kritische Gesamtausgabe* I/10, hrsg. Hans-Joachim Birkner et al. (Berlin/New York: Walter de Gruyter, 1990), pp. 117-143.

- Friedrich Daniel Ernst Schleiermacher, *An die Herren D.D. D. von Cölln und D. Schulz* (1831), *Theologisch-dogmatische Abhandlungen und Gelegenheitsschriften*, hrsg. Hans-Friedrich Traulsen unter Mitwirkung von Martin Ohst, *Kritische Gesamtausgabe* I/10, hrsg. Hans-Joachim Birkner et al. (Berlin/New York: Walter de Gruyter, 1990), 395-426.

- Friedrich Daniel Ernst Schleiermacher, *Amtliche Erklärung der Berlinischen Synode über die am 30sten October von ihr zu haltende Abendmahlsfeier* (1817), *Kirchenpolitische Schriften*, hrsg. Günter Meckenstock unter Mitwirkung von Hans-Friedrich Traulsen, *Kritische Gesamtausgabe* I/9, hrsg. Hermann Fischer et al. (Berlin/New York: Walter de Gruyter, 2000), 173-188.

- Friedrich Daniel Ernst Schleiermacher, *An die Mitglieder beider zur Dreifaltigkeitskirch gehörenden Gemeinden* (1820), *Kirchenpolitische Schriften*, hrsg. Günter Meckenstock unter Mitwirkung von Hans-Friedrich Traulsen, *Kritische Gesamtausgabe* I/9, hrsg. Hermann Fischer et al. (Berlin/New York: Walter de Gruyter, 2000), 203-210.

This book is dedicated to

Ute, Juliet,
Roy and Sophie

Contents

Preface

This extraordinarily well-integrated work, organized by University of Toronto professor Iain Nicol, is a concise collection, from 1817 to 1822 and 1831, of six essays, two sermons and one celebratory address. They offer, better than any other set of writings by his hand, Schleiermacher's faithful yet critical and innovative understanding of themes indicated in the title.

These items are translated here for the first time, eight from German (by Nicol) and one from Latin (the 1817 "Oratio" by Terrence Tice). Together they represent Schleiermacher at his ecclesial best: as epoch-making interpreter of creeds and confessions, as engaging preacher to a worshipping community, as university scholar in service of the church (as he emphasizes the 16th-century Reformers were), as official leader, as critically minded student of tradition, as sharp but loving debater on crucial issues, and as advocate of Christian community and church union.

In all these respects, though presented in much greater practical detail, I consider this volume to be an excellent companion to Dr. Nicol's translation and commentary on Schleiermacher's 1830 sermonic treatise on Reformation themes – *Reformed But Ever Reforming: Sermons in Relation to the Celebration of the Handing Over of the Augsburg Confession (1830)* (Edwin Mellen Press, 1997). Together the two volumes wonderfully breathe the latter-day Evangelical spirit of this great founder of modern theology.

In testimony to Iain Nicol's own like churchmanship, see the 16 distinguished essays in his honor presented in the *Toronto Journal of Theology* 18, no. 1 (Spring 2002), edited by Allen G. Jorgenson and Pamela McCarroll-Butler, under the apt title *Nowhere to Lay Their Heads: The Sojourning Character of Christian Doctrine and the Church.*

Terrence N. Tice
Professor Emeritus
The University of Michigan
December 2003

Acknowledgements

I am grateful to many people who in various ways have supported and assisted me in the production of this volume. However, I am especially indebted to the following co-workers, colleagues and friends: Kathleen Gibson, Chris Tucker and Elizabeth Kanhai of the Caven Library, Knox College; Dr. J. Dorcas Gordon, Principal of Knox College; Calvin A. Pater, Professor of Church History, Knox College; Ian Manson, Minister of Royal York Road United Church, Toronto; and to Philip Snider, graduate student in Classics at the University of Toronto, who provided a draft translation of Schleiermacher's Latin *Oratio*. For expert assistance with the translations I am deeply grateful to Edwina Lawler, Catherine L. Kelsey, who also spent invaluable weeks on the final revisions and formatting, and especially to Terrence N. Tice for his firm commitment to this project, his final translation of the Latin *Oratio*, and his painstaking refinements of my many awkward renderings. And, finally, to my dear wife Eleanor, my warmest thanks not only for her practical assistance in typing and proofreading but also for the support of her patient, encouraging and caring spirit.

Iain G.Nicol
June 20th, 2003

Editor's Introduction

The various writings of Schleiermacher translated in this companion volume to *Reformed But Ever Reforming*[1] are selected from among the occasional essays that he published between 1817 and 1830. For our understanding of the theological controversies that arose in the fourteen-year interval between them, both years are important. The first marked the 300th anniversary of Luther's posting of the *95 Theses*, the second the 300th anniversary of the presentation of the Augsburg Confession to the Emperor Charles V. Given the theological climate of this period, it was probably predictable that in themselves both occasions would offer opportunities for the re-kindling of old disputes. Less expected, however, was the coincidence of the 1817 and 1830 ecclesial and secular celebrations with the beginnings of a new development that was steadily growing in influence largely under Schleiermacher's guidance and leadership, namely, the movement toward the union of the Lutheran and Reformed churches in the state of Prussia. If at an earlier stage it seemed probable that controversies would arise quite apart from the matter of church union, it was with the addition of this new dimension to the overall situation that controversy became inevitable.

This coincidence of circumstances certainly did refuel some of the older debates about historical and ongoing differences between the Lutheran and Reformed

---

1. Ed. note: Trans. Iain Nicol, (Lewiston: NY: Edwin Mellen Press, 1997).

2

confessions. Yet it was also to evoke Schleiermacher's articulation of some re-
markably different perspectives on most of the key theological issues and church
practices that had been the cause of divisions in the past between Roman Catholicism and Protestantism on the one hand, and, on the other, within the circle of
Protestantism itself, between the Lutheran and Reformed churches in particular.
Now re-ignited by the move toward church union, among the most urgent questions that became front and center in the disputes that it evoked were those that
arose in relation to the authoritative status and binding function of the respective
creedal symbols of the two confessions. However, as the following selection of
questions indicates, it also soon became evident that this was an issue that had implications not only for the two churches. It was not an exclusively ecclesiastical
affair. It also involved potentially serious implications for the relationship of the
churches to the spheres of politics and academia, the two other areas of public life
with which they were interconnected and in which Schleiermacher himself was also
actively involved.

Over the many years since their separation after the Reformation have the two
churches not sufficiently matured to the extent that they have simply outgrown
their past doctrinal differences? In the interest of both parties should the union of
the two churches not be preceded by the ecclesiastical equivalent of a written pre-
nuptial agreement? Would it not be more fitting if the movement toward union
were to begin with negotiations about doctrine? Does the prospect of church union
not call for the formulation of a completely new confessional statement specifically
appropriate to the new community? In what precise respects should the authority
of such a document be understood in relation to the supreme authority of scripture? How may one take steps to guard against the possibility that a new confession, or for that matter any confession, could be employed in an exclusively judicial
way as a test of orthodox belief? Might the state possibly choose to intervene and
seek control over the affairs of the church by imposing a former creedal symbol on
the new union such as the Augsburg Confession? If this were to happen in relation

to the new union would the Reformed party not be put at a distinct disadvantage, or worse, possibly be completely overwhelmed by the Lutheran majority? Would such an intervention and imposition not affect the universities in that it might well involve the surrender of the cherished academic principle of freedom of theological teaching and learning? As one may see from the various items translated below, it was to these kinds of questions among many others and to the sometimes prolonged and heated debates that they provoked that Schleiermacher was to bring the fresh and provocative insights that were uniquely his own. It is well known that his contributions to these debates received a decidedly mixed reception by many of his contemporaries. Why this should have been the case may at least in part be attributed to the fact that Schleiermacher was already an ecumenist long before the advent of the Ecumenical Movement and the establishment of the World Council of Churches in the 20th century. However, the mixed reactions to his perspectives on these matters that were voiced at that time should not blind us to the fact that in this 21st century of albeit limping ecumenical aspirations to move beyond idiosyncratic denominational self-definition his vision "that they may be one"[2] as well as the grounds that he brought forward to support and sustain it are more relevant than ever.

This present collection directly reintroduces us to Schleiermacher in some of his many roles: to the preacher, the man who wanted to be nothing other than a servant of the Word, the congregational pastor and administrator, the moderator of synod, the scholarly academic theologian, and the university administrator. Perhaps to the surprise of some it also introduces us to Schleiermacher the controversialist and polemicist, the man who possibly may have been moved to assume these particular roles out of a sense of having been treated unjustly or perhaps even betrayed.

The specifically doctrinal and ecclesiological items that he addresses in these writings are much too numerous and wide ranging to be analyzed in any detail in a

---

2. Ed. note: John 17:11.

brief introduction of this kind. Still, it is not at all inappropriate to assemble them under the more general themes of creeds, confessions and church union[3] if for no other reason than that it is into these broader themes that these various smaller strands are woven. From among the many topics that could be selected from this volume for special attention in this short introduction the following three are of special interest.

First, the correspondence between Schleiermacher and Court Chaplain Ammon of Dresden. The detailed and lengthy communications with Ammon are probably the most sustained and devastatingly withering critiques that Schleiermacher wrote. In his *Schleiermacher: Life and Thought* Martin Redeker notes that these letters "may be one of Schleiermacher's sharpest polemical writings, attacking not only Ammon's position, but his person as well."[4] On the basis of even a cursory reading of this open letter and the supplement to it one immediately senses that this is the response of a person who had been deeply hurt and who, as already noted, perhaps even felt that he had been betrayed. What, then, were the circumstances that provoked Schleiermacher to respond to Ammon in the way he did?[5]

On 27th September, 1817, King Friedrich Wilhelm III issued an edict requesting that representatives of the Lutheran and Reformed churches hold a joint celebration of Holy Communion in the city of Berlin on October 30th, Reformation Sunday. It was in response to this directive that, as the presiding officer of the Synod of Berlin, Schleiermacher published its *Official Declaration* announcing the celebration and the conditions under which it would be held, thereby confirming the king's request. (See below, ch. I.) For one thing it is important to note that Ammon had earlier informed Schleiermacher, both "orally and in writing," that he supported the decision to hold this joint celebration of communion and that he had

---

3. Ed. note: Please see my editorial introduction in *Reformed But Ever Reforming*, vii-xxv, for a somewhat more detailed assessment of Schleiermacher's views on these themes.

4. Ed. note: (Philadelphia, Fortress Press, 1973), 191.

5. Ed. note: For many of the details of the chronology and content of the correspondence between Ammon and Schleiermacher I am indebted to the researches of Hans-Friedrich Traulsen and Martin Ohst, the editors of KGA I/10. See especially their historical introduction, XV-XXII.

also committed himself to cooperating in the matter of church union. Schleier-macher adds, however, that since this was a private communication between Am-mon and himself he had decided to make no direct reference to it in his *Send-schreiben* to Ammon.[6] Secondly, it is quite impossible to imagine that Ammon was completely uniformed about Schleiermacher's position on the matter of the joint celebration or about his active involvement in the movement committed to church union. Nevertheless, in a letter dated October 28th Ammon asked Schleiermacher to inform him of his position with regard to these developments. In this same letter Ammon went on to inform Schleiermacher that as editor of the *Magazin für chris-tliche Prediger* he had received numerous contributions protesting the union of the two churches but that "for good reasons" he had set them aside. (See below, 101-102.) Ammon failed to give any indication of what these reasons were.

Schleiermacher subsequently responded to Ammon in a letter dated December 3rd in which he criticized Ammon's action in laying aside the material expressing opposition to the union. As a supporter of the union Schleiermacher wanted to hear from all interested parties. Schleiermacher then goes on to say that he would welcome a clear indication of Ammon's own opinion about the service of communion that had already taken place and also about the developments that were continuing to evolve in the Prussian capital and elsewhere in the country. To this communication Ammon responded in turn in a letter dated December 12th.[7] However, Ammon chose not to extend to Schleiermacher the courtesy of a straightforward answer. Rather than acceding to his request by stating clearly his views in this private item of correspondence, Ammon went on to remark that he had already expressed his position publicly elsewhere. Where exactly? Ammon gave no information as to the publication in which it might be found. As Schleiermacher notes in the opening paragraph of his response to Ammon, it was only when he had completed his search of much of the currently available literature

---

6. Ed. note: See KGA I/10, 97, footnote to lines 23f.
7. Ed. note: The *Sendschreiben an Ammon* is Schleiermacher's response to this letter.

in vain and there after receiving a copy of Ammon's *Examination of Harms's Theses* that he finally located it.[8] This entirely unexpected turn of events came as a complete shock to Schleiermacher. Why did Ammon not consent to his request and communicate his views privately? Why did he choose to remain silent on the matter? Further, as Schleiermacher was to discover from Ammon's *Examination*, if Ammon was so vehemently opposed to the union of the two Protestant confessions why did he not warn him of what he perceived to be its dangers?

Had this limited correspondence ceased with his receipt of Ammon's letter of December 12th Schleiermacher would already have had sufficient evidence to conclude that in themselves Ammon's lack of honesty and evasiveness were disturbing and even shocking enough. However, on his reading Ammon's *Examination*, he was to discover that Ammon's dissembling attitudes indicated a deliberately devious strategy that amounted to an attempt to disguise something deeper and even more serious. Ammon's remarks on church union were to prove him right. In supporting the confessionalist and anti-rationalist Claus Harms's powerful and influential opposition to church union, Ammon, the hitherto Enlightenment anti-confessionalist rationalist, had performed a complete *volte-face*. Further, he had accomplished this feat while at the same time attempting to disguise the fact that his apparently sudden conversion to Harms's anti-union point of view in no respect represented any inconsistency with positions that he had adopted in his numerous earlier writings. Thus, having originally had good reasons to believe that Ammon had declared himself to be favorably aligned with the movement toward church union, Schleiermacher now found himself to be a man deceived.

In page after page of the *Sendschreiben* Schleiermacher chastises Ammon for the glaring inconsistencies and contradictions in his position, for his cavalier attitude to and use of Reformed and Lutheran doctrinal sources, for his reprehensible misrepresentation of both Lutheran and Reformed differences over ecclesiology and christology, for his superficial exposition of their respective understandings of

---

8. Ed. note: See below, 65, footnote 1.

the sacrament of the Lord's Supper, and for his sarcastic and virtually blasphemous mockery of the joint service of Holy Communion that was held in Berlin on Reformation Sunday. As Schleiermacher writes: "Should not the reverence that every Christian should have before the Lord's Table have restrained you from this attitude?" (See below, 104.) Leaving virtually no theological stone unturned Schleiermacher goes on with relentless irony and sarcasm to demonstrate that Ammon's tactics are academically dishonest, dangerously misinformed and misleading, and not least self-servingly duplicitous. As Schleiermacher was to say of him: "So does that little ship tack! So does the eel glide!" (See below, 99.) Then again: "If you had really converted to a theological position based on that of Mr. Harms, then the only respectable thing for such a man to do is candidly to acknowledge this, to refute his earlier opinion himself, and formally disavow each work written on the basis of that earlier opinion." (See below, 93.) Schleiermacher was clearly in no mood to mince his words.

In his supplemental response to Ammon's rejoinder acknowledging receipt of his *Sendschreiben* Schleiermacher informs Ammon that not unlike his *Examination*, his response "abounds in confusions and mistakes that would be so laborious and time-consuming for me to disentangle that I must leave this task to the readers themselves." (See below, 147.) Confronted yet again with Ammon's tiresome evasions, his apparently inveterate inability to give straight answers to straight questions,[9] his habitually careless and sloppy scholarship, his talent for talking in riddles, his remarkable gift for attributing statements to Calvin (and others) that Calvin did not make (see below 149f), and a book to Schleiermacher himself that Schleiermacher did not write (see below 160), it was perfectly clear that Ammon had taken Schleiermacher's chastisements with a grain of salt. It was at this point that Schleiermacher finally decided that he had simply had enough and brought the exchange to a close.

---

9. Ed. note: In his *Schleiermacher*, Friedrich Wilhelm Kantzenbach's lively and popular biography, Ammon is described as the *doppelzüngigen Dresdner*. "Fork-tongued" perhaps? (Hamburg: Rowohlt Verlag, 1967), 129.

A second matter that calls for some consideration with regard to the main themes that Schleiermacher addresses in this collection is the role of the Protestant symbolic books in connection with his understanding of the relationship between Protestantism and the Roman Catholic church. Much of his discussion of this question revolves around the important distinction that he makes between the two communions and the place that he assigns to the past and continuing function of the symbolic books in defining what he terms the "contrast" between them. For the purpose of this brief exposition of Schleiermacher's views on this matter and what we take to be some of the key questions that arise from it we shall derive our remarks chiefly from what he has to say about the issue in his *On the Proper Value and Binding Authority of the Symbolic Books,* (See below, Chapter VI,) seeking further clarification of these from his treatment of it in *Christian Faith,* §§19, 23-25, and 27. First, however, a sketch of the broader picture with reference to the status of the symbolic books in relation to scripture.

There can be no doubt about Schleiermacher's firm commitment to the principle of the authority and sufficiency of the New Testament for Christian faith and life. His most explicit statement about its normative status runs as follows: "The Holy Scriptures of the New Testament are, on the one hand, the first member in the series, ever since continued, of presentations of the Christian Faith; on the other hand, they are the true norm for all succeeding presentations."[10] This principle is one that Schleiermacher also frequently enlists in the material translated here in support of the position that the truth of all doctrinal statements, including those contained in the Protestant symbolic books, must be tested at the bar of this supreme rule. Thus the Protestant creeds and confessions must always be viewed as subordinate to the New Testament norm. They play a sub-normative role.

Nevertheless, although he readily affirmed this point of view he also had to address a cultural/historical situation quite different from that of the Reformation and

---

10. Ed. note: *Christian Faith,* §129. It will be recalled that for Schleiermacher the Old Testament plays no authoritative role in the formation of Christian dogmatics. See, e.g. *Christian Faith,* §27.

its immediate aftermath.[11] With the contending perceptions of late 18th- and early 19th-century rationalism and confessionalism the basic rules of argument and dispute about biblical authority in relation to the authority of subordinate confessional standards had radically changed since that earlier period in the sense that there was very little, if any, common theological or philosophical ground between the two parties. The highest compliment that most rationalists could pay to the symbolic books was perhaps that they should be honored as notable historic documents of the past but that they had ceased to be of any contemporary significance. On the other hand, among the confessionalists there were a good many whose highest compliment to them was to attribute to them an authority approximating that of scripture itself. If the one attitude represented a policy of abuse by neglect, the other came very close to symbololatry. Further, for among yet others on the confessionalist side there was another important ingredient in these controversies, one which from Schleiermacher's point of view could have posed possibly the most serious threat to church union. The issue that also had to be addressed was that of the adherence of some influential confessionalists to a policy that involved employing the symbolic books as instruments for establishing, or worse, imposing, uniformity in doctrine, public worship, catechesis and academic teaching. According to this view the symbolic books provide the only propositionally correct and authoritative canons and tests of orthodox Christian belief. Quite clearly, the danger inherent in this understanding was that if this view were to prevail, the only role left to the symbolic books would be an exclusively judicial one.[12] By means of the use of such an instrument, imposed by the church, or by the state, or by both church and state, the church would again be led into a legalistic captivity to the

---

11. Ed. note: In response to the confessionalists and with his keen sense of historical development Schleiermacher insists that one cannot treat the interval between the Reformation and the early 19th century as a period that has never been lived through or as though it could be wiped away "as with a sponge." See below, 162.

12. Ed. note: For Schleiermacher, no confessional standard is invested with the right to excommunicate.

letter, a situation in which there would no longer be any place for the freedom of the Evangelical spirit for which the Reformation had set the church at liberty.

In developing his own assessment and response to this situation one is given the impression that even though he seems to be more flexible and charitable toward the rationalists than to the confessionalists Schleiermacher simply invoked at least a temporary pestilence not on that which each house denied, but on that which they affirmed. (See below, 163-164.) In his *On the Proper Value*, steering a middle course between the two parties, he comes to the following two main conclusions about the status and function of the Protestant symbolic books.

For one thing, they have a declaratory function. If, as Schleiermacher affirms, the New Testament is "the first member in the series of presentations of the Christian faith," in a similar way, yet subordinate to the New Testament, as the first common possession of Protestantism its symbolic books are the first public expression of the spirit of Protestantism within the historical totality of Christianity. As Schleiermacher is also careful to point out, it follows from this assumption that it is not by appeal to the letter of these documents that all propositions in any system of Protestant doctrine must be confirmed but only by appeal to their spirit.[13] As presentations of the Protestant spirit, then, they are not to be understood as collections of doctrinal propositions that demand assent or as standards established to define and test orthodox beliefs. To view them in such a way is to misunderstand their original intention, which in effect is not to set forth an authoritative series of statements to be believed, but rather to give expression to the specifically Protestant form of piety (*Glaubensweise*) in contrast to the Roman Catholic way or form of believing. Focusing in particular on the Reformed confessions of the Reformation, though his remarks are equally applicable to the Lutheran symbols, John McIntyre expresses this aspect of Schleiermacher's perspective on the matter well when with reference to the declaratory function of these documents he writes: "This feature has to be emphasized... for we are always in danger of considering

---

13. Ed. note: See *Christian Faith*, §27.

their theological content, and using them as pabulum for the arguments about elements in the Reformed theological position, or as the basis for enlarging upon the differences that divided the several churches within the Reformation. *Beyond and above these differences* (emphasis mine) – and no one is denying them – there was a single unity of spirit..."[14]

Second, however, with their appeal to the authority of the New Testament the symbolic books also function at another level in demonstrating that certain errors of the Roman Catholic church represent deviations from this scriptural norm. Schleiermacher cites such errors and deviations in the following suggested formula according to which all Evangelical ministers might be required to subscribe to the symbolic books and to which all Evangelical Christians should give assent:

> "I declare that I find everything that is taught in our symbolic books against the errors and abuses of the Roman Catholic church, especially in the articles on justification and good works, in the church and ecclesiastical power, on the mass, on the function of the saints, and on vows, to be in complete agreement with Holy Scripture and with the original teaching of the church; and that as long as I am entrusted with the teaching office I shall not cease to expound these teachings and to uphold the orders in the church that are appropriate to them." (See below, 187.)

Whether or not this is to be understood as an exhaustive list of abuses Schleiermacher does not say. However, his insistence that with this formula "it is not at all implied that the positive formulations of those doctrines should not be open to correction" certainly should be carefully noted. Nevertheless, his stance is quite uncompromising. As he goes on to insist on the same page: "It is impossible for anyone to want to be a Protestant teacher who is not in agreement with the symbolic books in these matters," for it is "in these matters" that there is presented "the Protestant contrast with Roman theory and practice."

---

14. Ed. note: See his "Confessions in Historical and Contemporary Setting," in *The Presumption of Presence*, Essays in Honor of D.W.D. Shaw, Eds. Peter Mc Enhill and G.B.Hall (Edinburgh: Scottish Academic Press, 1996), 24-25.

For Schleiermacher, then, it seems that the appeal here is to the polemical[15] strain inherent in the symbolic books, one of the roles that with greater or lesser emphasis was clearly assigned to them in the Reformation and post-Reformation periods. Thus with regard to "these matters" that he cites in the above formula, the polemical role of the Protestant confessions is not to be understood as a merely temporary one or as one confined only to the Reformation and to the related events that were to succeed it. Their role in this particular respect is not exhausted. On the contrary, the polemical function of these documents survives and extends into the early decades of Schleiermacher's 19th century. So much does this seem to be the case that in an admittedly restrained yet nevertheless uncompromising form, it establishes the rules for his discussion of the relationship between Protestantism and Roman Catholicism and shapes his various assertions about the continuing contrast between them.

There are many questions that arise from this brief, but let us hope reasonably accurate account of the position that Schleiermacher adopts here that are as relevant to our own 21st-century ecumenical context as they were to his. With particular reference to our present ecumenical situation and specifically with regard to relationships between the Protestant churches and the Roman Catholic church, from a Protestant perspective the following selection may be offered for consideration. For example we must "rather have regard to the spirit (of the symbolic books) than cling to the letter,"[16] may it not be the case that by enlisting their past and continuing polemical role specifically for the purpose of defining the nature of the contrast this principle has been abandoned by the Protestant churches or at least is seriously compromised in current ecumenical discussions between the two communions? Or, as Schleiermacher's formula puts it: "As long as I am entrusted

---

15. Ed. note: The term "polemical" as employed here is to be understood in what Schleiermacher calls "its more general sense" as descriptive of debates about perceived differences over such matters as doctrine and church practices. For Schleiermacher's more technical definition of polemics, see his *Brief Outline on the Study of Theology*, trans. Terrence N. Tice, Atlanta: John Knox Press, 1967, §§54-62 (revised ed., Edwin Mellen Press, 1990).

16. Ed. note: See *Christian Faith*, §27.

with the teaching office I *shall not cease* (emphasis mine) to expound these teachings." Given our present context are we to understand that this expresses a determination to ensure that the existing differences between Protestantism and Roman Catholic theory and practice will be maintained come what may? Is the contrast, then, a temporary one, or is it enduring and permanent? In this same connection, do we consider Schleiermacher's criteria for contrasting that which is distinctively Protestant with that which is distinctively Roman Catholic to be just as fixed and changeless as any immutable dogmatic norm established by what he often referred to as the "traditional" Roman Catholic church? For the same purpose of establishing and defining such differences have we failed to enlist Schleiermacher's historical sensibility that operates on the insight that all institutions in history, including the church(es), are subject to change and development? Or, again for the purposes of contemporary debate and dialogue, have we failed to adopt his conviction that all doctrines, including those cited in the above formula, are similarly open to development, change and correction?[17]

In §24 of *Christian Faith*, in response to his own theological and ecclesial context, Schleiermacher was to note: "We cannot regard the tension (between the two communions) as already on the decrease." The observation is not exactly encouraging. Thus to the extent that he perceived this to be the case at that time he might well have been tempted to answer all of the above questions as follows: As far as the present circumstances are concerned, Yes, at least for the time being! However, by no means would this have been his final word on the matter, for in this same section of *Christian Faith* he also affirms that "the antithesis (contrast) itself, like every similar one within the Christian communion, must be regarded as destined some day and somehow to disappear." As to the "some day" of this confident statement it was clearly not given to him to know; neither is it given to us. However, with regard to the "somehow," or as to the ways and means presently at our

---

17. Ed. note: Whether or not Schleiermacher allowed the same freedom for such purposes to the Roman Catholic church as he did to the Evangelical church is debatable.

disposal for seeking to explore existing differences that currently divide us, the last two questions to the Protestant churches cited above call for much less ambiguous answers from them than are presently available. That is to say, with regard to *how* discussions between the two churches may be initiated, conducted, and where possible advanced, will be to a large extent dependent upon the readiness of the Protestant churches to formulate a more transparent theory of doctrinal development, one to which they will be prepared to commit themselves, and to define with greater clarity their commitment to the proposition that in the same respects as all other institutions in history churches too are subject to development and change. Such moves would not only assist the Protestant churches toward the promotion of their respective understandings of and relationships with the Roman Catholic church. They would also be of advantage both between and within the Protestant churches themselves especially in the present climate of tendencies toward denominational retrenchment and confessional redefinition.

Third, and finally, some brief remarks on Holy Communion as an act of confession. With reference to the joint celebration of Holy Communion between representatives of the Reformed and Lutheran churches held on October 30th, 1817, Ammon had put forward the view that negotiations about existing differences in doctrine between the two confessions should have preceded any such celebration and any further moves toward church union. Schleiermacher's response to him includes the reminder that if doctrine first had to be settled before the Christian community began there would in effect be no Christian church at all. In further developing his criticisms of Ammon's proposal Schleiermacher writes: "In our case the one method (that of doctrinal negotiation) has never proved successful; why should we not simply proceed to the other and begin with a deed? Nevertheless, I do not have to content myself with saying this, rather, it can indeed be made immediately evident that the other way is impossible." (See below, 109-110.) These remarks and others to the same effect scattered elsewhere in his *Sendschreiben* to Ammon immediately call to mind a similar one that Schleiermacher had made with reference to the 1830 celebration of the handing over of the Augsburg Confession, one which was not to escape criticism. In this connection he wrote: "Indeed, in general the celebration has value not in that the document was drawn up or in the precise way in which this was done but in its being handed over. It is not the work that is celebrated but the deed."[18]

The point that Schleiermacher is making with regard to both of these examples is essentially that confession as action or deed not only normally precedes but also takes precedence over confession as creedal document. Expressed somewhat differently one might say that confession as document or as symbolic book first has its source in confession as action. In distinguishing between these two forms of confession it should also be noted that confession as action is never self-generated. It is rather the case that confession as action always arises in the form of a person's or of the church's *response to,* say, divine revelation or the divine command.

In this sense it is in obedient response to Jesus' "Do this in remembrance of me"[19] that the church celebrates Holy Communion. "We do this," as various Communion liturgies put it, "according to the holy institution, example and command of our Lord Jesus Christ." In and through this action-in-response of Holy Communion the church as the body of Christ confesses that its very being consists in the communion with Christ of the many who are both his members and members of one another.[20] Hence it is the sacrament of the new covenant, of the new creation, and of the new community that embraces and embodies a distinctively new kind of belonging to God and to one another.

---

18. Ed. note: For further details see Schleiermacher's Foreword to the Augsburg Sermons in *Reformed But Ever Reforming*, 1-3.
19. Ed. note: Luke 22:19.
20. Ed. note: See e.g., I Cor. 12:15; Rom. 12:4; Eph. 4:25.

In his espousal of the cause of the union of two hitherto separated churches it was to a vision of this new kind of belonging that Schleiermacher was committed. What, then, could have been more appropriate for the two churches than to "begin with a deed," one that enabled them to confess and to celebrate the gift of their oneness in Christ?

I

Official Declaration of the Synod of Berlin
Concerning the Celebration of Holy Communion
which it will hold on 30 October 1817[*]

At the request of the honorable Consistory of the Province of Brandenburg, the entire German clergy of this capital city, of both Evangelical confessions, assembled together on the first of October in order to come to a final decision about their forming a union in one synod.[1] Now, after this resolution was passed, pending approval of higher authority, and we had bound ourselves together in a far closer way than ever before by this means, there arose the proposal from one member of the assembly that we might now also wish to come together in a joint celebration of Holy Communion, perhaps not simply at one time and in one place, but also according to one form, and indeed in such a form that no one from either party could take offense at. It was further proposed that since we had postponed our synod meeting until the 11th of November we might undertake this observance

[*] *Amtliche Erklärung der Berlinischen Synode über die am 30sten October von ihr zu haltende Abendmahlsfeier* (Berlin: Realschulbuchhandlung, 1817); SW I.5, 309-325; KGA I/9, 173-188.

1. Ed. note: See endnote #24 to the fourth discourse in Schleiermacher's *On Religion* (1821) for his advocacy of a synodal polity. In the earlier years of his ministry, from 1794, he had served with a bishop.

already at the Reformation Jubilee, and designate the second day of this festival for the purpose. Both proposals were passed with almost complete unanimity, and even the few doubts that were still raised have in the meantime been settled of themselves.

At our invitation, the local faculty of theology had immediately agreed to this celebration, and the French clergy also declared their willingness to do this. Later, in consequence of a wish of His Majesty for an assembly at another location on the seventh, this celebration was transferred to the day before the festival, and other official bodies joined in the celebration. After this, independent of our negotiations, it was decreed at a higher level[2] that the Lord's Supper would be administered at the Reformation festival itself in all the churches of this capital city, solely in accordance with the form that has been accepted for our celebration. Now, all of these matters are well-known elsewhere and are of less relevance here. However, for the action that we have taken we believe that we owe a common and reliable explanation, partly to our congregations, apart from that which any individual gives to one's own congregation, and partly to the whole Protestant church, chiefly because often such matters otherwise receive neither full nor careful publicity.

Hence, as far as our congregations are concerned the first thing about this action is that there is one aspect to it that is less immediately pertinent to them. It is well-known that we ministers[3] have always lived in fraternal concord with each other without regard to confessional differences, but by means of making a beginning with the synodal polity we have never been so closely united as we are at present. Now, since just as in our being united here it is as united together that we are to build up the church so as to have the most immediate and vital influence of our spirits on each other, so we had a heartfelt need also to edify ourselves in each

---

2. Ed. note: The king issued this decree on September 27. (See below.) Generally, Schleiermacher took umbrage at the king's – and his ecclesiastical advisors' – meddling in affairs that belonged to the churches.

3. Ed. note: *Geistliche*.

other's company by means of the most noble thing that Christianity has to offer, without any separation or disruption. The fact that this celebration was not connected with the inauguration of our synod assembly was for the most part due to its postponement, and is in itself a matter of chance. Thus, insofar as this action was originally to be entirely for ourselves and among ourselves, it concerned our congregations only to the same extent as does everything in the life of a pastor[4] that should be evident to them as the fruit of the pastor's genuinely Evangelical sensibility and in agreement with the doctrine that the pastor proclaims. Moreover, to this extent all of us who freely joined together for this celebration immediately had the joyous conviction that our congregations of both confessions would take no offense at us for having departed from the hitherto existing form for the sake of this one, for given all our instruction they should be reasonably well-versed in distinguishing what is essential in Christianity from what is non-essential.

In this case, however, everything essential is preserved in the sacred action, whereas only that which was non-essential was altered in the interest of serving a higher purpose. Or is it not a genuinely Evangelical Holy Communion when every dubious notion about transubstantiation and sacrifice is set aside, when the sacred meal is administered in both kinds, when in the name of Christ the servant of the Word does what Christ himself did in breaking the sacred bread and in dispensing the sacred cup? Nevertheless, if the public instructions that we have already in part offered on this matter and shall in part still continue to offer on the basis of this same understanding still prove to be insufficient for some, then we at least have to declare that any person who takes secret offense at this action, to which we were immediately very much impelled by the most intimate love among brethren and by the deeply felt needs of the times, must oneself bear the blame for this discontent, in that we are all convinced that each of us, when any child of his church[5] turns to

---

4. Ed. note: *Seelsorger.*
5. Ed. note: *Kirchenkinder.* This term refers to any of Christ's "children," including adults.

him in trust, will be in a position to relieve this person's doubts and effectively convince this person of the genuineness of this action.

In addition to this consideration, however, this celebration indeed originally also had another aspect in virtue of which it was to have direct reference to our congregations, and it was for its sake that we were also not opposed to the greater spread and publicity it acquired but rejoiced in a truly spiritual way over all the things that made it a glorious event. That is to say, in spite of the fact that at the time when we passed this resolution the king's decree of September 27th had not yet been issued, and in spite of the fact that we did not know – though since that time this is what has happened because of a directive from a higher level – that the congregations would immediately be given such ample opportunities to follow our example, at the same time it was indeed already our intention to set them an example. We wanted above all to encourage all those who would find themselves in the same situation as we – who, as called to live together in the most intimate union of their hearts, had nevertheless been formerly accustomed to being separate from each other in their partaking of the sacrament because of the different confessions – so that like us they would be united under a form of the sacred meal such as would abolish this disruptive division. Moreover, we hoped that this joining would gradually take hold and spread and that indeed sooner or later it would also appear to the congregations to be worthy of acceptance, so that just as for a long time various Reformed Christians have been uplifted[6] in services of worship in Lutheran congregations and *vice versa*, and Lutheran Christians have had their children baptized and instructed by Reformed ministers and *vice versa*, and their marriage ties blessed, this final dividing wall[7] would now fall also, and in that Christians of both confessions also united together in the Lord's Supper a wholly reconciled and undisturbed church community would embrace both parties, both now and in the future.

---

6. Ed. note: *Erbaut*. Literally, "edified."
7. Ed. note: *Schiedewand*. See Eph. 2:14.

Yet, as much as it is our heartfelt wish that this example of ours should achieve a good and widespread success, we nonetheless call "good" only that person who comes from a pure and peaceful heart, and it is also for this reason that even by our example we are far from wanting to rule over anyone's conscience or from wanting to rush any single person whose heart and mind is not yet decided in this important matter. This is so, for even if we quite generally advance the conviction that no sincere Evangelical Christian who calmly grants us a hearing will take offense at what we are doing, we can in no respect so generally demand in such a way that everyone should immediately consider themselves ready to participate without thoroughly probing the matter and weighing it in the way that is appropriate for a free Evangelical Christian so that their consciences will not come to be confounded. Moreover, we would rather prefer that this change of form and this union, however close to our hearts they may be, would gain general currency at a later stage than that any hesitant heart and mind should complain that on account of being not entirely free in one's participating in new forms one's peace and devotion in this most sacred occupation of a Christian should be disturbed.

Hence, in that this form of the sacrament that is mutually appropriate to both confessions is offered to all the congregations in our city, now our sincere intention is the following. If the entire congregation does not accept this new form because it freely desires it but to a certain extent members within a congregation are left insufficiently instructed or convinced and prefer the hitherto existing form, in no respect do we want to place them at a disadvantage in relation to the others as to our care and love. Rather, we want to have them be especially recommended to us so that we may win them over gradually to the conviction that we perceive to be the better one. Further, in order that the bond of love between us and them might not appear to be disturbed we shall also partake of the sacrament alternately with them according to the form to which they have been so long accustomed. Thereby we shall also demonstrate to them in the clearest way that according to our conviction in certain particular aspects of this sacred undertaking no modification of faith and doctrine needs to be connected with this change. On the other hand, we also expect from both parties in such congregations that they will remain attached to each other in the same love of brethren. With Christian modesty, friends of the accustomed form should consider that if this work of union – not one that has newly begun but simply one that has been undertaken once more – is of God, they will not hinder it, but that if it has proceeded from human purposes then it will fall to ruin of itself. However, those who devote themselves wholeheartedly to the new form should consider that everyone stands and falls with their Lord, and as appertains to those who are strong in faith they should sustain those whose whom they think to be weak in faith, so that there will be no splitting into parties and no division. In cordial love and solemn earnestness, this is what all of us declare to our dear congregations.

Further, as concerns the whole Protestant church, we owe it an explanation of our proceedings and purposes to the extent that this undertaking also meshes together with work already begun here and in certain other places, but still untouched elsewhere, to unite the two former Protestant confessions in one undivided Evangelical church community, in that this work will certainly not be completed by what we do but will nonetheless be more definitively initiated and begun. Now, in that our immediate aim depended upon establishing a form of Holy Communion that could be common to both confessions, we did not think it necessary anxiously to weigh whether one party would have to sacrifice or adopt approximately as much as the other so that no one could complain, for such a task can never be satisfactorily resolved. Rather, it leads too easily to attaching equal value to what is important and to what is of no significance. Just as little did we think that we had to reconcile the different notions held by the two confessions. When it comes to full union of the two churches, it can depend all the less on making dogmatic adjustments. Why? First, the items of doctrine in which they differ are not even generally or altogether uniformly accepted in either church. Second, these differences are rather to be found only in each church's body of doctrine and are of far less importance than some of the differences that occur between theologians of the same church. On this account, dogmatic differences no longer pose any obstacle to communion between the two churches.[8]

The same consideration also applies to this one point of controversy with regard to the doctrine of the Lord's Supper. The difference has arisen on the basis of different interpretations. If people were once zealous to the point of mutually slandering and splitting off from each other over this difference, that was no praiseworthy thing. If it is now as good as forgotten by many Evangelical Christians for lack of instruction or because of indifference about the matter, this too is no praiseworthy thing. The more ardent does zeal become in Christianity once again, as indeed we hope, the more these differences too will again become prominent, and we did not want to proceed to eliminate them by means of disputation as has been attempted at other times. Rather, in that we assume that they will continue to persist we simply want to establish the fact that Christians of both persuasions can harmoniously and devoutly partake together of the Lord's Supper. In essence, this can be achieved when the entire liturgy of Holy Communion emphasizes the commonly acknowledged principal points and omits the controversial subordinate points and when the distribution of Holy Communion, instead of polemically reminding one of the contrast between the two parties, finds the words of Christ himself sufficient – words from the different interpretations of which arose the different opinions of the Lutherans and the Reformed – and in which each individual is also able to gain awareness of one's own full notion. This is the one thing that at present seems to us to be essential wherever any such unification is to take place, though in the future, once it is more firmly rooted, all the biblical statements that deal with this sacrament will be able to be used alternately in administering it without disadvantage. Everything else, such as the form of the bread once blessed, which of course must be broken in accordance with the words of Christ if they are

---

8. Ed. note: See endnote #14 of Schleiermacher's *On Religion* (1821) for a discussion on corruptions of dogmatics.

being spoken, whether it is more like the ordinary bread of the Reformed church or the wafers of the Lutheran church, and also whether and in what way attention is drawn to its consecration, or how the Lord's Table around which those who partake of Holy Communion gather is adorned, these and further things of this kind do even at present seem to us to be matters of complete indifference.

Above all, we so little intended to establish all the details regarding how the sacred action would be carried out on this day as a general pattern for all those who have the union at heart that neither were we ourselves intent on everywhere following exactly what was similarly done in Nassau-Westphalia prior to our undertaking and possibly elsewhere before that, nor did we ourselves come to any consensus about all the details. Rather, in firm trust we left these details to the worthy brethren who would serve at the altar on that day. We are much more of the conviction that these matters are everywhere best determined according to what the dominant disposition and prevailing circumstances in each place make of them, and we think that such freely established differences do not necessarily have to be brought under one and the same form in that their undisturbed persistence unquestionably demonstrates best how little depends on these externals. Therefore, we also now declare that when there is agreement only about what is essential to the rite, the action will be wholly in accord with our spirit and understanding, and even if the external forms depart from ours in any significant way, the one is just as dear and of value to us as the other.

As far as the further consequences of our action are concerned, we are not yet in a position to judge how much and how quickly the example we have set and the subsequent decrees from a higher level – owing to which no one should indeed feel compelled or rushed – will prove to be effective. Yet, even if initially the congregations agree only in part to the new form for Holy Communion while the two older forms still continue to exist alongside them, and even if congregations in areas where only the one confession is indigenous do not feel themselves induced to adopt the new arrangement for a long time, sooner or later there will inevitably come a time when there will be a number of congregations that will wholly adhere to this new form. Thus, in such congregations Holy Communion will no longer be celebrated in its earlier form, nor will it in any respect be celebrated any longer according to its old form by the pastors of such congregations. The point will also be reached, however, when at the same time, the two hitherto existing forms used in the Reformed and the Lutheran churches will continue to remain if not within our own territory then outside it. In the interest of this time, already at this point we consider it advisable to explain publicly and candidly the nature of the relationship that will then have to exist between congregations that have adopted the new rite and the other Reformed and Lutheran congregations both within and outside our territory, and between such ministers and the other Lutheran and Reformed clergy both within and outside our territory so that – instead of widening communion among the churches, as we wish – this communion is still further restricted by misunderstanding of our good intention or others' narrow-mindedness.

That is to say, for a long time the congregations of both confessions within the State of Prussia have already been united with each other in a closer way than is true elsewhere, partly in individual cases by their making use of the same places of worship and to a greater extent partly by their being commonly administered and governed. Nevertheless, at the same time, together with those congregations in the rest of Germany, in the northern kingdoms, and in those scattered about elsewhere, the Lutheran congregations of our territory have formed one and the same Lutheran church. Together with congregations in the rest of Germany, in Switzerland and Holland, Poland and Hungary, and others scattered elsewhere the Reformed congregations have formed the one Reformed church. Moreover, this is also a bond that we have hitherto cherished and valued; indeed, it has been indispensable; for how often do individual families and persons change one land for another, and how often do travelers pass through other lands and want to be acknowledged and accepted as members of the church there?

Until now, all this process has taken its natural course. Wherever they arrived the Lutherans remained with the Lutherans, the Reformed with the Reformed. However, now that even legally among us it is the partaking of Holy Communion that is the only sign of the difference between the confessions, one rightly asks what is to become of this association when there are towns and areas in which the different Reformed and Lutheran forms of Holy Communion are no longer to be found? To note, just one further point: Quite frequently, ministers, and excellent ones too, are called from one land to another, and this blending can prove to be a great blessing in that thereby spiritual gifts and views are often communicated where they were lacking formerly, and one-sided outlooks that have become ruinous are counteracted in a way that would not be possible if every established church were completely isolated. Thus, how little we can wish for such isolation, how little for our part we make it our objective to form a third separate church in addition to the Reformed and Lutheran churches that exist alongside us are matters about which we here wish to make our public declaration.

Thus, we confirm that if there will be congregations in our diocese that will be wholly devoted to the new rite, in which what differentiates the Lutheran from the Reformed has disappeared, we shall also admit to our Holy Communion and receive into our church community any members of a congregation that is still Reformed or still Lutheran who come to us and who feel that their consciences are not bound. We shall do this without hesitation, whether it will be forever or for a certain period of time, without in any way interpreting this action to them as involving any modification of their confession of faith or as involving a transfer to another church. On the other hand, we also live with the hope that when members of our congregations that are devoted to the new rite go elsewhere where this rite is not used, the Reformed and Lutheran congregations will acknowledge and admit them without demanding that on that account they should be regarded as having separated themselves from our Evangelical community.

Similarly, we declare that we shall never have any objection when a minister who has himself formerly conformed to the old Lutheran or Reformed rite – provided only that he himself does not feel bound by his conscience – is called to be pastor of a congregation in which this difference no longer exists, also that we shall never regard this as a matter involving any modification of doctrine or of faith, no more than we are of the opinion that any one of us has now modified his doctrine or his faith. In the same way, we will not reproach any one of us, inasmuch as he does not feel himself to be bound by his conscience, or regard him as having separated himself from our Evangelical community when he allows himself to be called as pastor of a congregation in which the difference between Lutheran and Reformed still exists.

Thus, in this way and for our part, and also for the future, to all Reformed and Lutheran congregations that are still divided, and as long as there shall be any such congregations within or outside our territory, we extend the hand of brotherhood for an undisturbed and lasting communion within the church, for every situation that will present itself, as it has until now. Moreover, with regard to the fact that with this we offer and wish for nothing new or unprecedented, we appeal to the example of the community of the Evangelical Brethren, which is also a union of Christians of the Lutheran and the Reformed confessions who celebrate Holy Communion together according to a rite that is satisfactory to both parties. Reformed and Lutheran Christians are always admitted into these congregations without there being any question of their modifying their confession, and members of these congregations also equally partake of Holy Communion with Reformed or Lutheran congregations. However, if despite our declaration and this clear example, our congregations that are bound to a deviant rite should be regarded anywhere as if they had established a new confession of their own, and if an effort were made to exclude us on this account from communion with the continuing Lutheran and Reformed congregations, admittedly quite against our expectations, and if our best intentions are confronted with a narrow-minded zeal, then, quite naturally, we shall heartily regret this. However, without arousing any controversy over such behavior, we shall bear it with Christian gentleness and patience and shall live with the hope that such endeavors will find but little sympathy and will on the whole remain ineffective. And now, in the hope that we have satisfactorily explained all that is necessary, we ask that God might bring this good work to completion without controversy or confusion.

II

Sermon on the Second Day of the Reformation Jubilee Festival, 1817[*]

Praise and thanks be to God for having given us his Word
to be our lamp on the path of life.[1]

My devout friends, from time immemorial it has been acknowledged that on specific occasions it is necessary and uplifting to recall the memory of great events,
not only to rescue from oblivion those matters the immediate traces of which have
indeed been dispersed and made to vanish as the times have changed, but also to
heighten and revive anew the feeling for that which is still ever present and which
continues to have its effects, and it is this latter point that defines the purpose of
the great festival of these days.[2] This is so, for just as in every moment we all
breathe the air of heaven and live only in and through it, but indeed find it to be

[*] "Am zweiten Tage des Reformations-Jubelfestes 1817" (Berlin: G. Reimer, 1818); SW II.4
(1835), 67-76; and (1844) 98-109. Ed. note: This sermon was preached at Berlin's Church of the
Triune God on Saturday, Nov. 1, 1817. An earlier English translation appeared in Dawn De
Vries, tr., Friedrich Schleiermacher, *Servant of the Word* (Philadelphia, Pa.: Fortress Press,
1987), 87-99.

1. Ed. note: Ps. 119:105.

2. Ed. note: The theme, taken from Mt. 18:5-6, is given in the text: "That we want to be
helpful toward young people's having free use of the divine Word and that we want to educate
them to that justification which comes from faith."

wholesome and invigorating and we drink it in more copious draughts so as to become more intimately and richly conscious of this situation in life, whenever heaven laughs with joy, so in the same way, and for all that we live daily in the free enjoyment of the glorious benefits that fall to Christianity on account of the Reformation of the church, all of us can and shall count it a great blessing of God that God has spared us to join together in this tercentenary celebration so that we can let ourselves be filled in a more intimate way than can occur in ordinary life with the feeling of the great blessings that have come to us from this event, and so that by recalling the divine dispensations and by bringing to mind these cherished instruments of the Lord we shall become more actively and joyfully conscious of our relationship with them and with the great energy of their time with all its strains and struggles.

However, just as the individual person on whom the gifts of God are bestowed more abundantly should not have the benefit of them for oneself alone but should share them and impart them to others, then in the same way, a generation upon which a day of glorious remembrance has come should not take delight in the divine blessings for itself alone, but should also be intent upon transmitting its delight to generations to come and as far as it is possible raise them up to the same consciousness.

Moreover, it is also a remarkable characteristic of everything that is great and noble in human affairs that those who have laid the foundation for them have always been the friends of youth and have always looked especially toward the coming generation with its desires and aspirations. This is so in that indeed, when it is simply a matter of casting aside an external yoke or of successfully surmounting a momentary danger, then it is the thought of ourselves and of our contemporaries that can inspire us and keep us valiant. In contrast, when it is a matter of the renewal of the inner life and of establishing a new form of well-being for humanity, those who have had this most at heart have always understood and felt that they had to place their hopes chiefly on the generation to come. This is why the Redeemer himself was the first friend of children, and he knew well that if these did not hold firmly to his Word then his appearance on earth would have been in vain. This was also why in the great work of refining Christian doctrines and practices the blessed man of God Martin Luther and his associates were so very particularly suffused with painful feelings about the coarse and gloomy condition in which the coming generation was growing up, with so few resources to awaken the dormant divine spark and hence it was to them that they devoted a large part of their endeavors. Suppose that in equal measure the same spirit had inspired all their followers and pupils and all those who shared the advantages they had gained, and that everyone had always been intent upon forming the coming generation to be more free and pure, pious and strong than had been the case in their own experience. Then how much more widespread among us would be a faith that is firmly rooted in the heart! And how much more general would be a joyful life, vigorous in God and worthy of the purified doctrines! Well then, if we and our fathers must thus have failed in various respects with regard to what the Christian owes to the future generation, it is not without justification that our young people are placed before our eyes here today, they being the precious object of our love and care and of our most sacred obligations, the heirs of all our goods and blessings to the extent that we share these with them and initiate them into taking possession of them and enjoying them. Hence, there can be no more dignified conclusion to this day of high celebration than the sacred vow to fulfill this calling worthily and eagerly. To this end may God bless our devotion in this hour.

Text: Matt. 18:5-6. Whoever receives one such child in may name receives me; but whoever causes one of these little ones who believe in me to sin,[3] it would be better for him to have a great millstone fastened round his neck and to be drowned in the depth of the sea.

---

3. Ed. note: The text of the Luther Bible used by Schleiermacher is *wer aber ärgert*, i.e., "but anyone who vexes one of these littlest ones."

32

These words stand in the closest connection with what we have just been stimulated to think of. Here our Lord says to us quite clearly and openly that the person who is greatest in the kingdom of heaven[4] is not the one who even in the purest and most spiritual way cares only for one's own soul, but the one who receives children, and that the most culpable is the person who vexes them.[5] To receive them means to receive him, and indeed this is the greatest thing that can be promised to a Christian as a result of one's endeavors. What, however, can it mean to receive children other than to receive them into the kingdom that the Redeemer has established? What can it be that vexes them, other than, in this respect, to neglect them or indeed to hinder the tug of their own hearts from moving in this direction? Hence, these words remind us of the obligations that are incumbent upon all of us with regard to young people. So, in order to tie this matter more closely with our text, we shall simply concentrate on those features that especially concern the good things that have been entrusted to us by means of the church's reform.

We can trace this reform back chiefly to the recovery of the free use of the divine Word, also to the fact that Christianity's great doctrine of the fruitlessness of all external works and of justification by faith alone[6] has been established anew among us. Accordingly, our reflection today will fulfill its end in two resolutions, namely, that we resolve to be of assistance to young people in the free use of the divine Word, and that we resolve to bring them up in accordance with the righteousness that comes from faith. We ask that the Lord's blessing attend this twofold reflection.

---

4. Ed. note: Mt. 18:1.
5. Ed. note: See note 3.
6. *Gerechtigkeit*. Both "justification" and "righteousness" translate this term. The point is that we are made righteous, acceptable to God, only by grace through faith. It is God's doing; our works do not achieve this status. See also Schleiermacher's sermon on Gal. 2:19-21, entitled "On Righteousness based on Faith," in *Reformed But Ever Reforming: Sermons in Relation to the Celebration of the Handing Over of the Augsburg Confession (1830)*, tr. Iain G. Nicol, Schleiermacher Studies and Translations Vol. 8, (Lewiston: NY; Lampeter: Edwin Mellen, 1997), 65-77.

[I]

Based on the historical accounts that in these days everyone has sought to bring to mind anew, all of us know how deep in darkness the Word of God had already been buried for a long time prior to the reformation of the church. Among those learned in scripture it was already studied in the original languages rarely enough, but in the mother tongue used by the people what was made available was as good as nothing at all, and the little that most people did hear was nothing more than the still garbled and misunderstood material that was made the basis for sermons. In addition, the flourishing of the important work of reformation manifested itself chiefly in the great eagerness with which many thousands of people received Luther's translation of holy scripture. Nevertheless, my devout friends, the feeling for a situation is never quite the same as when it first arose once it has become a habit and a requirement. We cannot directly share in the feeling of our predecessors when, as it were, the Word of God lay new and fresh before their eyes. Instead, on a day such as this we indeed have to try to imagine in as lively a way as we can what new light must suddenly have dawned on them concerning the nature of Christianity, how the once dust-covered and obliterated image of the Redeemer was suddenly placed before their eyes, and how in all its capacity to evoke their love engraved itself on their hearts. What is more, do you not think that young people too would have been deeply stirred by these impressions? Do you not think that they would have asked with longing about that whereby every heart is so uplifted and spiritually satisfied? Then, should fathers and mothers not willingly and joyfully have led them to the treasures of the divine Word and have invited them too to gather and enjoy them? Of course this is what they did! And so, my dear friends, even if we cannot transpose all of the inspired feeling of that time into our own lives, Oh, at the very least we shall want to guard ourselves against acting in this matter with a contrary sensibility and spirit.

For this reason, I consider it to be my most urgent duty today to draw your attention to a pernicious error that has crept into our dealings with young people. We have persuaded ourselves – and for most people this has certainly arisen from a good intention – that our young people can first understand holy scripture only very late, and that if we were to present it to them too early in part they would thereby simply be robbed of the desire and love for it in future as well, and in part the reverence and awe with which they should one day approach it would thereby be undermined in advance. To be sure, indeed, there is a dangerous abuse here, and certainly it is a serious outrage when we degrade holy scripture to our children and reduce it to a dead, indifferent clamor of words! May we not, however, have thrown away the use with the abuse or the blessing with the outrage.

What do we mean by saying that young people are first to be capable of understanding the Word of God? Are we to take it in the full sense that they are first to be capable of grasping everything from it that can be presented to them in all its interconnections with precise definitions of every single word and phrase, so that neither too much nor too little of it will remain in their souls? As indeed we all know quite well, this understanding of the divine Word is of course only a matter for experts on scripture, and even for them it is a task to which their endeavors are continually devoted, since they do not yet boast of having completely fulfilled it. Thus, if we should have to wait for this, we would have to revert entirely to the practice of the church wherein scripture is not left universally and freely open for the use of every Christian. Furthermore, in this case we who are proclaimers of the Word of God also could not appeal to the particular experience of the Word of God among the greatest number of our hearers but would simply have to refer them to what we say about it; and if you free Evangelical Christians shudder at this thought, for us who are your teachers it is even more intolerable. So, this cannot be the meaning. You are all satisfied with a less than perfect understanding of the matter, and you are not surprised that this is a book from a distant time and derived from language foreign to us. On the contrary, the meaning is that young people should wait only until they are at least capable of this imperfect understanding that parents and teachers can give them, and indeed, since everything is to be traced to God and to a person's relationship to God, until they can conceive the thought of the Supreme Being.

Yet, my dear friends, who can conceive this thought? Does the eternal one not dwell in unapproachable light?[7] Do we not know and feel that our notions of God, however much we may try to refine them and make them fit exactly, are indeed never satisfactory to ourselves, and that they always contain some element of image or figurative expression? Are we then to keep young people at a distance from the divine Word because their ideas are still somewhat more childish than ours? Further, given that we are constantly becoming conscious anew that no one can come to the Father but by the Son,[8] why would we want forcefully to keep them back from him who himself called the little children to himself? There certainly does develop in our children a need for what is more elevated and divine, and along with that need also the capacity to satisfy it, much sooner than those who listen mostly to such hesitations might believe. Why should we not believe this too? Shall we count it as nothing that the activity of the divine Spirit in us is plain for them to see? Does it mean nothing that our own piety stimulates presentiments in them that can not thereafter be completely suppressed? Shall we then count it as nothing that through baptism they have already been received into the community of Christians? Certainly, if they understand our admonitions and instructions, and if sin is also born in them out of their desire, and if they become aware of the difference between obedience and disobedience so that their conscience is also stirred, and it is God's voice in human beings that teaches them to ask the question of God, in this way they will also soon understand in all its implications the glorious statement from Paul's Letter to the Romans – which is well-nigh the most difficult book of the New Covenant – regarding the law in the members that is at war with the

---

7. Ed. note: I Tim. 6:16.
8. Ed. note: Jn. 14:6.

law in the mind.[9] Indeed, even the heart of a child can apply this portrayal to itself as soon as there awakes in it the conflict between the spirit and the flesh. It too has its sighs and tears amid which it asks: "Who will deliver me from this body of death?"[10] Moreover, if we only take note of these moments, we too will soon be able to teach them to understand the answer even if at first only in the way of a child, namely: "Thanks be to God, who gives us the victory through our Lord Jesus Christ."[11]

Is it not the most delightful and agreeable occupation of motherly love devoutly to observe how human powers gradually unfold in this young creation, and also obligingly to assist every initial stirring until finally the entire heart and mind has opened up and joyfully puts forth its shoots and buds? Further, what in turn is most sacred about this very process if not to observe the first traces of receptivity for the one thing necessary, for the first sign of longing for a higher life? Finally, when we do take note of this, what can we do better than to advance to meet it with the pure milk of the divine Word?[12] Thus, if we thank God the Lord today more ardently than ever for the blessing of God's Word, well then, let us also make a vow not to hinder or delay its wholesome effects! Let us acknowledge the sacred obligation not to withhold the Word of God from our children and not to be too hesitantly cautious about it. Let us rather offer them from it whatever can awaken the spiritual life in them, whatever can still the longing of their hearts in good time under fatherly and motherly guidance, so that we shall receive and not vex them.

And you, dear children, now that in these days as well you have been informed about the occasion for today's momentous celebration, consider what a sacred treasure was the Word of God for our forebears and still is today for all of us. Consider what kind of great and excellent men the Lord especially had to shape and equip to extract the Word of God from the dust of oblivion; and let what you

---

9. Ed. note: Rom. 7:23.
10. Ed. note: Rom. 7:24.
11. Ed. note: Rom. 7:25; I Cor. 15:57.
12. Ed. note: I Cor. 3:2; I Pt. 2:2.

have heard and read about this readily attend you and be set before your eyes when you read the divine Word! You yourselves will feel now that it is much too significant and sacred to be treated in the same way as other human books. You occupy yourselves with many of these books only so that you will not fill an idle moment without profit. Never snatch at the Word of God in this way, only when you feel an urgency and a need that can be calmed only by means of it. Other human books will be given to you so that you can learn certain good and useful things from them, but when it comes to the Word of God certainly do not believe that anything is achieved from it if you merely learn from it. Rather, whatever you take from it and make your own is of no help if it does not move your heart but simply lies dead in your soul. However, when such a passage rises in your soul as a warning impulse, make note of it, and if it confirms a prohibition issued by your parents and teachers, if, in turn, you discover therein the admonitions of your mothers and fathers, become then all the more vigilant and attentive. Do this, and to your spiritual well-being you will in good time sense the power of the divine Word in your hearts, and your love toward it and reverence for it will ever more increase and be firmly established within you.

However, my dear friends, as we see gathered before us for this important celebration children who are chiefly from our schools, we certainly cannot thank God enough on this occasion for the fact that in the period of pernicious quibbling about divine things and of ruinous control over wholesome institutions the connection between church and school among us has not been dissolved as well. This we do, for it is only on account of this connection that a large number of our young people have reached an early acquaintance with the divine Word, and we can have no doubt about the blessed influence of this acquaintance. Where this acquaintance is lacking, how much more easily is the germ of goodness repressed, how much more easily are young people plunged into all sorts of confusions, and how few of them in fact return to the path of life after their pious sensibility has been humiliatingly stifled! So, filled with heartfelt thanks, let us then promise most solemnly in-

sofar as it is up to us, to bring up our young people in the proper fear and knowledge of the Lord and to impart his Word to them early on so that it can be a light
upon their path. [13]

[II]

Now, the second great blessing of the Reformation of the church was that reli-
ance on external works, which unfortunately had also crept into Christianity, was
broken, and the great doctrine of justification by faith was established. That in
which the essence of this doctrine consists, is so often quite rightly the subject of
our reflection. We find it so magnificently expressed in the statements of those men
of God whose memory fills us in these days, and it is so much the subject in our
powerful and edifying hymns that I do not think it necessary to speak to you about
it as though it were something with which you are unacquainted. However, the
question that we have to answer is this: What does it mean to bring children to this
doctrine? In this regard, furthermore, the first and most important thing is this: that
we should be extremely attentive in preventing any other kind of righteousness
from developing in children so that they will be kept receptive to the one righteousness that alone counts before God. We must surely feel that this depends very
much on us, for it is through our expressions of approval and disapproval that the
consciences of our young people are in fact initially formed. Moreover, in this respect too I have to issue a warning about a very widespread error. In every society
a great deal must be done or left undone if one member is not to disturb another
but each person is to exist at peace within the whole and all of this is of equal value
whether it be done willingly or unwillingly and whether it be the truth or a pretence. The case is the same with a great deal that has to do with what human arrangements, laws, and customs require and prohibit in civil society. Moreover, it is
much the same case in domestic life, and even more, of course, when a greater

---

13. Ed. note: Ps. 119:105.

number of children are gathered for instruction and for exercise of their powers. Now, patently to the extent that these arrangements are either maintained or violated, the task will be made easy or difficult for parents and teachers. Hence, it is natural that violators will have to be reprimanded and punished, but those who are obedient will be praised and awarded. Yet, unless we are very careful, precisely herein lies an all too natural temptation among our young people to place too great a value on what is in fact merely external and thus to strive after false righteousness. So, this subject cannot be recommended enough to the attention of all Christian parents and of all who are involved in the guiding of young people, for the fact that rewards and punishments are attached to this external aspect of conduct will never vex our children or lead them astray as long as we but lead them to view rewards and punishments as something merely external and as long as they but take note that the child who is punished can also be loved more and the child who is rewarded less, and thus that for us there exists something superior to these external virtues.

Yet, if children see that all of what we bestow in the way of love, attachment and sympathy is continually shared mostly with children who are externally obedient, pleasant and conscientious, will they not be vexed then, and will their awakening conscience not be confused and the work of the divine Spirit in them disturbed? Will they not then be led astray, if not by being led to their fear of punishment or by a limited urge for honor alone, at least by regarding their natural sense for law and order and external legality as superordinate? Furthermore, is it then not we who are to be blamed for the fact that they are heading in the direction of a false and perverted righteousness? Will it not be our fault when in days to come they will set an empty and false reputation over against the spirit of punishment? Oh, let us then apply all diligence so that we will not fail to do the right thing here! If today we give thanks to God in the most heartfelt way for having taken from us all vain honor and instead letting us share in the righteousness that comes from faith, let us also solemnly promise to guide our young people on that same path, insofar as it is up to us to do so.

They look to us. Let us always show them that to all external actions we grant only external recognition but that our hearts are attentive and listen when something different and better stirs within them. Also, to the extent that they are able to sense what exists in our lives that comes from faith, let us show them that that for which we have to thank God most is that we have no fonder wish than to receive them too into the community that shares this disposition. Let us show them that they are then and in that measure dearest to us when their hearts are open for this, when this fills them with reverence, and when in their lives too they are ready to be led and guided by this spirit. In that way we will certainly do our part so as to receive them and can confidently leave the rest to divine grace.

As for those of you, dear children, who already take part in the shared life of instruction, take this word well to heart. If you feel how sincerely we rejoice in these days that we have been set free from the erroneous impression that human beings can satisfy God and themselves by means of external conduct, bear in mind that you can just as little satisfy us or yourselves in this way. Do not be surprised that in all external arrangements we shall continue to demand obedience and conscientiousness of you, but that indeed our joy in you and our best hope for you are based on something quite different from this obedience and conscientiousness. If you live vigorously and joyously in your own circles, then soon there will also develop in you a common feeling exactly the same in content. You will soon note that those who do something good based on obedience and conscientiousness are not those whom you love and respect most. This is not at all because you still to some extent take a certain delight in disobedience but because pride in this external conduct can occur only when the better sort is lacking and because once this pride arises and one is thus satisfied with being externally beyond reproach one cannot have any desire at all to grow in true goodness. If you take pains, however, to ask yourselves whether you have God in your hearts and whether you are truly and lovingly devoted to those who represent God to you, then you will soon observe that being able to do this is God's Spirit and gift in you, and with us you will also bear a desire that this Spirit and gift from God will be firmly established and maintained in you. Accordingly, God preserve you so that you will not be ensnared in any external sanctity until you too become receptive to the righteousness that comes from faith.

Yet, my friends, as we think above all of our young people today, all of us will certainly find cause to rejoice especially that by God's grace our civil and social life has also made significant gains in that there is little occasion for anyone to rely on the external aspects of their actions alone, even if only to win other persons' respect and love thereby; that in its entire form civil and social life increasingly makes the impression that our people consists of those who seek their merit and reassurance only in the possession of those blessings that come to them in faith and through faith, and that the purpose of all external laws and regulations lies simply in letting these efforts have their way ever more freely and to establish them ever more securely. May all empty pretence increasingly die away and be carried to the grave, may all our confidence rest only on the concord of our hearts and minds, based on what is good, and may all respect increasingly be given over to true German love and fidelity and to genuine and simple godliness. The more we build in this sense, the more we will be formed as a Christian people, and the easier it must also become for us, in that the whole form of life is in accord with our teaching, with our guiding our young people in such a way that when a germ of the divine life emerges it will surely be nourished and quickened. As a result, they will press forward to the true freedom of God's children, which consists in a person's surrendering oneself as a servant of true righteousness free from all inflated illusions and vain pride. Accordingly, today our vow is this: to continue to refine our life so that the great good deed that we commemorate today will be handed down to each future generation even more fully.

42

Truly, Lord God, you alone are wise. As your whole world coheres so that nothing therein may be lacking, even if that which remains is to stay as it is, so it is with your decrees in every generation of human beings. Hence, we also feel how all those good and excellent things in which we rejoice are connected with the great good deed that we commemorate today, and how everything is ever more formed toward being a great work of blessing worthy of our most heartfelt thankfulness and deepest devotion. Oh, may all who share in this blessing be also truly filled with the feeling of the condition of degradation from which they have been delivered by the faithful servants of your Word, and may they hold firmly to the good things that they have gained at such a cost. To you, Lord, who have never forsaken your church, which, we in all faith hope, you especially up-build and bless now to your children's consolation and joy, to you we especially commend the church on this day. Today, the more we look to the past and are thus mindful of changes that occur in human affairs, the less can we keep from thinking that even in the future days of sorrow and of darkness and confusion could return. Yet, the Spirit of your Son whom you have sent us has continued always to hold sway in his community. The more widespread the darkness is, the more vigorously does your Spirit rush forth from place to place as the fiery Spirit who chastises the world and gathers together those who have gone astray.[14] The more peacefully that light and freedom rule, the more gently does the Spirit hold sway among the faithful as the Spirit of truth and love[15] who lays hold of the treasure of the Redeemer and illumines it to his own. In this way, may he abundantly hold sway among us too, may he speak and instruct through the servants of the purified Gospel, and may he be with all those who are busy with the generation to come. As your Son himself has said, we can do nothing greater than receive little children. If they receive your Word from us and are led toward a Christian life, then we too shall live and work on among a worthy generation, then we shall rejoice not only in

---

14. Ed. note: E.g., see Mt. 3:11-12 and Lk. 3:15-17.
15. Ed. note: Jn. 15:26 and 16:13; also I Jn. 4:6.

the past but also in the future, and we shall attain our share in the glory of the Lord, who is with us to the close of the age.[16] May it be so. Amen.

---

16. Ed. note: Mt. 28:20.

III

Address Celebrating the Third Centennial
of the Reformation of the Church by Luther
at the University of Berlin
held on 3 November 1817[*]

[I]

Most excellent and illustrious men, most eminent in all ranks, most favored colleagues and most beloved students,[1] I hope none of you will be surprised that, in
the third century since the restoration of evangelical truth, I, of all people, should
speak in my own person, I who favor the teaching of Zwingli more than that of
Luther, from whom this day nevertheless receives its name and honor. I hope you
will not be surprised, for on these highly festive days we devoutly celebrate the
memory of that event which is common to both Luther and Zwingli: that is, the
happy restoration of the supreme authority of sacred scripture in matters concerning Christian faith and life, the complete overthrow of the superstition of arbitrary
works and external merit, the casting out of all intermediaries of faith in God save
Christ alone, the wresting from Christian worship of the species of pagan and Jew-

---

[*] *Oratio in sollemnibus ecclesiae per Lutherum emendatae saeularibus tertiis in Universi-*
tate litterarum Berolinensi die III. Novembris A. MDCCCXVII habita (Berlin: Unger, 1817); SW
I.5, 309-325; KGA I/10, 1-16.
1. The original Latin text is translated and notes added by Terrence N. Tice, with assistance
from Philip Snider, graduate student in Classics, University of Toronto, and Catherine L. Kelsey.

ish priest, and the removal of all cause and occasion for struggle between church and state. Nor did those noble-minded men, full of the divine Spirit and equal in dependence on the eternal Word and in mental fortitude, who, through such great darkness, cut for themselves and others a path to the light, ever think it fit to break off ecclesiastical relations with each other. Indeed it would be ill considered in this rightly undertaken celebration, if, in this same place, we were to celebrate the Wittenberg theses of Luther as the first act of the Reformation today and then, some years later, celebrate the pronouncements of Zwingli in Zürich or the Tigurin Colloquium,[2] though the two sets of views are different in doctrine. We who do not cling to its subtleties repented a short while ago of all these differences, which some would have wished to bring to light once more.

Indeed, neither Luther nor Zwingli must be celebrated today but rather the work of our most good and great God and the divine Spirit, which work is most worthy of eternal memory. This is so for, indeed, when disgust with priestly perversity and turpitude had entered not only into them but also into a great many people of all walks of life throughout the world and when images of better conditions had made their appearance, the Holy Spirit effected a desire to emend religion in their souls. If this desire had not preceded the reformers of religion, they themselves would not have been able to accomplish anything. Thus, many distinguished men such as Luther, Zwingli and others eventually offered themselves as a vanguard for the disparate and timid multitude. Since this would occur within the borders of northern powers and wherever in Germany numbers of Reformed churches live in common with Lutherans, these people would not refuse commemoration of the church's Reformation in common with the Lutherans. Surely you do not think it right to reject this practice at this time when you see a com-

---

2. Ed. note: In 1523, shortly before the first Zürich Disputation held that year, Zwingli published as its basis a set of 67 "Schlussreden" (Pronouncements or Theses). These comprise the first systematic treatment of doctrine in the German language and were his most comprehensive work of theology. Under his direction the Zürich reformation was already in full swing in 1523-1525. The Marburg Disputation (1529) signaled unbridgeable differences between Zwingli and Luther, especially over the Lord's Supper.

monality and communion occurring between the two churches and when unity of worship is maintained in such a way that the hope shines forth in this period that eventually the abundant disagreements among our forefathers will be buried in oblivion.

Who, then, is able to bring it about that I, who have been made dean by decision according to university regulations,[3] should fear lest I should not be a worthy enough speaker today because I am connected to the confession of the Swiss?[4]

[II]

Nevertheless, perhaps it would have been better if our forbearers, since the foundation was laid equally by both parties, would together have established the day for holding the centennial, even if it were only arbitrarily. They could have done so out of concern that otherwise some events would be celebrated all by themselves, practices that would belong to the one group, but another event would be different for the other group, so that the nature, scope and seriousness of this occasion would not be declared with sufficient aptness. On the other hand – for I should say what I think, though I do understand that this observation will be pleasing to no one – even if the differences between the two confessions should come to be dismissed, if you were to consider only the things done by Luther and his followers in Saxony,[5] it certainly would not be fitting in my judgment for this centennial celebration to be established for this day, seeing that when he put up his theses in 1517 Luther had not yet entered upon the reformation of the church. This is so, for it does not seem to be sufficiently accurate to say that whatever Luther would have

---

3. Ed. note: After the founding of the Friedrich Wilhelm Universität in Berlin in 1810, Schleiermacher was made the first dean of the theology faculty.

4. Ed. note: More generally, Schleiermacher refers to the Reformed confessions, more specifically to the first confession of Basel (1534), and the first and second Helvetic confessions (1536 and 1566) among others. The English texts of these confessions and Zwingli's 67 articles are in Arthur C. Cochrane, *Reformed Confessions of the Sixteenth Century*, Philadelphia: Westminster Press, 1961.

5. Ed. note: From 1518 Luther was under the protection of Frederick III, Elector of Saxony, in which the town of Wittenberg lay.

accomplished with his friends after this event, he would have moved on from this initial struggle differently, as he himself said: namely, had the Roman curia conducted itself a little more cautiously even then, all the ecclesiastical disturbances that had arisen would have been settled very easily. What if Luther himself had not only not refused to return to communion with the Pope but had even been inclined to the view that papal authority must be recognized?[6] What if he had honestly believed in the miracles that were said to happen among the images of the saints? Surely then this pursuer of the Roman church would have to be said to be among the most faithful of its adherents. Rather, the day that seems to me must be chosen is the one on which together with the masters and youth of Wittenberg he burned the papal decree and the excommunicating bull against him, about which even he himself said: "Now, at last, I begin to do serious things. Those that were done earlier were just a game."[7] Moreover, he said this rightly, for by this deed the Romans were no longer able to consider peace, and the Roman pontiff pointed this out in the same letter in which he declared that he did not want the church to be overturned from Luther's speaking these words. Out of true passion concerning such things and impatient of delay, our forbearers desired to place the centenary of the Reformation as early as possible. So, it was thought that since they had already submitted to this passion, it would not be right for us to change the day now.

Yet, if we look closely at the matter, it does not seem suitable that this consideration could help us and our address today. We may certainly agree that what pertains to general evangelical piety has played an important role in the celebration, very richly and fruitfully so, and we may recognize that since the assembly was held in those days perpetual prayers for the safety of our church were poured out and vows to God were made that were fitting for conferring benefits on us in this place and on this day. This being said, it is proper for us now to take up that part

---

6. Ed. note: Zwingli was also an adherent of the Pope at that time but had completely broken with papal institutions by 1523. In 1519 Luther made a decisive break with Rome and papal primacy in his disputation with John Eck.

7. Ed. note: The burning occurred on December 10, 1520, and Luther never sought to return thereafter.

of the argument which touches more closely on the universities and the development of doctrine. To serve that purpose, the memory of matters that were accomplished on the day before the Kalends of November 300 years ago gives us an opportunity that must not be discarded. This is so, for if the theses that the blessed Luther affixed to the church door in Wittenberg for the purpose of debate were indeed the beginnings of the church's Reformation, it must be admitted, my listeners, that the work that must be celebrated forever had proceeded from the doors of academe. From the moment you will have arisen and you will have reflected among yourselves, ask: How much is entrusted in the universities to assure that the church be increased and promoted? I think you would then readily agree, after all the rest is taken care of, to my discussing this point.

However, there are two other points especially on which the safety of the church depends: discipline and doctrine. Accordingly, as soon as people had said goodbye to Roman authority – because almost all of the bishops, who were likewise princes of the Empire, were then standing as one apart from the parties of the caesars and the popes – it became impossible to preserve episcopal authority in the Evangelical church that was arising in Germany, though this was later accomplished in Sweden and Denmark without any loss to the church.[8] So it was necessary to resort to the secular princes for help to overcome faults in the church, to establish improvements in divine worship and to increase overall handling of discipline in the sacred domain. Nor thereafter was anything accomplished to the detriment of the nascent church when magistrates of free cities and princes, who were accustomed to moderate use of power (namely, Frederick the Wise, John Con-

---

8. Ed. note: In Sweden apostolic succession was retained in 1534, and the church long continued relations with Rome. Only in 1593 did it adopt the Augsburg Confession. In the Swedish Constitution of 1809 it was required that the king and members of the government must be members of the established Church of Sweden. In Denmark reformation was swifter, beginning with the declaration of religious freedom at the Diet of Odense in 1527 and adoption of the Lutheran Confessio Hafnica in 1537. In the 17th century draconian rules were promulgated forbidding Roman priests to practice at pain of death, and then all property was taken from Roman converts. Later, in laws set forth between 1849 and 1852, total religious freedom was restored and the Lutheran church disestablished.

stans, and John Frederick the Magnanimous), conducted early affairs among the Evangelical churches, for the honesty and modesty of these men was joined to their constancy and generosity. Frederick especially achieved the name Wise for the reason that he himself did not think himself to be very wise. Therefore, ecclesiastical matters were renewed neither suddenly nor tumultuously but as gradually as possible. Christian people, struck by the force of truth, voluntarily sought improvement in worship. Moreover, if magistrates or princes were challenged concerning these innovations anywhere, they answered that they themselves understood these matters less, that theologians must be heard, and they themselves listened to the theologians.

Later on, the situation did indeed change completely. After the supreme authority of the Emperor was diminished, and the princes of the Empire increased to nearly royal power, almost no part was left anywhere for nobles or for cities in administration of state affairs, nor did any proposal prevail except by decision of the kings and the princes, to which the church itself at length yielded. It did so in such a way that no one could easily say what would happen concerning the evangelicals or why these kings and princes were present in assemblies of Christians responsible for establishing and preserving sacred matters. No one could say why the secular leaders should prevail as heralds of the Word. Finally, no one could say why princes ought to be the guardians of the church or why even the highest bishop could not dare try exactly to define the church's rights. Nor did it help much that theologians were accustomed to being counsel to the princes in these matters, because what courtiers hear and report can soften and sometimes crush even a strong spirit.

Luther, in fact, did not once speak with Frederick the Wise, nor did he perform any service among his counselors. Therefore, he was all the stronger in speaking truth and was preserved in his own dignity and freedom. Moreover, where the countenance of the prince threatens or where the prince himself has less concern about sacred matters, what friend or minister would be so brave that in his accomplishing things he would desire not to promote the prince's cause simply because it would be unpleasant to misrepresent something to him? Even if his conscience were altogether sound, at that point it would not be sound in purity and strength and his soul would not be sound. George Spalatin[9] was a learned man, eloquent, very friendly with Luther, and he was not timid. Nevertheless, you could not count many instances in which he helped his friend or his cause. Instead, Luther sharply scolded him when he offered his hand and counsel to the Elector for the purpose of suppressing some book when he himself had written more vigorously on the same subject, though without exception in those days it was not easy for anyone to dare take action on one's own. Rather, all things whatsoever were entrusted to the princes and their ministers.

The situation had been this: If the prince were pious and hardworking, assigning his own things to each person in turn, then the churches could flourish by their own strength. If he were contemptuous of the Christian faith, desirous of vainglory, more confident in meting out magical revenge than in dealing with the religion of human beings, then ecclesiastical matters would fall from bad to worse, the protection of divine worship would be neglected, ancestral religious institutions would be turned to other uses, the churches would be despoiled, no one would care about proper learning of the divine Word among ministers, and unworthy men would encroach upon sacred affairs. We see a lamentable example of this situation in the years before that most courageous and most fortunate liberation of Germany.[10]

In contrast, it can happen that if the prince is zealous for theological matters beyond the norm for a prince, is devoted to certain opinions, and is ardent and endowed with an overhasty and fervid mind, so that a rein is put on preachers making them less able to hand down sound doctrine and candidly to admonish their hear-

---

9. Ed. note: Georg Burkhardt (1484-1545), born in Spalt, humanist and reformer; a very close friend of Luther and allied with him in the work of reform especially in Saxony.

10. Ed. note: Reference is to the successful withstanding of the Napoleonic takeover of German territories a few years before.

ers, then in their performing those very rites the just freedom of the churches would be put at critical risk. At length it would surely shame the entire Evangelical church that these matters were entrusted to the power of individuals or of a few men, especially those who would be turned as much as possible to very different matters, matters that do not belong to human authority. Rather, for aids and supports these matters look to divine grace. These aids and supports must be judged and ordained by the Holy Spirit, which presides over and is common to all "according to the measure of Christ's gift."[11] Christ never promised that he would will to dwell in princes and nobles of the earth instead of indwelling everybody.

Things concerning this assuredly very grave matter that our most august and compassionate king has very recently established in the Evangelical church of this kingdom will cure that evil. He sets forth a worthy example for contemporaries and descendants, one that will be imitated. I speak of the institution of presbyteries in all evangelical sectors and the calling of synods at different levels, the demands and decrees of which, on their own authority, will confirm any honest and just prince who ever refuses to fall under any suspicion of arbitrary power in sacred affairs. In time, therefore, the church will be secure.

[III]

Now I shall briefly set out how this situation relates to universities. That is to say, legitimately constituted bodies of clergy would restore sacred discipline and the safety of the church, as much as can be done among things human, placing the church outside all danger that would have to arise from the mind of a single individual or from the minds of a few men. The work of these bodies, moreover, is to receive all our petitions and take counsel concerning them. There is a need for two things: first, for correct ideas, then for practice and experience in sacred affairs. Indeed, experience gradually comes during their performance of ecclesiastical ser-

---

11. Ed. note: Eph. 4:7.

vice.[12] However, as to right ideas, which necessarily precede such practice, wherefrom are they to be communicated to them? Wherefrom can they be instilled in the minds of youth, if it not be in academia? So, I do not know on what grounds I could speak with the pride with which a great many theologians of this age are accustomed to slighting practical theology.[13] This slighting seems to me quite capricious and clearly dangerous, so that it cannot possibly be done with genuine pride. Truly, I do not know why the present stunted and depressed condition of the Evangelical church, from which this attitude has arisen, would not be prolonged and even turn for the worse.

Moreover, the blessed Martin[14] did not hesitate to arrange music for Christian gatherings, to compose sacred music, to write a summary of Christian doctrine appropriate for the use of ordinary youth and to hold this more dear than almost all of his other writings, also to visit churches and cities, the countryside and villages with Philip, Pomeranus[15] and other theologians possessing the utmost authority and right doctrine. In Switzerland Zwingli also prescribed as much to those who did not disdain such practice. Thus, it would not have been possible for such practice to be unworthy for anyone choosing to hand down the doctrine and precepts belonging to these ideas. Moreover, unless Luther, with that same liberty and noble frankness in which the university at Wittenberg excelled from its very beginning, had provided guidance for his listeners concerning spiritual matters and sacred ends, surely he would not have engaged such a number of those who supported his bold ventures and the hard work of reformation, which was very risky.

---

12. Ed. note: Here, as in Schleiermacher's practical theology, "service" refers to the direct leadership of a congregation, chiefly by the clergy, thus to ministry.

13. Ed. note: See Schleiermacher's *Brief Outline of Theology as a Field of Study*, translated with essays and notes by Terrence N. Tice (Lewiston, NY: Edwin Mellen Press, 1990), xv 230 p. There he places high value on practical theology as the "crown of theological study" and holds the fostering of good leadership in church government and service as its basic aim.

14. Ed. note: Martin Luther (1483-1546).

15. Ed. note: Philip Melanchthon (1497-1560) and Johann Bugenhagen (1485-1558). The latter was pastor in Wittenberg from 1523 until his death. Another close associate of Luther, Bugenhagen played a prominent role in organizing the Lutheran church in North Germany and Denmark. He also assisted Luther in his translation of the bible.

Consequently, when he separated himself from the Pope, they would not have been involved in all that ensued with him. On the contrary, although the beginnings achieved by only a few men would have borne some result, that outcome would have been suppressed at the very outset.

Therefore, let us imitate this signal man of that time. At last, as this third century comes to a close, let practical theology rise up from oblivion and contempt. Let that most important part of theology be cultivated and increased in the university, which shall then aim itself at laying out the office of ecclesiastical service and its rules. No one would then wish or be able to engage in this office without conducting oneself in accordance with proper ordering and governance of the Evangelical church overall.[16] Theologians alone are not sufficient for this activity, nor do I call upon theologians alone today. There is need in it for lawyers, politicians and philosophers[17] as well. Therefore, following the example of the friendship and sociality[18] that existed among Luther, Philip and Hieronymus Schurf,[19] let the masters of these disciplines augment the work of theologians. May the law of the Evangelical church be sought again from its theoretical and historical sources, and let people do their reforms there in accordance with the reason of our times. In this approaching fourth century, let our universities defend these changes, a work worthy of our labor and most fruitful for the future.

---

16. Ed. note: Schleiermacher divided practical theology into rules for church service and church government. In his time, both parts were chiefly, though not exclusively, the responsibility of clergy in their role as leaders of the church. Theologically educated clergy he calls "theologians."

17. Ed. note: Schleiermacher did not mean specialists in philosophy alone. He deemed philosophical mindedness to be a general characteristic of being university educated. Accordingly, to this day most doctoral degrees are in philosophy (Ph.Ds).

18. Ed. note: "Sociality" is a term in Schleiermacher's ethics for a situation of free social interchange, along with the family, the state and learning (in schools, the university, science), one of the chief institutions of a society in general.

19. Ed. note: Schurf (1481-1554), Professor of Jurisprudence at Wittenberg, acted as Luther's legal counsel at the Diet of Worms (1521), at which Luther defended his views before Emperor Charles V.

[IV]

I now proceed to another part of my address, which has to do with doctrine. The whole basis of this work of reformation lay in the doctrine of renewal, in that Zwingli and Luther wholly rejected the common accustomed type of theological demonstration and refutation, which was derived from positions held by the fathers and doctors of the church. Thus, if anyone should wish to refute them these two men demanded that scripture alone be the judge of the controversy. That uncommon demand, which so struck all who favored the cause of reformation that it aroused desire and care for the sacred books, and, in turn, among the learned both effort and enthusiasm were employed in collecting, interpreting and comparing. As a consequence, theological doctrine was brought to such great perfection as no mortal had ever seen. From this source, the interpretive arts and criticism then flowed, in the use of which the Evangelical church has always eminently distinguished itself.

If anyone should compare in part what is held and what is fulfilled in this respect by evangelicals and in part what is neglected and omitted by the popes, it would not be difficult to decide which side excels in building a fuller account of doctrine and explicating distinct notions. The one side collects traditional notions in a temporal series, declares each to be a dogma in that it is seen to be singular in nature, puts it into writing, and adheres to it. The other side, based on writings from the earliest period of the church, which writings are indeed full of the Holy Spirit but which also contain the seeds of dogma, tries to form the dogmatic material into an interconnection of Christian doctrine and, at the same time, to restore an accurate image of that early age.

Moreover, the issues then arise as to whether it is more excellent to separate day to day theological study from other studies and ecclesiastical service from this study or not to admit anyone to sacred ministry unless that person is well versed in biblical interpretation and sacred philology properly conjoined with profane studies of antiquity, so that each candidate is able to pursue a variety of efforts within this area in turn.

Yet, among us these studies also saw changes when, not long after the blessed Luther's death, a situation ensued that was very different from that in which Luther and his allies jointly contributed to study and care of the sacred books. Changes occurred wherein the task of fulfilling Christian doctrine by all parties together dissolved and degenerated into scholastic arguments in a contrived form of writing that proved to yield no help to healthy interpretation so that it was now possible for interpretation to be neglected altogether. Nor were all who were engaged in interpretation able to enjoy the investigation of Christian antiquity. Instead, they chose to watch for comments of value in writing and discussion of contemporaries. Indeed, without a doubt that very time saw a decline in matters evangelical in themselves, because words were being valued over virtue, formulae were being valued above religion, so that hatred and envy were tearing the church apart. Thus, nothing was lacking to nourish evils that customarily germinate in the enthusiasm for partisanship. Then, since people are accustomed to rush to the opposite of any such evil, something very different arose, namely disrespect for Christian doctrine. This happened because while, to be sure, doctrine may arrogate to itself the splendor of the divine light, scholastic doctors can also envelope that light with darkness, by which I refer to the zeal for casting doubt, for arguing, for equating all things divine with things human, and finally for impudently, impiously mocking whatever refers to divine revelation. These evils not only proceeded against the Roman church, but in the earlier part of the 18th century also arose among us as well, far and wide.

That disease no one would have believed would take root in Germany. We see this phenomenon in studies of our theologians that were falsely promulgated and arose through abuse of the critical arts. In part, however, it crept up on us from contact with the frivolous French, in part as the progeny of English pride, for those things on which learned men and theologians among us tended to hesitate concerning historical and philosophical arguments were by far a different sort compared with what contemporaries would be able to detect from the witticisms of the French and the great noise-making of the English. Yet, why should I say more, since I would not so much demonstrate these things as recall them to your memory?

None of these evils, though they would disturb and slow the progress of doctrinal work, was able to deter anyone observing matters of religion from adhering to the Evangelical church. Certainly our own time has now grown away from the earlier irreligious skepticism and proud bluntness of statement. Nor, however, should the church seek glory for itself from the fact that things religious and Christian history are treated less carelessly today. That happy substitution occurred in the manner I have indicated, all of which relates closely to the main subject of my address just as all that I have drawn out concerning the reforming events that we commemorate does. To be sure, so that in treating errors of this sort we are not led to a defense, which can certainly be devised but which serves to the detriment of letters, the firmest remedy, and best means of defense, if anyone should be persuaded to it, is to be placed in that very freedom of teaching and learning that is the greatest glory and most valuable property of universities that flourish in evangelical lands.

I say property, because universities, which are much older than the Reformation of the church, from that time on were divided into two types. One type comprised those of the popes, whose universities were forced more and more to resemble schools, where what was necessary to teach to anyone and what was necessary to learn were warily ordered by rules and regulations. The other type comprised those of the evangelicals, which, as I have mentioned, were ennobled by freedom of teaching and learning. As I recalled in passing, such freedom may have seemed to favor bad practice. It has indeed done so where it is permitted to anyone who has taken an academic step up to teach anything at all, and in this way many badly judged things are handed down. Also, where anything at all is allowed for any student to hear and to learn vain boasters take advantage of the inexperience of youth, and youth harm themselves by aspiring to activities for which the strength of their minds are not yet sufficient. On that basis, errors have inescapably been born and propagated.

Nevertheless, all these results, when compared to very clearly good ones that also issue from freedom of teaching and learning, must be held to be of scarcely any importance, and for several reasons. First of all, who is that most learned person who, when the right to teach is confined to narrower limits, is so unwearied by frequent repetition that could be avoided that he would not muster disgust for the resultant teachings? Who is the person that tedium itself would not pursue into the hiding place of the muse and impede such efforts, so that he would be less inclined to promote newly discovered doctrine? Moreover, if doctrines should come to be divided among different parties and opposing schools, and if one portion of them that sets itself above *res publica* should gain assent, how could it not happen that, should every freedom of teaching be restricted there, an opposing party would always rise in turn?

In such a circumstance, universities that were subjected to Roman authority neither would produce men notable for their learning nor would correct and develop their doctrines. Rather, they would have left them to be handed down imperfect as they were just as, for instance, the Aristotelian school of philosophy which once occupied the cathedrals holds its place up to the present century. In contrast, whoever is quite learned and wise among us would be able to wander more broadly in the fields of doctrine and to hand down a great variety of doctrines to listeners. He would be able all the more to examine what methods and theories they follow, also to examine what is uppermost in his own mind, then even to examine the discipline he holds dear before all else. He would then return to his labors fresh for some while and strengthened in many ways. Moreover, if princes and their ministers or the heads of juvenile institutions belonging to one party or another should ever make an approach and refuse appointments of professors unless they agree with them, then for the sake of that other party the teachers should, of their own will, rise up in protest and draw the minds of youth under their care with them.

It is necessary in support of this freedom of teaching that the freedom of learning should indeed occur as far as we who perform that service are accustomed to for ourselves, so that we would refuse to demand students' fealty to what we say. Accordingly, whoever teaches youth in his own place in this way will do so as if among those who would listen to a person who is devoted to an opposing opinion about the same thing. Further, we should act in our teaching in such a way that students should have before them what they can perceive, not what they would have to conjecture. Then, if yesterday's report of opposing opinions would simply drive out today's, one would have worked in vain.

By these things we would use such situations as examples by which students can learn to learn and can compare for themselves what natural plan exists for investigation and examination. Gradually they will thereby become more confident in themselves, so that later they may shuck off the reins of authority of whatever kind. Exercise of this freedom would also help those very youth while engaged in their ordinary studies, so that in choosing masters to whose discipline they would be especially attached, they might already indulge their genius as if they were taking in greater gulps of living air and the very serenity of heaven, so that they might excel the more splendidly. Thereby they should mature more quickly from the habit of youthful admiration and imitation into the virile strength of their own minds.

From that freedom between masters and students, things are born that customarily happen between professors and students, namely a bond of intimacy and friendship. Such experiences do not allow masters to grow old. Students are corrected and strengthened more by paternal counsels than by strict respect and rigorous discipline. We have a shining example of such intimacy in Luther, who was surrounded by a sword-clad throng of students at Wittenberg. He advanced to the disputation at Leipzig spurred on by the urgent desire of his students, refused to

60

hide any longer but came into the light from his retreat at Isencensus.[20] Who among you does not know this?

Thus, you, my listeners, will judge with me concerning this freedom of teaching and learning, which indeed students demand so earnestly and rightly, whether it is greater than the great freedom of writing and reading by as much as speaking is more effective than the written word. Surely you will agree that it is very precious, and you will rejoice that it is inborn and securely fixed in our universities to such an extent that people might be able to destroy universities but they would not be able to restore or preserve them after the freedom of teaching were lost. For this reason, leaders of cities have concluded that if anyone among them, led by severity of spirit, were to censure student morals and simple delights in freedom a little more sharply, and if they were to have books approved or disapproved by censors, then people of the city would want to have pious doctors bound with even more unjust rules. In this light, a leader would indeed not dare to remove any freedom in academic teaching.

Since you have strongly protected this freedom through all the vicissitudes of time, it would not seem necessary to warn you. Nevertheless it is my task to warn you, so that in the very name of this freedom you may celebrate the Reformation of the church with us and so that on this very important and holy day you may bind yourselves quite religiously to your wish to use this freedom in such a way that the right idea of this freedom in things divine and things human, which is gained with constant watchfulness among the good men of this age, by persistence, fortitude and commitment to truth, may be preserved whole and be extended in others forever as much as it is in you.

---

20. Ed. note: Luther disputed John Eck, a Roman Catholic theologian, at Leipzig in 1519, arriving from his protected retreat at Isencensus castle.

[V]

Therefore, as to the Evangelical church, which we reckon as the mother of such goods, which has been managed by wise laws and institutions and has conformed to them over these four centuries, may it flourish for a long succession of years to come, and may it continue to grow, also being commended by us today to the power of the divine providence wrought by God's eternal power, by our heavenly Savior, and by the fortunate direction of the Holy Spirit. I pray that the kings and princes and the magistrates of free cities may preserve and strengthen this church with a kind spirit, also that they may cultivate and observe its precepts with an obedient heart and that if any danger should threaten from any side, strong and vigorous persons shall never be lacking. I pray, too, that all doctors of evangelical theology and pastors of congregations may be, like the blessed Luther, upright ministers and propagators of the divine Word, and then heralds to all human beings and sycophants of none.

As much as is possible, may the University stand on its own merits as the fortress of liberty and learning, the bulwark of Christian truth. From day to day, may it mete out a greater breadth of doctrine, and in whatever good arts of human history and of forming well warranted notions its members may practice in their own right, may they never cease to turn these good arts to the use of the church. This latter wish I would extend to all in all but especially to our own University, in which under the auspices of the most august king of this realm, in this place that it has begun to occupy[21] and in honor of its own most generous founder. May the University hold strong, and may the number of its students ever abound, who would go forth from here as learned and pious men, and may they serve the church and their country with a grateful heart.

---

21. Ed. note: Since its founding in 1810, the Friedrich Universität at Berlin has occupied a stately royal palace, as it does to this day.

On this solemn day, on which we celebrate with pious hearts the memory of the church and its sacred doctrine, which was renewed by a doctor of theology, it seems appropriate in accordance with the custom of our predecessors to exercise a particular right that is granted us by our most generous king. I speak of the conferment of the highest honor in theology, with which pious men who deserve well with respect to sacred letters and the church are customarily adorned. Thus, by the decree of the University's officers, I, F.D.E. Schleiermacher, Doctor of Theology and Professor *publicus ordinaries*, and Dean of the Faculty of Theology, by the power vested in me in this year by the University's officers do present these following very learned men to receive the doctoral degree.

First, Carl Immanuel Nitzsch, master of philosophy, who formerly read at Wittenberg, now of the seminary for evangelical ministers, in view of the fact that in this very place, on this very day, our most august king has ordered him to be installed as professor and third deacon at the Church of Mary, and who has published excellent evidence of theological learning.

Second, Justus Godfrey Hermes, who must be cherished not only by his own congregation and ministers at the Church of St. Gertrude in our city but also among us all because of his evangelical integrity, purity of doctrine, simplicity and especially the sanctity of his discipline and life.

Third, John Geibel, the most deserving Reformed pastor at Lübeck and a most eloquent advocate for the bond of brethren among Christians.

I hereby make them Doctors of Sacred Theology, I announce their creation, and I propose that they be adorned with the privilege and honors attached thereunto.

Finally, a word on behalf of our youth, who are to us most beloved. So that some part in celebrating this day should be yours, we have ordered you to try sketching the image of Philip Melanchthon, whose memory on this day is recalled as among the first rank. Thus, after this sheet of paper is shown I will announce the name of that one among you who has not only presented his little work of art with diligence, given the shortness of time, but has also done so acutely and ingeniously beyond the strength of his youthful age. He is Herman Olshausen Holsatus, to whom are given from the royal treasury 100 gold nummi struck in memory of this celebration, and I add over and above this award 10 aureii displaying Frederick, and I admonish him that he pursue the same diligence that he has now proved to us in his own studies.

Now, at the close of my address, I pour out prayers to our benevolent God that the performance of this Republic of Letters and of the Evangelical church may turn out happily and with good fortune, that God may move the minds and spirits of very learned men to deserving fine recognition from this institution of letters and Christianity, that God may direct them to such honor by the divine Word, and that God may illuminate by God's own light this very upstanding youth and his comrades and all of us who are present, to the end that the students under our care may be broadcast and propagated as the most abundant fruits in their country and throughout the Christian world.

IV

To Court Chaplain D. Ammon

on His Examination of Harms's Theses[*]

Reverend Sir, you will perhaps have already been wondering why I did not immediately respond to your friendly letter of 12th December of last year. However, the figurative expressions in which you mainly spoke were so unclear to me that I chose rather to postpone my response until I would have read that to which you referred me, namely, how you had publicly expressed yourself on the matter of church union, which is the main subject of your letter. To be sure, this too actually should not have delayed me for so long. Nevertheless, you had given me so little account of where I should find your remarks on the matter that since I seldom receive the latest news on the most recent literature, I had to resign myself to waiting. Then I noticed only recently, when I received your *Examination of Harms's Theses*,[1] that this also included your opinion on church union that I had sought so long in vain.

---

[*] *An Herrn Oberhofprediger D. Ammon über Seine Prüfung der Harmsischen Sätze* (Berlin: Realbuchhandlung, 1818); SW I.5, 327-407; KGA I/10, 17-92.

1. Ed. note: Christoph Friedrich Ammon, *Bittere Arznei für die Glaubensschwäche der Zeit. Verordnet von Herrn Claus Harms, Archidiaconus an der Nicolaikirche in Kiel, und geprüft von dem Herausgeber des Magazins für christliche Prediger*, Hannover/Leipzig, 1817. This text is included in KGA I.10, 429-443. Claus Harms, *Das sind die 95 theses oder Streitsätze Dr. Luthers, theuren Andenkens. Zum besondern Abdruck besorgt und mit andern 95 Sätzen als mit einer Uebersetzung aus Ao. 1517 in 1817 begleitet*, Kiel, 1817. For a detailed discussion of the theological and personal circumstances that gave rise to Schleiermacher's *An Ammon* see Hans-

Now, if I am to relate everything with the same openness and candor that I have always demonstrated in our small correspondence with each other, I honestly admit that your praise of those *Theses* and your account of the efforts they have produced took me very much by surprise. In general, here, very few of these efforts have come to my attention, even though in our territory for a long time we have been proving ourselves to be neither very careless nor excessively apathetic or indolent on the matter. However, for a few days there was some discussion of these *Theses* on both sides. Since this discussion was calm and moderate in both praise and blame, either there are no Sadducees, outright sinners, or political casuists among us or our people want to be stimulated by means other than those *Theses*. You will also find the same calm and measure, most Reverend Sir, in what an estimable and promising young minister among us said,[2] though unfortunately only about one portion of the *Theses*, and in fact I too would know of nothing better to wish for Mr. Harms than that these *Theses*, which have so many weak points, would soon be forgotten.

I respect Mr. Harms as a man who is well-disposed, clever, truly Christian, and inspired by a noble zeal, and I am gratified that his influence is so extensive. As a minister he will certainly always be blessed, and my only wish is that friends and enemies will leave him in peace to settle down in the position that suits him. Even so, all along I have had occasion to be critical of him in certain matters, for catechisms with ten new commandments and sermons without a biblical text are bound not to please me. I would never make use of the catechisms, and as a ministerial supervisor I would certainly not tolerate having sermons with no biblical text. Hence, when I received notice of these *Theses* I was immediately anxious about how this esteemed man would have extricated himself from this

---

Friedrich Traulsen and Martin Ohst, eds. KGA I/10, XV-XXXVI, and also the former's *Schleiermacher und Claus Harms*, Schleiermacher-Archiv, Vol 7, Berlin-New York: Walter de Gruyter, 1989, especially 117-138.

2. Ed. note: The reference here is to Karl Heinrich Sack's *Für die Vereinigung der lutherischen und der reformierten Kirche. Wider die 21 letzten der 95 Sätze von Claus Harms*, Berlin, 1817.

matter. Even the form, which I know something about from my own past experience, is rather clumsy and risky; and then, in addition, to attach himself with his own *Theses* to Luther[3] and indeed to present them as a version of Luther's theses and offer them to meet the exigencies of our century as though the spirit of Luther should remain totally the same, this seemed to me to be a very bold and almost presumptuous business, and I was curious about what Mr. Harms would indeed bring us that would have the same unity, the same importance for the contemporary church, and from which he could demand and expect the same influence.

When I received them I naturally sought first of all for some well worked out parallel with Luther's *Theses*, but I immediately had to abandon this search, in that it is already stated in the inscription that, unlike Luther's, these *Theses* do not focus on one issue but are directed against all sorts of "deceptive and confused knowledge," expressions that already revealed to me that they have very little in common with Luther's language at its core, since indeed knowing can neither deceive nor confuse. Moreover, you, dearest Sir, further compound the man's sins of this sort by letting him speak of a reason that takes the moon for the sun. In fact, Mr. Harms soon begins to make for himself a pope against whom his *Theses* are to be directed, or rather two for one, reason and conscience. However, neither does he focus on these with their respective claims as firmly as Luther did, nor does he handle them as carefully, and in this way he separates their Tetzels[4] and their Curialists[5] from themselves as Luther did. Yet, patently reason and conscience affect Mr. Harms far more closely than the Pope of Rome affected

---

3. Ed. note: Luther's *95 Theses* were posted on the door of the Castle Church in Wittenberg on 31 October, 1517. The opening sentence of the preface reads: "A disputation of Master Martin Luther, Theologian, for the elucidation of the virtue of Indulgences."

4. Ed. note: The principal abuse which evoked Luther's *Theses* was the sale of indulgences by the Dominican Johann Tetzel to finance the building of St. Peter's in Rome.

5. Ed. note: the term *Curia* refers to the administrative and judicial institutions of the Roman Catholic church that discharge the functions of the papacy. Curialists are office bearers who belong to the *Curia*.

Luther, and it can hardly be said that even with his eyes he has seen such things from them as Luther saw from his Leo.[6]

To put it briefly, with their to-ing and fro-ing about shared and local deficiencies, about things near and far, about matters known and unknown to the author; with their half-truths expressed in oracular sayings, and their riddles that are not worth the trouble to solve, with their motley style with its blending of mannerisms, and with their straining after luster and wit, these *Theses* have made very little impression on me, save for the regret of seeing that here the author, who otherwise has already produced so many fine things, has acted rashly and in error. They did appear to me to be not at all like flashes of lightning, which even if they do not really ignite always have the power to strike and kindle, but like rockets, most of which in part refuse to soar and in part burst too soon, and of which only a few complete their beautiful and orderly course though even these are then but a fleeting outdoor fire. Moreover, these theses had to lose all the more behind Luther's *Theses*, with their profound seriousness, their simple power, and their pious gentleness. Now, however, that you, Most Reverend Sir, should regard all of these ninety-five *Theses* without exception as long-established truths, this was something that took me quite by surprise, partly because some of them are very obviously false, and partly because only recently I was able to recall some items from your *Dogmatics*[7] that were by no means in agreement with these *Theses*.

Allow me, then, to address a few questions to you, indeed not by following any particular order but simply as they occur to me. Do you in fact really think, Most Revered Sir, that by separating the theory of virtue from the doctrine of faith Calixt[8] committed the grave sin of enthroning conscience and that Kant actually elevated it to this status? In your book on *Christian-religious Morals*[9] were you

---

6. Ed. note: Pope Leo X (1475-1521). Elected Pope in 1513 he was responsible for Luther's excommunication in 1520.

7. Ed. note: The reference is to Ammon's *Summa theologiae christianae*, Göttingen, 1803.

8. Ed. Note: Georg Calixtus (Kallissen), 1586-1656, generally regarded as the first Protestant theologian to separate dogmatics and ethics.

9. Ed. note: The reference is to Ammon's *Vollständiges Lehrbuch der christlich-religiösen Moral*, Göttingen, 1806.

still in fact not of the opinion that the very same Kantian formula was not at all different from the claims of Jesus himself, with the consequence that if Kant had enthroned conscience, then, according to your view at that time, Jesus himself did the same? Moreover, if it is so sinful to separate the theory of virtue from the doctrine of faith, have you not done the same thing in that you have written a work on morals that is a book entirely separate from your *Dogmatics*? Then, by again giving us your *Dogmatics* without re-incorporating the work on morals into it have you not acknowledged that there is still some benefit to this?[10] In his well-intentioned zeal Mr. Harms certainly seems to confuse two things, to separate ethics and the doctrine of faith, and to separate conscience from the Word of God. To adopt the language of Mr. Harms, it is only by means of the latter move that conscience is enthroned. Yet, in no respect did Calixt do this, for his theological ethics is very much based upon the Word of God. However, that the doctrine of faith according to the Word of God and the theory of virtue according to the Word of God are separated from each other, and Calixt did no more than this, is something to which you definitely still consent. Why, then, do you permit Mr. Harms to discredit this good man and all his followers, yourself included, and not rather inform him that even he himself sanctions the same thing in his ninth thesis? That is to say, if faith has an Antichrist other than action, then surely it will also be good to oppose each of these Antichrists with one's own stronghold of doctrine.

Furthermore, is then this a long-established truth for you, namely, that the Christian religion must be completely rejected, if it is to be rejected, insofar as it is not in agreement with reason, thus that is to say in no respect in agreement with it? Indeed, you cite only the conclusion of this thesis but in fact you do not contradict it, and this implies that it does belong among the long-established truths. Here, according to Thesis 34, reason is certainly supposed to be the reason that is one's

---

10. Ed. note: This is the stratagem Schleiermacher himself adopted for the 1821-1822 and 1830-1831 editions of *Christian Faith*.

own mental capacity,[11] something that religion neither teaches nor about which it needs to be instructed. However, according to §18 of your *Dogmatics* the best proof of the truths of revealed religion is the conformity of doctrine with the mental and rational nature of human beings. Evidently, this seems to be only the other reason, the collocation of all mental powers that are distinctive to human beings. Yet, this only appears to be the case, for your paragraph nonetheless speaks of proofs and recommends throughout that investigations are to yield the truth. Thus, as a proof that agreement must be one that is known, and among all the mental powers that are distinctive to human beings only the particular mental capacity that we call reason concerns itself with investigations and proofs. Hence, in fact, your whole proof is a matter of reason, or at least you will have to concede to me that reason, as one's own mental capacity, belongs to those powers that are distinctive to human beings, and therefore that if the truths of revealed religion are to be in agreement with all of these powers, with rational nature as a whole, then they may not contradict that particular mental capacity of reason either.

Moreover, at least now, in that I have had to speak so awkwardly about this matter, do you then not sense how deficient is the language that Mr. Harms has selected and developed for such theses? Or is this twofold use of the word "reason" also a long-established truth and is it not the case that the sum total of mental powers that are distinctive to human beings is never called "reason" but only that sum total of powers is called "rational" because by means of the supervention of that one power that is actually called reason all of these powers have become different higher powers so that actually there is no double use of language here? In contrast, in Thesis 38, when "reason," heartily and genially deporting itself,[12] speaks for theses that are meant to be posted alongside Luther's with the intention of defending them, this is certainly an unprecedented use of language, a usage that makes me see stars. The same thing happens to me when in

---

11. *Geistige.* Ed. note: In this context some emphasis is obviously placed on intellectual ability, but Schleiermacher then quickly adverts to the entire collocation of mental powers.

12. *Herzlich und gemütlich.*

Thesis 39 "reason" has its mode of understanding[13] and the heart too has its distinct mode of understanding, and each of the two with what belongs to it is turned toward a different world.[14] Now, it is clear that no one will readily attack such theses, but if they were supposed to be defended then even every genuine Lutheran would have plenty on his hands. Why precisely do you, Honored Sir, give all those who take pleasure in clear thinking about such things, the pain of declaring that these matters now subjected to such wordplay are to be taken as long-established truths, especially now that you see what happens when no fixed order is intended? This observation would have made a splendid epilogue, but it has now come to me prematurely in the middle, for I still have some questions about it.

That is to say, does Thesis 37 also state a long-established truth, for it is indeed stated often enough, that there exists a peculiar desire to preach the new faith from a chair that was once occupied by the old one? Should this perhaps be said over the grave of Luther whose chair had also been occupied by the old faith and who did not descend from it when he gave it up? Would you want to post this thesis in Duke George's capital city?[15] Do you also subscribe to Thesis 50 and expect that it will have a significant influence in ensuring that with the help of the symbolic books no one will be able to distort the firm Word of the bible? Is this a matter that can be attended to in this way if the symbolic books are not, as Thesis 83 also states, "the fixed norm for all interpretation and all dogmatic speculations beyond which no one may venture without separating oneself from the church?" To be sure, this too is clearly long-established fact, as long-established as that upon which I still heartily insist, namely, that any church that affirms this point as a matter of principle is not Evangelical but is of a traditional nature like the Roman church, no matter how many dogmas and practices it may have changed. However,

---

13. *Verstand.* Ed. note: For the most part, "intellect" translates this word here.

14. Ed. note: Schleiermacher is himself engaged in wordplay here, as in some other passages. Here the association of feeling with reason is proleptic to a later argument that a predominance of feeling or intellect is not to be assigned to different churches.

15. Ed. note: Namely, Dresden, the city in which Ammon held office.

I always did believe that on this point you were my partner in faith; yet if you really affirm that, how do you explain all the critical comments on church doctrines in your *Dogmatics*? I ask this, for if the result is not always clearly evident, everyone can surely see that in many instances church doctrines would be quite otherwise posited if your conviction were in complete agreement with the symbolic books. Certainly I am not mistaken, for in §153 of your *Dogmatics* of 1803 it is stated in plain language "that it would be a very fine thing if false teachers were to be held to the terms of their duty by means of an obligation to the symbolic books if only there were always agreement between the various books that are here and there acknowledged to be symbolic and both the genuinely divine Word and the confession of those in our own time who are considered to be wise and pious." To be sure, in §160 in the most recent edition the following is added to these statements: "and if they are purged of obvious mistakes," and a new note quite intentionally has us being engaged with these "obvious mistakes"– discourteous expressions, spurious etymologies, and minor errors of various kinds. However, these are indeed mere additions, and they cannot allay the essential misgiving about agreement with the confession–something that unfortunately is not seldom lacking of those who nowadays are considered to be pious and wise and among whom we indeed count you as well. Then there is the fine conclusion to that note: "Given the such great value of these books, who would choose to be offended by such minor flaws?" Surely this conclusion is not intended to make us believe that these minor details were the only things about the symbolic books to which you and others who in our time are considered wise and pious have to take exception, for if you had reached a different opinion on this point and thought that it was either not a question of agreement between the symbolic books and the confession of the wise and pious of the present day, or that they were of themselves already in agreement with the symbolic books, you would have omitted the main passage. Thus, with regard to this Thesis as well as to the 83rd, to which you likewise seem to give your assent, I cannot conceive how you can take them to be a truth, certainly not a long-established one or even one that is brand new!

Do you also hold it to be a truth, a long-established truth, Most Reverend Sir – taking the following words only in the usual sense – that when a preacher "takes the path from intellect to the heart the words 'our Lord and Redeemer' are like 'friend and servant' in letters?" In what sense? Is such a preacher perhaps the same as those who let their congregations hunger and sorrow in some remote region of false belief? Is everyone whose nature it is to find the surest way to the heart through intellect immediately one of the discredited rationalists? Moreover, are there not also sincere rationalists whom one would treat unjustly if one were to regard their saying "Lord, Lord,"[16] to Christ as merely an empty compliment? Here I am aware of not advancing my own cause, and although I know that opinions about my way of thinking theologically are very divided, though based on various misunderstandings, I am nevertheless aware myself that I do not belong among those who are to be reproached with what Mr. Harms calls "the new faith." However, this wholesale rejection, as superficial as it is harsh, disgusts me, and I do not understand how you, Honored Sir, can extol it and commend it to us so unconditionally. In my view, anyone who wished to post his *Theses* over against Luther's, no matter how much this person might rightly be angered by certain deficiencies in the church, should indeed have been suffused with the feeling, just as Luther, the vehement Luther, had purged himself of all passion before he wrote his *Theses*. This person should have prayed for God's grace in the struggle against perversity and repented of all vain conduct. Then this person would have written something better than epigrams that lose their sting when grasped with the slightest courage; then one would have felt more than one does now that everything was intended simply for the honor of God and informed by Luther's memory!

---

16. Ed. note: Matt. 7:21.

Thus, finally, although I am passing over a number of things, I ask that you permit me to refer briefly, perhaps as occasion offers, to the final Theses, which you praise so especially as the most powerful description of the life of the different western churches which you truly expound with affection, even though with regard to these theses I do not understand how you can be in agreement with Mr. Harms. Right from the start, I do not know whether it is willfulness on Mr. Harms's part in his zeal against the Reformed that he calls the Catholic church "evangelical-Catholic," as if to suggest that as the "Reformed" have respectably borne this name one could just as respectably grant it also to the Roman church, or whether it is a slight negligence on Mr. Harms's part not to have kept in mind what the term "evangelical" intends to say precisely in its contrast to the Roman Catholic church.[17] However, as a leading theologian you should not have committed the double injustice, first, of allowing Mr. Harms to proceed without reprimand when he calls the Roman church Evangelical, and then, of claiming this name for the Lutheran church alone whereby some who are misinformed could be misled into thinking that this is something new that the Reformed church should lay claim to them as well.

Still, let us leave this issue and attend to the matter at hand. As you explain it, the distinction between the character of the Roman and the Protestant churches is to be accounted for by differences in predominant feeling and predominant intellect. This is a matter of long standing, and although I would not exactly care to grant it I indeed wanted to let Mr. Harms proceed with his commitment to this mode of representation. Yet, the way in which he presents this mode of representation, with Word and Sacrament as contrasts, really means that he is making a distinction not between Catholic and Protestant but between Catholic, Lutheran and Reformed, so that it is then the Lutheran church alone that according to the "*medium tenuere beati*"[18] is the bearer of salvation and heaven in itself, and whether the others may also be said to be bearers of their own glory is something

---

17. Ed. note: See especially Schleiermacher's discussion in *Christian Faith*, §§ 23-25.
18. Ed. note: "the blessed hold to the middle way."

that you leave to us to determine more precisely. Thus, the Catholic church is shaped chiefly with reference to the sacrament and less so in accordance with the Word. Does this then mean that it has little of the Word, or that it requires the Word less, or that it operates less by means of the Word? I cannot grant this. Does any Protestant church apart from the English church have such a collection of prescribed prayers and have such commitment to their frequent repetition, whereby they are evidently presented as the principal means of religious formation, as the Roman church does? On the other hand, is it not quite readily satisfied when each Catholic Christian partakes in the one reiterable sacrament once a year? Does it not, then, hold to the Word in a pre-eminent way? Nevertheless, let it be granted that the Roman church does hold less to the Word than to the sacrament, now it is being stated of the Reformed church that it holds much more to the Word and thus less to the sacrament. I cannot agree with this notion either, but having established the nature of the relationship between the two in this way, what now becomes of the Lutheran church? The answer would have to be that it holds equally to both Word and sacrament, but what does this mean? If it as little possesses and makes use of the sacrament as the Reformed, and equally as little of the Word as does the Catholic church, then clearly it is inferior to both. Or does it possess and make use of the Word just as much as does the Reformed church, and yet also just as much of the sacrament as does the Catholic church? This, then, would imply that it actually bears the entire nature of the Catholic church in itself, for the fact that this latter possesses less and makes less use of the Word is merely its limitation. Can you accept and praise this? Or finally, if it is Mr. Harms's intention to stick very closely to the middle way and state that the Lutheran church indeed holds more to the Word than does the Catholic church yet less so than does the Reformed church, then, to be sure, more to the sacrament than does the Reformed church yet less than does the Catholic church, then surely he can demonstrate to us what this holding less to the Word consists in. Does it hold less to developed dogmatics? Is it less committed to preaching and singing? Is it less committed to the instruction of youth through the Word, and if so, does it take pride in this? Or is it less committed to the reading and use of the bible? Moreover, might it not also be just as difficult to demonstrate that it is more committed to the sacrament than is the Reformed church, for the Lutheran church's possessing more external practices is what Mr. Harms calls "sacrament"? Or, if we are to have a thorough understanding of the matter, are the sacraments celebrated with more devotion and ceremony in the Lutheran church than in the Reformed church, and do they prove to be more moving and more effective in the Lutheran than in the Reformed church? Indeed, Honored Sir, you come to the aid of these *Theses* of Mr. Harms, which you designate as particularly excellent, with the help of a brief explanation. However, allow me to say a few further words as to whether the explanation turns things around instead of clarifying them and as to whether it is in and of itself correct, quite apart from Mr. Harms.

You declare the notion of being committed to and being formed by the Word to be due to the predominance of intellect, hence you state that the Reformed church lives and operates within a Christianity of intellect. Is this the opinion of Mr. Harms? Certainly not, for otherwise he could in no sense call it glorious but would have to condemn it as unchristian. This is so, for if the Word is conveyed to the heart only through intellect − and does it in fact have any effect if it is not conveyed to the heart? − then according to his 46th Thesis the Redeemer can no longer be acknowledged. Further, you associate external action with the sacrament, and in this way you explain this being committed chiefly to the sacrament as the Christianity of perception,[19] which lays hold not of intellect but of feeling and imagination in such a way that the mind is eased and the heart improved. Yet, according to Mr. Harms's view of the matter the effect of the sacrament in its distinction from the effect of the Word is not explained in this way. The reason is that if the Word is in no respect whatever conveyed through intellect, then it must also take hold of feeling and imagination, otherwise I do not

---

19. *Anschauung.*

see how it can find access. Hence, by means of its being committed chiefly to the Word and formed by the Word, this taking hold of feeling and imagination must also be at the disposal of the Reformed church. Thus, Mr. Harms cannot be satisfied with your explanation, for it misses the point of his distinction, and I would really like to know how he thanked you for it. However, is your explanation in itself right?

First, the criticism that Mr. Sack[20] has already leveled at Mr. Harm's view to the effect that it is un-Protestant is also to be found in your explanation when you state that the Lutheran church is placed at as great a distance from both the Reformed and the Catholic church. This point is also implicit in your explanation, in that without making any distinction you state that internally the wiser and the better of all three confessions are even now already equally united in spirit. Is this really true? Is there for you no more intimate circle of religious thinking and sensibility in which you can ally yourself with the Reformed but not with the Catholic, or rather with the latter only in a wider circle? If you experience your relationship to the Redeemer, most profoundly as this is expressed in our doctrine of justification[21] by faith, then is there not a sense in which you can extend your hand to the Reformed as those who are like-minded yet not extend it to the Catholics, not even to the wiser and better among them? If so, there would have to be wiser and better Catholics who must also complain that the declared doctrines imposed by their church are not in agreement with their own confession. Yet here, where the matter at issue is the churches, this cannot be what you mean.

Accordingly, do you really want to deny me that and insist that when it comes to religion, in your wisest and best moments the Catholic stands just as close to you as does the Reformed? Moreover, with your appeal to this point also in connection with church union, do you suppose that any union of the Lutherans with the Catholics would be subject to the same condition as would their union

---

20. Ed. note: See footnote 2 above.
21. *Gerechtigkeit.* Ed. note: This famous term is ordinarily translated "righteousness" in accordance with biblical usage. See sermons in the companion volume to this one, namely, *Reformed but ever Reforming,* trans. Iain Nicol, (Lewiston, NY: Edwin Mellen Press, 1997).

with the Reformed? If they were to provide perfect congregations and perfect teachers, the matter would be resolved, on the one side as on the other. Yet, does it not follow from this realization, my dear friend, that none of the three churches has any distinctive perfections that give the one any advantage over the others, but instead each simply has its particular imperfections, which it need only set aside so that they can immediately be ready for union? This is how it seems to me, but this does not appear to be your opinion, for according to your explanation the Lutheran church does have some distinctive perfections and the Catholic church too – at least you do not depict for us any imperfections that belong to it – so that only the Reformed church seems to have to acquiesce to its own distinctive imperfections! However, let us see how matters stand with regard to those perfections! I shall not review everything, only the main points.

"The Lutheran church ... conjoins faith and love by means of the intimate connection between Word and sacrament." I certainly do not wish to deny you this; however, my only question is whether it has this conjoining by virtue of its distinction from the Reformed church? I take this question with the utmost seriousness, Honored Sir. For me, and certainly for many, it is a matter of conscience, for precisely among those of us who pursue the union of the two churches I for my part certainly know that I shall always be committed to the Reformed school of theology. However, if you can demonstrate to me that in this school as such there exists a principle such that it prevents or denies the most intimate connection between Word and sacrament, I, at least, shall immediately withdraw from this school and wean myself from everything whereby I adhered to it. Then I would do so also because of the union, toward which until now I have cooperated quite unrestrainedly and from the purest intentions. However, if there does exist a separation of faith and love in the Reformed church and if this is integral to its spirit – no matter how many individuals may assume themselves to be above it, all because they do not carry the spirit of their church within themselves–then indeed we would have to take the utmost care not to infuse our

Lutheran brothers with this separation. Moreover, if the reason for this evil could not be detected yet the evil itself would have to be conceded, then at least the union would not have to take place, leaving the Reformed church on its own in this unfortunate separation. There is no need for this, however. The points that distinguish the Reformed church from the Lutheran church are so easy to see that the reason for this evil will certainly not elude our joint efforts. Accordingly, just point out what the evil is, demonstrate to us in our words or works or both that if among us faith and love are not entirely separated, they are less intimately connected with each other than in your church, so that we of the Reformed position may first take care of this before our union takes place! You must know what it is, and in my name as well as in that of many of your partners in faith and mine I demand of you the proof.

Until you provide it, let me be comforted by the other statement in which you ascribe excellence to your church, namely, "that in the imperfect church militant on this earth it is always either feeling or intellect that is predominant." Thus, if I, being Reformed and therefore determined for predominance of intellect, unite in the most intimate way with a Lutheran Christian, to be sure then I will fail to discover in that person the absolute union of intellect and feeling that is supposed to correspond to Mr. Harms's commensurateness of Word and sacrament, for according to your last statements this is nowhere to be found. Rather, it is the case either that intellect is predominant in this person too, and if so we shall then find mutual consolation, or that feeling is predominant in this person, and then we shall come to each other's assistance. But how? According to your earlier statement, if feeling is dominant in a person then that person belongs to the Catholic church, and if it is by intellect then to the Reformed church. Thus, according to these final statements, what, then, is the status of the most glorious Lutheran church? In effect it would be nothing at all. Rather, in it some Catholic and some Reformed, and it would exist in a condition of oscillation between the two, and precisely in this oscillation would lie its excellence. If this should be your opinion clearly you must to some extent qualify the earlier passage; but if you do this, you will then also be unable to give assent to Mr. Harms's last Thesis, which declares that everything in the Lutheran church develops from within itself. Instead, one rather would have to believe that everything will gradually develop out of it and that those within it who are disposed toward Catholicism on account of a predominance of feeling will also become more and more truly Catholic. Moreover, in support, you could cite the experience that actually almost all Protestants who have gone over to the Catholic church have come from the Lutheran church: for example, Stollberg, Schlegel, Müller, Schlosser and Werner.[22] From among the Reformed no one immediately comes to mind, and it would also be expected that Lutherans with a disposition toward being Reformed on account of a predominance of intellect would really be Reformed in any case.

Still, once more I cannot really believe that this is your opinion. Just as for myself I am then poles apart from your opinion but can in no respect solve the puzzle wherein – according to your view that if everywhere in the Christian church either feeling or intellect is predominant and that the character of the Reformed church consists in the predominance of intellect while that of the Catholic church consists in the predominance of feeling – wherein, then, according to your opinion, the distinctive character and excellence of the Lutheran church is supposed to consist. Instead, I await the solution from you alone. As I have stated, I do not at all think of the matter in this way. For me, the Catholic church stands on one side and the Protestant church on the other, and the difference between the two Protestant confessions seems to me to be trifling in comparison with that difference.[23] In passing I would also note that I take it to be contrary to prevailing practice and contrary to a proper relationship here to talk about the Catholic confession alongside the two Protestant ones, for the Catholic church has offered

---

22. Ed. note: Most notably, Friedrich Schlegel, (1772-1829), most prominent and influential figure in the Berlin "romantic circle." Schleiermacher was to develop a firm friendship with Schlegel during part of the "romantic" phase of his career. Schlegel converted to Roman Catholicism in 1808.

23. Ed. note: See e.g., *Christian Faith*, §§ 23-24.

no "confession" to anyone, and we cannot attribute one to it. This expression is fitting for the protesting churches instead.

Now, I also think that it is because of this disparity that the two Protestant confessions conduct themselves toward each other quite differently from the way you present them and that it would be much easier for them to unite with each other than for one of them to unite with the Catholic church. Moreover, in this respect I think I have Luther on my side. Or do you think that if in accordance with Luther's wish Catholic theologians had also come to Marburg he would just as easily have allied himself with them on fourteen such principal points and continued to dispute only the fifteenth?[24] On the other hand, to you this situation appears to be quite different on account of the great imperfections of the Reformed church to which you repeatedly refer, for you have almost nothing good to say about it. If it is firmly committed to self-contained concepts and to a geometrical conciseness of argument, then–apart from the reference to geometry, which for one thing is not at all appropriate for such matters and concerning which I also would not know of its having crept particularly into Reformed theology in the period of mathematical philosophizing – that is a great honor, one that I do not at all dare immediately to apply exclusively to the Reformed church but that I gladly put up with from such an expert when the domain of scientific theology is at issue. Although in that context you too hardly consider it an honor, in that your *Dogmatics* favors a more skeptical analysis of concepts rather than demonstrating their firm closing. Yet here, my dearest friend, it is by no means a question of scientific theology but, as the entire context demonstrates, one of the immediate activity that brings illumination to the mind and improvement to the heart. Moreover, this being the case, there the notion of hardened concepts and

---

24. Ed. note: The reference is to the Marburg Colloquy of 1529, a conference involving Luther, Zwingli, and other Reformation leaders designed to develop doctrinal consensus among various Protestant parties. On the fifteenth article (on the nature of Christ's presence in the Lord's Supper), Luther and Zwingli disagreed vehemently. Their failure to reach agreement on this matter was to have seriously negative consequences for relations between the Reformed and Lutheran churches for centuries to come.

geometrical arguments should indeed arouse more fear and abhorrence than praise and admiration. I do not think, however, that you will find more demonstrative sermons or sermons that protest against everything that cannot be demonstrated or popular textbooks in the Reformed church than in the Lutheran church.

You then say that "the Reformed church scorns" (to scorn is in itself always an expression of rebuke) "any element in worship that is to give rise to contemplation."[25] Indeed, hardly the correct expression, for that response can be wholly internal. Moreover, the Reformed church does not scorn such practices out of some distinctive repugnance toward them. Rather, it uprooted them in its original zeal particularly because in all modesty it had no confidence in itself but in the interest of surety instead wanted to uproot everything to which superstition and false piety had attached themselves. Therefore, even since that time, especially in those areas in which it is not closely surrounded by Catholics and has nothing to fear from their influence, it has again adopted certain elements of this kind such as the organ and church music. Indeed, according to Zwingli's own teaching, then also it could again accept images, because under such changed circumstances even the mere appearance of their being venerated can no longer arise.

Then you also impute scorn for "the lively movement of imagination and feeling" to the Reformed church. How was it, Most Honored Sir, that when you wrote this the name of Lavater[26] did not occur to you, a man who is decried more than anyone because of his religion of the imagination, and did the thought even occur to you that he acted against the spirit of his church? Did you not think of Menken and Ewald and Krummacher?[27] You will say that these are exceptions. Yes indeed, they are the most distinguished and renowned exceptions, but

---

25. *Das Beschauliche des Cultus*. Ed. note: The word refers to the direct and prominent effect of what is beheld on the senses. Thus, it can sometimes be translated "contemplation."

26. Ed. note: Johann Caspar Lavater (1741-1801), Swiss Calvinist pastor, theologian, philosopher and poet.

27. Ed. note: Ed. note: Gottfried Menken (1768-1831), Evangelical theologian, from 1802 pastor in Bremen. Heinrich Georg August Ewald (1803-1875), one of the most notable Orientalists of the 19th century. Friedrich Adolf Krummacher (1767-1845), Reformed theologian and pastor.

nonetheless enough people of a similar kind are attached to them, and for the modest size of the Reformed church that number is certainly not trifling. Did you not think of the entire French Reformed church, which distinguishes itself in its endeavors to apprehend imagination and feeling through speech? Indeed, since you praise Calvin's *Institutes*, I confess to you that it is an invaluable book for me also, because even in dealing with the most complex material Calvin never neglects to make reference to the religious sentiments associated with it.

Further, as for the "rigidity and stringency that, if the Reformed church were ever to rule, it would be a severe impediment to genuine tolerance and gentleness." What do you mean by this? Since, with us in the German lands no ecclesiastical power extends beyond the territorial boundaries, the rule of the Reformed church is indeed not merely a matter of a possibility that had not yet come to pass, rather this church actually still prevails in four Reformed cantons of Switzerland and it has also prevailed for a long time in Holland. When you consider how the Arminian controversies[28] were conducted, and in spite of the different outcomes compare them with the crypto-Calvinists and others in the Lutheran church, then you will indeed not be able to say that the former demonstrated a lesser capacity for toleration and gentleness. This is so, for the fact that it was preferable that the Arminians should be permitted to form a distinct sect is not something that you can consider intolerant or harsh. Still, why should we not proceed to a yet higher level and compare how right at the very beginning both parties conducted themselves toward each other with regard to the matter of toleration and gentleness. On page 20 you quote a statement from Luther, one that you should rather not have cited.[29] One should just as little rouse the passionate words of great men as the slumbering lion; every time they awaken the effect can only be destructive. Moreover, this statement is one that you could have allowed to sleep the more peacefully, since

---

28. Ed. note: The reference is to the Dutch theologian Jacobus Arminius (1560-1609), and the Remonstrants who accepted his revision of the Reformed doctrines of predestination and grace. The teachings of Arminius and of the Remonstrant Articles (1610) were firmly rejected by the Synod of Dort (1618-19).

29. Ed. note: See KGA I/10, 438, 9-15 for Ammon's quotation of Luther.

84

two years later in Marburg Luther was indeed more charitable toward the Reformed. However, now that you have quoted it I want to supply you with a statement from Zwingli that deals with the same matter and with which it can be compared: "We do not readily depart from great men, especially those who flourish at the present time and who are so blessed in their writing that they seem to have given the world a different form. Only one thing I request and that is that what we shall impart here will be viewed according to the rule whereby we always weigh their writings. Accordingly, it is solely on this basis of reading the writings of others that we see the disposition from which an author seems to have written, for in the discourse itself every intention comes to light. Hence, wherever we see anything written from love toward God and our neighbor, there we close our eyes to some things."[30] These indeed are the purest principles of genuine tolerance and gentleness. The same things are in fact demonstrated in the way in which the Swiss theologians in Marburg offered and sought a relation of brethren in that after they had discussed the main points they were able to regard the Lutheran view not as an error, for the sake of which the ecclesial communion could have reservations, but only, as they expressed it, as a "weakness." You will also find the same tolerance and gentleness in the Swiss confession,[31] by means of which the former group had hoped, though in vain, that what was left unfinished in Marburg would be completed.

Where, then, is all this one-sidedness and imperfection that you ascribe to the Reformed church to be found, and how can you maintain the position that you have advanced that the one is the Christianity of the intellect and the other the Christianity of the heart?[32] Of course, Mr. Harms goes much farther still, for when he explicitly states in the 87th Thesis that the Reformed church too depends on the bible according to its own received interpretation just as well as does the Lutheran

30. Ed. note: Schleiermacher's own footnote here refers to Zwingli's *De vera et falsa religione commentarius*, p. 195, Zürich, 1525.
31. Ed. note: The reference is to the First Helvetic Confession of 1536.
32. *Verstand/Gemüth*. Ed. note: In Schleiermacher's own usage *Gemüth* refers to mind and heart together, to the psyche, not to "the heart" alone.

church, in the 82nd Thesis he nevertheless expresses the opinion that reason has prevented the Reformed from extending their church and that the union of the Reformed church with the Lutheran church would involve a reception of reason into the Lutheran church, then indeed according to Theses 87, 88 and 89, it even appears as though this would involve the adoption of the religion of reason, that is to say, of religion stripped of reason or of religion. Surely this would be the most terrible of situations! This is so, for if the Lutheran church, not having admitted reason into itself until then, were now to admit a religion stripped of reason, what a complexity of unreasonableness would arise from this! Or, if the Lutheran church, not having admitted reason into itself until then, were also to admit a religion stripped of religion, what a total vacuum for reason and religion would arise from that! You will surely grant to me that Mr. Harms has no control over the language that is appropriate to theses, and that the truth that he intends has been seriously harmed on account of the oblique way in which he expresses it.

As concerns the perspective on the Reformed church that Mr. Harms has expressed here, I readily take a lenient view. His zeal has overtaken him. Moreover, he is already in a difficult position over against those who are indifferent and those who are not Christian. Hence, I can find it quite natural that he readily keeps anything new at arm's length when he does not rightly know whether it would be regarded as hostile or friendly. Moreover, in the same way as he once opposes the Altona Bible,[33] it can easily happen to him that when anything seems to him to be sinister, he sees it as analogous to this bible. He lives in a territory that is entirely Lutheran and in which he has no immediate relationships with the Reformed. Hence, I can also easily forgive that he knows the Reformed church only from hearsay and that it is on account of this that he has gained an erroneous notion of it.

However, as for you, one of the foremost among the learned theologians of our Fatherland, I cannot let you off so easily. You have obviously not repeated this

---

33. Ed. note: A version of Luther's translation of the Bible published in Altona in 1815.

view after him, but when you confess yourself wholesale to Mr. Harms's *Theses* as though to long-established truths, you should indeed have honored the truth and should have told Mr. Harms that in this matter he is mistaken, that Reformed Protestantism is just as little a religion of reason as is the Protestantism of the Lutherans. You should have told him too, that if Luther could not switch to the opinion of the Swiss with regard to the doctrine of Holy Communion, because for him the text was too powerful, it was for this very same reason, that the text was too powerful – and less because of its consequences and severity – that Calvin could not choose to abandon his more rigorous view of the doctrine of election. On the basis of your superior knowledge you should have informed him that the Reformed church is certainly as well-formed as is the Lutheran church, and according to his sense of things almost better so, because comparatively speaking, in several regions the final decision in matters affecting the clergy is not left to a person who is not a minister, and in relatively more places Reformed souls actually choose their pastors. You should have told him that it would have been better if he had rather not brought up the point about the religion of reason, in that on a rough calculation the result would show that so-called rationalism has haunted the Lutheran church far more intensely and more audibly than it has the Reformed church. Or would you not also agree that this is so?

Now, after I had discovered all these surprises and taken them into account, you will find it natural that I should have sought some reason for them and that I asked myself and others how it could have come about that you could have approved of so many things about which you must be differently and better informed and that are also in conflict with the convictions that you have put forward in public. This puzzle was certainly not easy to solve. However, if I am to continue with the same candor that I have shown till now, I should not conceal from you the fact that some people surmised that it was on account of Mr. Harms that a new light had dawned on you and that in joyful gratitude for this you were also struck by the youthful urge to commend things that could not appropriately be commended. Naturally, I was unwilling to submit to this view, and I replied that although you could have been taken unawares in this way this was not in the least so, that overall you had already reflected too long upon Christianity and the Christian church from every perspective, and that you were too harmonious in your influence upon it from the pulpit, the podium, and the writing desk to have been so easily converted to such contrary views, rather, whatever it was about the *Theses* that could be true for you must surely have been stated in your writings already a long time ago, even if in a different form, and therefore could not have made such a strong impression on you that you were now so dazzled by that new light as likewise to take what is wrong in the *Theses* to be true.

Yet, even with this commentary I did not prevail, rather, the response of those people to me was as follows: There are some things in your writings that seem to contradict precisely the main points in our *Theses,* and since you had so much to say in praise of these main points, some change that necessarily altered your convictions must have taken place very recently. Hence, it could indeed well be the case (as they pursued their images further) that it was in Harms's mirror that you first saw reflected how you had been shaped until now and that from the silent cloud some coarse hail also fell on the bare skin around your neck and shoulders. For just look, they said to me, the examiner would surely also have to share in the displeasure expressed in the 24th Thesis over the devil's having recently been killed and hell closed over, but in §72 of Mr. Ammon's recent *Dogmatics,* though only in the form of a note but one that in this book indeed cannot be ignored, the devil is deemed to be a matter of poetry, and in §73 Mr. Ammon is raised above all doubt in the view that moral evil must be derived from natural causes, whereas in §71 it is only the familiar third person plural that discusses the doctrine of the devil. Thus, at that time Mr. Ammon, they surmised, himself must have put the devil to death, at least to some small extent, and with good intentions simply preserved the remains in alcohol.[34] Yet now, they said, the situation is different, for no one has demonstrated to him more forcefully than Mr. Harms that he has rendered himself an accessory to murder. The same is the case with regard to hell. In §§177 and 178 it is indeed not exactly closed over, but in fact it has a convenient back door through which one can re-exit, and as far as Mr. Harms is concerned this comes to pretty much the same thing. Therefore, they concluded, this is also why even Mr. Ammon felt himself affected and so withdrew into himself.

They went on to take note of the 18th and 21st Theses, which state that if the concept of divine punishments completely vanishes, God is no longer even the court usher of conscience, and that it is much worse to help oneself to the forgiveness of sins than to allow them to cost money. This too, they indicated, could have affected Mr. Ammon rather deeply, for consider the following. If according to §§ 124 and 125 of the new Summa the notion of the forgiveness of sins is merely an image, though one not devoid of content, and if the outward consequences of sin of themselves lose the form of punishment when the inward condition of the heart and mind is improved, if guilt is gradually effaced through growth in virtue, if, according to Thesis 125, the active obedience of Christ is effective only as a glorious example and guilt is gradually taken away only through faith in the dying Redeemer's innocence and holiness – such faith being understood simply as a splendid means to improvement – and, finally, if the representative action of Christ places even before cruder eyes the Redeemer's tenderness, then one can just as well help oneself to the forgiveness of sins and Mr. Harms scarcely can have had anything else than such a theory in mind. However, they added, no one has yet put it to Mr. Ammon in this way, and what formerly could not be set right for him by all the orthodox systematic theologians whom Mr. Ammon has thoroughly studied has now been straightened out by Harms with his few thorny

---

34. Ed. note: Compare Schleiermacher's own critical treatment of belief about the devil and hell in *Christian Faith*, §§45, 72, 75-78, and 119-120. See also his 1830 sermon on the theme "That we have Nothing to Teach Regarding the Wrath of God," in *Reformed but ever Reforming*, tr. by Iain Nicol (1997), 141-154.

words. The long-established truths could strike him in his heart and mind only with a new "flash of lightning."

It is the same, they said, with Thesis 45. Here it is declared a Mohammedan position that God is denied a son because he has no wife, a point about which Mr. Ammon certainly had some pangs of conscience at first for in the *Dogmatics* he frequently mentions Mohammed with great respect. Later, however, it must especially have struck him that there was an analogy here between this point and the fact that at the beginning of his treatment of the doctrine of the divinity of Christ it is noted that certain authors spoke of God's son and daughter, also the fact that he could not refrain from including Plato's jest: "and in no respect whatever did the man appear to me to be a god, but certainly did appear to be divine,"[35] which in the first edition was quoted in his conclusion to the entire doctrine of the Trinity as a means of defense against scholastic sophistry, even in the new edition, albeit not as his opinion but nonetheless quite intentionally.

Likewise the 74th Thesis, that many thousands were no better than the disciples of John and could say that they had never heard that there is a Holy Spirit, must have made Mr. Ammon anxious for his pupils and readers, they pointed out, for he has not told them much that is reassuring on the matter. Although the old edition of his *Dogmatics* does not intend to deny that the Holy Spirit is God by nature, it is unable to discover the grounds for its individual existence or to distinguish the Spirit of holiness from that of the divine omnipotence. Moreover, where it becomes a matter of exhibiting the Holy Spirit in the work of sanctification, according to §123 the "*doctores ecclesiae*" evidently teach that the effective cause of sanctification is the Holy Spirit alone. However, since every human capacity is dependent upon the hint of divinity, in no respect does this call into question the critical remarks in §§ 126 and 127 to the effect that the origin and development of human virtue must also be attributed to the gracious

---

35. Ed. note: Plato, *Sophist*, 216. "He is not a god at all, but divine he certainly is, for this is the title I should give to all philosophers." B. Jowett translation, reprinted in *Great Books of the Western World*, Vol. 7, 1952, p. 551.

will of the deity. Yet this, they said, is something that occurs in a mediated and external way, by means of instruction, example, and a variety of life-situations, a view that is not much different from that of the Altona Bible. However, all kinds of objections against anything immediate are raised and answered in such a way that reason and conscience themselves may still be said to be the power and voice of the deity and thus the theologian too may continue to maintain that the sanctified condition of our hearts and minds is a work of God. Hence, at this point the Holy Spirit gets hidden away again, any distinctive activity of the Holy Spirit is wanting altogether, and it is impossible to ascertain whether one exists or not.

The new *Summa* certainly presents the church's doctrine of the third person in greater detail, and in the whole locus on the Triune God it refrains from the captious titles of *epicrisis* and *observationes criticae*.[36] Yet, there too in §58 it is still considered probable that the sacred writers accepted a distinction between body and soul in God, and the *Summa* concludes that its intention in not having readily sought any wisdom above and beyond revelation was so that it could very gently lead us back from the Holy Spirit to that probably original notion of the soul of God.

Now, my discussants indicated that §§132-134 on sanctification teach exactly the same thing, namely, that the person gifted with reason also has the capacity of will to choose and to desire divine gifts that are pleasing to God. These paragraphs are also content at least to bring out this point, that our intellect and heart are also dependent on the deity, hence they too must be sanctified for it. Further, as my discussants go on to say, should we perhaps want to search out the special activity of the Holy Spirit in the creation of holy scripture, then indeed in its presentation of the church's doctrine of the divine Word in §137 the new *Summa* also calls the sacred writers *theopneustous*[37] and declares the external Word to be a great gift of

---

36. Ed. note: "critical summary," "critical observations."
37. Ed. note: See II Tim. 3:16 where "all scripture" is referred to as "inspired" (*theopneustous*), lit. "God-breathed."

God. However, it was already noted prior to this in the *consectariis criticis*[38] in §11, where the few adherents to *theopneustie* are dismissed, that the concept of inspiration could not be brought to bear upon the human soul without posing the greatest moral risk, and in §12 sufficient reassurance was found in the fact that with the purest trust the sacred writers had attributed their sacred meditations to the will and authority of the deity in faith assured of the deity's consent. All of this then fairly well agrees with what is presented in a note to §12 in the German version of the *Glaubenslehre*[39] namely, that these holy men had themselves sought the essence of revelation in free reflection and that rational and even self-discovered ideas and teachings are from God and in conformity with God's will. In this manner, the Holy Spirit disappears again even here. Thus, at this point it must surely have struck Mr. Ammon that he had still brought his hearers no further than the point at which the needy disciples of John also stood, and suddenly he felt it was high time for him to commit himself in greater earnest to the symbolic books and to adopt their concerns so that the firm Word of the bible could not be distorted.

Yes, my informants continued, Thesis 10 against conscience and Thesis 34 against reason also had to strike him deeply, a man who, as was noted already, declared that reason and conscience are independent voices of God and who at §138 indeed states that reason and conscience actually read the divine rule within themselves. Does this not mean, moreover, that they write it down and that reason has need of the external Word only because apart from experience it is still bare and hence can easily be led astray? Thus, the more it clothes itself with experience the less will it be in need of the external Word and so will be capable of being all things in all.[40] Furthermore, as for the wickedness and unbelief that must arise from this situation, no one has urged this view on Mr. Ammon to such an extent as have Mr. Harms's *Theses*, they thought. This is why he now tacitly distributes the

---

38. Ed. note: "critical consequences."
39. Ed. note: The reference is to Ammon's *Inbegriff der evangelischen Glaubenslehre*, Göttingen, 1805.
40. Ed. note: The allusion is probably to Eph. 1:23.

judgment of condemnation on every assumption of reason into religion. This is why he now especially rejects parallels from what is heathen, parallels that seem to be as comparable to the biblical sayings as one egg is to another and that are so abundantly scattered about in his *Dogmatics*. This is why he condemns the historical exegesis that indeed so apparently dominates the *Dogmatics*, not only in the arrangement of biblical doctrine but also in the *epicrises*, and he condemns it with expressions that are more likely to be found in Jean Paul,[41] since they are not located in Harms's *Theses*.

This part of the discussion perhaps would have continued for a long time in this way, using similar demonstrations that you had only recently changed your entire view and that it was Mr. Harms who had been the cause of this. However, since these good friends jumped back from the 74th Thesis to the 10th, thus leading me to suspect that this would involve a whole new series, I interrupted them and affirmed that no matter how many such arguments they brought forward they would never convince me that you had changed your whole theological opinion only because Mr. Harms had prevailed over you.

My reason was that even if I were to grant that in that you unconditionally approved of Mr. Harms's *Theses* with all their truths and half-truths, apart from a few details that in this respect were not worth discussing, you in fact would have to condemn a great deal in the Latin and German versions of your *Dogmatics* and *Morals* and indeed even in your *Biblical Theology*[42] if we wanted to examine it as well. So, either you had not noticed this, because your attention had chiefly been directed toward something else, or your change of mind could not be so recent but would have occurred earlier and would have to have been submitted somewhere to people of learning or to the greater public, and perhaps we would have to look more to your publications in German and to your most recent sermons in order to find the first expression of this important change. This would be advisable, for if

---

41. Ed. note: Jean Paul, pseudonym of Johann Paul Friedrich Richter (1763-1825), Romantic novelist, philosopher.

42. Ed. note: The reference is to Ammon's two-volume *Entwurf einer reinen biblischen Theologie*, Erlangen, 1792, and to his three volume *Biblische Theologie*, Erlangen, 1801-1802.

you had really converted to a theological position based on that of Mr. Harms, then the only respectable thing for such a man to do is candidly to acknowledge this, to refute his earlier opinion himself, and formally to disavow each work written on the basis of that earlier opinion, except to the extent that as historical documents they always retain a but greater value. Any man who may be just a small light in the church could in the stillness indeed revert from one system to another, but a man of such a reputation as yours must in no respect do such a thing. Thus, anyone who maintained that it is not simply because of your failure to sift the more dogmatic element from the more ecclesiastical more precisely that you seemed to accept much that is in contradiction with your earlier remarks should at least not expect me to believe that it was with the *Examination* of the *Theses* that you first came forward with this opinion; rather, in plain clear language this person must identify the transition for me somewhere else in your writings.

Then, however, others began to speak, because they saw that I was vacillating, and, thinking themselves to be more confident of what concerned them, they replied: It is obvious, as even a child can see, that in the *Examination* of the *Theses* you did not want to have been regarded for the first time as a supernaturalist or as strictly orthodox but took it as a known fact. The whole tone in this document is evidently not that of a man who has himself been struck by hail and who is still in pain because of the spots it has hit. It is rather that of someone who already has previously taken shelter at the right time and who now has no sympathy with those imprudent and careless people who, paying no attention to differences in the seasons, still go about in thin clothing and to their greatest misfortune defy the hail-laden cloud.

Indeed, they did speak of the conversion of rationalists in the Lutheran church – in comparison with whom the poor Zwinglians and Calvinists are after all still the true heroes of the faith – as an enterprise in which it was known that you had worked most diligently with the entire range of Evangelical teachers. In no respect did you present it as a new opinion that the *theios aner* [43] at which the old *Summa* feared it had to lead, is not sufficient, that one could take Jesus to be a divine human being and could be a Mohammedan as well, and therefore, like Mohammed himself, there also remain forever deprived of any participation in the benefits of the Gospels on account of one's unbelief in the Son of God, and indeed very rightly so. Rather, this matter was brought forward quite incidentally, as though it had already stood just as pointedly and firmly in your textbooks for a long time. Thus, in this matter these people were evidently mistaken that it was because of Mr. Harms that you had only now made the transition to these views. It was only I who was more than strange in that I had taken the matter so earnestly and strictly and had demanded a public disavowal from you.

These discussants then asked: Could one not just as easily advance the opposite maxim? When he who is a small light in the church changes his theological views he indeed is in the fortunate position of being immediately able to make his exit with the truth, and of course this is more convenient by far. It cannot be disputed that it is indeed much easier for such a person to remove one's own textbooks and either to compose a new one or to commit oneself to some unfamiliar one than to revise them so artfully and to change course so gradually in all one's publications that no one can correctly observe what has happened or that one person could think that something has happened and the other that nothing has happened. However, a man in your situation is surely obliged to adopt such a procedure at some point; placed in a position like yours, in the controversy between rationalists and supernaturalists now when all the evidence indicates a strong tendency to return to the stricter theories of revelation, in these circumstances what would be more desirable and more urgent than placing oneself between the two parties in such a way that it may seem that one can belong to both, to the one party by virtue of things that are long-established and are not

---

43. Ed. note: "divine man."

effaced and to the other party by virtue of views that are artfully interpolated in other places.

It is well-known to us, they went on, that you have a different way of going about things, if not to settle the controversy between the rationalists and the supernaturalists then at least to show that it does not exist for you. Now, this is simply your way, however, and about you my interlocutors say that you always want to have something peculiarly your own but that in the end you will nevertheless achieve nothing in this way other than to render yourself disreputable to both parties. Yet, the whole aim of Ammon's style, they said, is to make both parties right and at the same time so to confuse their controversy that they have to ask themselves whether they themselves rightly know what they want. Moreover, as long as no arrogant and unrefined person intervenes – something indeed that in these mellow days and against such a man can in no way be expected – then this way of going about things is infallible.

Hence, they continued, since you are indeed somewhat artless in such matters, if we are to expose this whole feat for you, then just look up the Foreword to the new *Summa*. Here, on the one hand, you find a rejection of reason in relation to Scripture, because as such it is unable exhaustively to set forth the content of divine truth in general concepts, and thus, you think you have a theory according to which revelation has a distinctive content. However, in that at the end the author then states that he has remained entirely faithful to his old principles and in this way directs you to the Foreword to the first edition, what you then read is as follows: "What is positive is related to general concepts only as the individual and particular are, it includes in part only clarifications with the help of examples and factual claims, and in part communications conveyed through the intervention of wise people to those who have not yet discovered it through the guidance of reason and of the nature of things." Accordingly, it would be a splendid thing indeed if the supernaturalist and the rationalist, taken together, could both interpret this matter in common, though in the process finding some ways of speaking that are especially suitable to each one. Of course, either one can do the interpreting in such a way as to counter the other, but the author's reputation and his friends will already see to it that this will not happen.

Reading further in the new Foreword, my discussants pointed out, you will discover that the edition is enlarged only with some notes on history and earlier theology and by a few paragraphs that still seemed to require the proper ordering and sequence of doctrine. Now, as far as the notes are concerned, at the note on the symbolic books you yourself have already made a little test of what sort of effects can be attempted if this course is taken. In contrast, as far as the paragraphs are concerned, put to the test the first two that have recently been added, namely §§27 and 28. There, inserted between the paragraphs on the rule of faith and on the mysteries you will find a discussion about irrational and rational super-naturalism. Now, the natural sequence and ordering of doctrine would surely have required that this material would have been inserted within the doctrine of revelation, but then in that context could have remained the same as it has already been stated that everything stayed as it was, namely, that the doctrines of the biblical authors are based on their own meditations.[44]

So what is it, then, that is asserted in this discussion? Irrational supernaturalism is rejected. This is something for the rationalists, but in what does it consist? In this: "that nothing in Christian theology is accepted as true that is not found in Scripture in just as many words." Accordingly, we are all at once introduced to a point of contention that is quite alien to this present time, and even our supernaturalists are content to put up with the idea that this irrationalism, in which in and of itself there is nothing supernatural at all, is being rejected. Then in the following sentence the rationalism that consists in the notion that the entire content of Scripture is reduced to its conformity with the nature of things and with the highest findings of reason is for its part also rejected, because reason is to take its knowledge of God only from Godself. In contrast to this position, moreover,

---

44. *Meditationen.*

formally and explicitly accepted, rational supernaturalism maintains "that indeed God's revelation through Christ does not in the least contradict sound reason, but on account of the immense extent of God's truth revelation by far surpasses it."

This certainly sounds very definitive, and so the supranaturalists, though Mr. Harms not yet, to be sure, must now count Mr. Ammon as completely one with themselves. Moreover, since he has not altered his principles, he too has certainly already labored with them for a long time on the conversion of the rationalists by means of the Latin and German versions of his *Dogmatics*, though they have not much noticed it, while in his heart always disavowing the pride of rationalism, though never saying so quite openly. It is quite fine that the order of doctrine required saying at this point that the respect due divine revelation is violated by the license of rationalism, and that the pride of rationalism has already long been condemned by the symbolic books, since in subsequent sections not even the slightest trace of it is to be found! Moreover, this is why I also think that the rationalists will gradually recover from the hefty blow. They rely above all on what is stated in the Foreword about the relationship between what is positive and what is general. They already suspect something good from the remark that true deism also owes its origin not to philosophy but the Christian religion, and they reflect about whether in the end it is deism alone that goes beyond human reason.

To be sure, my interlocutors point out, it should also be the doctrines of Christ and of the salvation that is to be obtained through him that go far beyond reason, but when they then look for them they will discover that Mr. Ammon indeed spurns rationalism's pride but still loves its humility. If only rationalism is not given prominence in generalized, arrogant statements, and if only respect for divine revelation is not violated by them! Yet, if rationalism retreats into such individual doctrines, Mr. Ammon then puts up with it, for what then is it in the doctrine of Christ, as you also find it in the new *Summa*, that goes so far beyond the limits of reason? Certainly not the historical note that groups Jesus together with Moses and Mohammed for us and that distinguishes him only by the sentimental aphorism of Chateaubriand that Mr. Ammon would gladly place at the apex of all Christology: "that at the tomb of Jesus Christ even the highest truths of faith seem to condescend and to become perceptible to even the simplest hearts and minds."[45] Certainly not the ambiguous remark on which criticism alights "that the Word that was in Jesus came from heaven." Certainly not a generous but indeed merely provisional tolerance for the thorny ecclesiastical doctrine of the person of Christ. Certainly not the result of the analysis of his prophetic office, in which all the others are taken finally to converge: "that Jesus, who accomplished so much by means of teaching, was endowed by God with wonderful insights and powers?" Every rationalist can indeed acknowledge this! Moreover, just as little do what others have already suggested with regard to the doctrines of the forgiveness of sins and justification go beyond reason!

Nevertheless, the discussants indicated, it is in the doctrine of the Triune God that there are to be found some important changes that have to do with the second person. In §55 the doubt that was expressed in §50 in the old *Summa*, that the kernel of various doctrines seems to be found among the sacred writers themselves is now absent, and in place of this, supported by numerous biblical passages, there is the conviction that the holy authors of Scripture expressly attribute divine names, attributes, works and honor to the Son. The following paragraphs refrain from using the dubious headings "ecclesiastical doctrine" and "critical remarks," which to be sure in such an article can easily lend themselves to heterodox interpretations,[46] and it is expressly admitted that the bible presents this entire doctrine of Christ not allegorically but in the most serious way and that the most important gifts are attached to it.

---

45. Ed. note: The editors of KGA I/10 note that the quotation is from Chateaubriand's *Les Martyrs*, Paris, 1809, III, 17.

46. Ed. note: Much of the present essay is a preliminary indication of procedures Schleiermacher is about to follow in publishing *Christian Faith*. Although a great deal of what he presents there is critical of various doctrines promulgated ecclesiastically, as of biblical interpretations and views of various theologians, usually he weaves all these considerations into his presentations of doctrines of faith that have currency in the Evangelical church and does not divide the three parts from each other. On the complex relation between "orthodoxy" and "heterodoxy" in the development of doctrine, see *Brief Outline*, §§203-212.

As my discussants said, this is how the supernaturalists are already won over, failing to notice that after this, in the doctrine of the Redeemer and of the ordering of salvation, very little indeed depends on the higher nature of Christ. So does the little ship tack! So does the eel glide! Is it not a wonderful feat to satisfy the supranaturalists with well-timed general remarks, and where it is less noticeable, the rationalists with particular remarks that would amply make amends for their seeming loss? Moreover, only the person who has failed to note this maneuvering can believe that it was in his *Examination* that Mr. Ammon wanted to present himself as an orthodox[47] symbolic theologian for the first time.

Surely, they went on, *Examination* is a continuation of this conciliatory procedure, and indeed a hasty one at that. With clouds of hail from the northwest, the coat is wrapped around as tightly as possible against the storm; there emerges into prominence loud and clear the firmest attachment to the symbols, especially when Mr. Ammon places the Augsburg Confession on the same level with the bible; and he considers those who place Jesus and Mohammed not all that far apart from each other to be so utterly beneath and behind him, and then indeed is so strict as to allow himself to look down on every latitudinarian with a most unbending contempt. The charges against the rationalists are bold and severe, but they are quite deliberately derived from points that cannot be directly identified in his earlier remarks. That the spirit of the age is a spirit of light and perfection, that the religion of morality is the only conciliatory and ennobling one, that one cannot really know whether God exists, that making oaths is blasphemous, that marriages at different intervals would establish family happiness – none of this is to be mined out of the rationalistic corners of Ammon's *Dogmatics*. However, neither have the rationalistic theologians maintained this, nor will they recognize themselves in the image of the boastful Novaturienten.[48] Just as when it is said that in theology, the biting reason of the one rationalist is hectic, that the intoxicated reason of another

---

47. *Rechtgläubiger.*
48. *Novaturienten.* Ed. note: Ammon uses this term in his *Bittere Arznei;* see KGA I/10, 434-435. It seems to refer generally to those of a rationalist persuasion for whom only that which is novel is of value.

is reeling, and that the dreaming reason of a third rationalist is affected with a sweet madness, they will think that this applies only to individuals who have lost their way; but there is no need for them to admit that the mode of thinking necessarily leads to any one of these confusions. Thus, there is still some consolation for them this time too. Indeed they will find certain general expressions that will even allow them to right themselves if here Mr. Ammon "wants to leave undiscussed how the written Word is related to the enlightened conscience," for they well know how he has discussed it elsewhere.

So, they concluded, you see how these matters stand: that Mr. Ammon has in fact followed another maxim from the one that you wanted to make generally valid, that he wanted gradually to acquaint us with his change of mind, and that with his earlier indirect remarks he has earned the right to present himself now as a long-established participant in this way of thinking. Moreover, if he considered it necessary to come forward now with a better defined and more sharply articulated confession, and if it seemed expedient to him now to state freely and openly that the Augsburg Confession is his banner, one from which he would as little depart as from the bible – whether this is because of the firm experience that the churches of rationalist preachers are becoming empty or because the people cannot be content with superintendents of the church who are devoted to the new faith, for what reason – then simply admit that he could not do this more brilliantly than by attaching himself in this way to Mr. Harms's *Theses.* It is only to be feared that the occasion for this decision was not the most agreeable, in that it is unmistakable that the entire document reveals an unpleasant irritability, an ill temper, which in a strange way has raised the man's otherwise even and calm style and drawn it in the wrong direction.

So, my Dearest Sir, you can see that in my simple helplessness I had to listen to all of this, and it is perhaps even more simple-minded of me to relate this to you in turn, but this is how I work, and especially under such general circumstances I shall not let go of it. Only, do not chastise me by asking me who, then, were the people who declared all this against you. I would rather take everything upon myself, for I honestly do not know how to give an exact account of what others have said about this matter or of what my own conflicting thoughts were. Surely you will already know how one feels when one is pulled from one side to the other in such a way, and how disorderly the interchange can be! Unfortunately, through all this exchange of views I have not in fact come to any clearcut understanding of the matter; rather, concerning the subject of our exchange of letters, what remains left for me is the main question that I do not know how to answer for myself. It is this question that I now want to put directly before you and discuss with you in no way other than in my own person.

The question is this: How and when did you become so bitter and vehement against the union of Protestant congregations of the two confessions that has begun in various places and also with us? I confess to you that I would rather have expected heaven's collapse than this, for I could not have anticipated it from your letters to me and still less from your earlier remarks on dogmatic points with regard to the sacrament. Of course, Most Esteemed Sir, it was you who began to mention this matter between us. What could you have intended in doing this if you did not want to tell me what your honest, heartfelt opinion on the subject was? In fact, you only informed me that for good reasons you had set aside all the protests against the union that had been sent to you.

Now, of course, if you did this so that you could come forward with this vigorous and brilliant protest alone and so much more emphatically, that may have been a good reason. However, if the matter does lie so heavily on your heart, you should have considered not only yourself but me as well. If spiritual well-being is at stake here, and you cannot know how soon even the spiritual well-being of many Christians who otherwise stand under your supreme direction will be at stake, then just as on your own you turned in a friendly way to me, you should also have given me a friendly warning so that I might not share the blame for this outrage because of my participation. For this, since you have permitted me to chastise you where and how I wanted – for until now I have not yet chastised you but simply attempted to interpret – I would indeed like to chastise you at this point.

Indeed, after I had protested against your setting matters aside, because it seemed essential to me that this important issue should be discussed from all sides, and after I had clearly challenged you to state your whole opinion on the subject, even in your second letter, which includes your rather obscurely presented parable of the two princely brothers, I really cannot find this harsh judgment that you express in your *Examination*. I could not believe that you consider the matter to be so dangerous and corrupting of the soul, but only a difficult one, one that you believed could not easily be completely resolved to everyone's satisfaction.

Indeed, I would like to demand even more of you. You are well informed about what is going on here and elsewhere, as your document clearly intends to give us to understand, though it is stock full of anecdotes and allusions to anecdotes that I do not know to be either true or false. Moreover, you also most certainly thus knew, in timely fashion what people had in mind elsewhere and especially here as well. Finally, you have no lack of connections of all kinds and are certainly a master in the art of making the best of them at the right moment. On these grounds, would it not have been worthy of a leader of a large church, "which is furthermore regarded as a model of orthodox Lutheranism," to turn in all earnest with a warning to our influential ministers or our ecclesiastical superiors, to put forward the danger, to advise urgently against it, to guard your conscience, and to declare most firmly that for your part they could expect not the slightest cooperation but only the most measured resistance? Without anyone having been able to accuse you of meddling in other people's business, and with your so firm, unshakable conviction, do you not think that this would have been worthy of your authority and your position? Or is this something that you have done already, of course not toward me but wherever it was worth the trouble, and is it simply that I do not know about it? Well then, direct me to those to whom you have turned, and

I shall readily take back my chastisement! Indeed, if this is so, and your well-informed remonstrances and well-intentioned warnings have been scornfully rejected, then perhaps I could at least in part also excuse the tone in which you speak on this matter, for certainly, in and of itself it is inexcusable and is worthy neither of the matter itself nor of your person.

Right from the outset one thinks that one is listening to a Catholic for whom our festival was a vexation. What, then, did you have against the innocent paeans to take such offense, among which some have proved to be very good as well? Or against academic hoods, which indeed were also worn in the years 1717 and 1617 when there was no talk of union and no need for any thunderclouds against the religion of reason? Why, precisely at the celebration of the Reformation, should divisions of the army not hold a church parade when it otherwise belongs to their order to do so? Where laurel wreaths might have played a role I certainly do not know, but if in some places civil servants otherwise do not exactly go to church regularly, why do you ridicule them for having done so on this day? Is it not better than their having failed to do so on this day too? Further, having craftily spied out – whether in your own vicinity or at a distance I do not know – that on this day renowned scholars communicated again for the first time since their first communion, why do you not rather rejoice in the stillness and hope for some good effect from this awakening action? Why would you rather, in this passage in your document, point fingers at people here or there? I do not think that this is worthy of you.

Now, to be sure, none of these remarks seems to have anything directly to do with church union but only with the Reformation festival. However, I think that they would hardly stand there if they were but to ridicule only the hasty embraces among the brethren, embraces that patently refer – and this you will not care to deny–to the Holy Communion that was jointly celebrated by the ministers of this

104

area.[49] Is this mockery worthy of you and of the matter itself? Should not the reverence that every Christian should have before the Lord's Table have restrained you from this attitude? In accordance with your conviction you can take this action to be a mistake; then it deserves your reprimand, namely the reference to what is holy should have checked your mockery.

Why do you then call these embraces among the brethren hasty? A Judas-kiss is slow or it is a studied display; these were not so, nor have I yet heard that they did anyone harm. They were rather the natural expression of the fact that this action had corresponded to their idea. Each participant recalls it with joy, and as should be the case, by means of this meal of love many a bond has been tied, many an obstacle has been cleared away, and numerous hearts and minds drawn closer to one another. If afterward we had some solid controversies about this at our synodal assemblies, as there should be and is self-understood, and if we discovered many difficulties and tackled them at the most contrasted end points, in the process we also felt the blessing of that action, a blessing that diffused moderation and eased the return for anyone who claimed to lose one's way. Moreover, do you, you who have told us so often both in German and in Latin that in the last analysis when it comes to the sacrament of the altar everything depends upon its spiritual efficacy, do you forget yourself to such an extent as to say in mockery to us – to us who sought to receive such a blessing for an important and momentous undertaking – that we could just as well have gathered together for an ordinary meal and there too express the love of brethren that we hold in common? In spite of the fact that I do not have the honor of being known to you personally, you will also certainly know that I am one of those joyous people who on that account knows full well how much a genuine lifting of the spirit and a true warming of the heart can occur even at an ordinary meal. However, I feel the shame of your comparison so much that I shall say no more about it other than that I am so deeply sorry that even here you hide behind Luther, seeming to want to follow the

---

49. Ed. note: The reference is to the joint Lutheran/Reformed celebration of Holy Communion held at the Nikolai Church in Berlin on 30 October 1817.

great man particularly in a matter that he spoke about somewhat incautiously when he was roused by passionate zeal and for which you yourself have otherwise criticized him.

With obvious reference to this con-celebration of the Lord's Supper, with what right do you state that the Reformation festival was celebrated like a new play? Does this apply to the sharing of this Supper among us clergy on the 30th or to that of our congregations on the 31st? In the first instance, who is it that you readily want to brand as a comedian and a dissembler before Germany's eyes? Name him! and to whomever it may apply, let him be on his guard, but do not denigrate randomly or give free rein to whispering slander. That is indeed not fitting for such a man! Or is it simply on the grounds of your own experience that you assume that among a certain number of ministers there must necessarily be some hypocrites? Then I offer you my condolence for this knowledge of human beings just as I equally do for the way you make use of it. Or is it our congregations that you have in mind? If so, wherefrom do you get your knowledge of them? What kind of opinion of them do you presume? What kind of skill does it take that a man like you embraces an antiquated cry that would like to be issued audibly once again but for quite different reasons and that barks at Berlin as at a new Babel?

Then again, how do you associate the undertaking of the work of union with the trivial statement that human beings are born actors? In fact, what reason do you have to presuppose that for anyone – I shall certainly not ask whom you mean – a play was at issue on this occasion? For my own part, I have always considered this to be among the worst of manners and not at all to be considered appropriate in good society: to throw down insinuations that are too imprecise to call anyone to account for them but which therefore arouse all kinds of suspicions, from which something is always bound to stick, for what other intention can one imagine of such a procedure? The most natural chastisement for such behavior, however, is this: that it should quite openly be revealed for what it is. Moreover, since you have permitted me to do this, I shall now carry it out. As I have stated, this tone you take in your discourse, one that I do not propose to pursue further in all its tracks, could not be explained even on the basis of the presupposition just pointed out. On the contrary, since this presupposition might not be correct, namely, that you took accommodating steps to warn us and you along with your warnings were rejected, this very tone should almost spare me the trouble of discussing the matter with you any further. Yet, I cannot let you off so completely that I should not try to demonstrate to you how indefensible your reasons are, how many misunderstandings you have jumbled together, and how many unfounded insinuations are to be found here, whereby your readers, if they are not accurately informed, must inevitably be led astray.

Your principal reason for opposing the union of the two Protestant confessions into one undivided church appears on page 22 and reads as follows: "From the beginning of Christianity until our present day the communion of the altar was based not on communion in unfaith or on half-faith, but in total and complete faith." When I transpose this into an unmalicious, simple statement what it is to mean is this: that from the beginning of the church a full communion in faith was also integral to the communion of the altar. Can you affirm this? Have there not at all times in the church been a great many controversies over points of faith that yielded no actual schism and produced no mutual excommunications? Is that written only for those who know of no deviations in faith other than those that in the history of the church come under the very blunt label of heresies? However, you certainly know better. Indeed, in your new *Dogmatics* you are especially pleased to quote statements that contain significant deviations in points of faith from people who have never been accused of heresy or excommunicated! Moreover, how does the matter stand even today? Are there not many deviations in faith that do not involve any breach of the communion of the altar? If for some time you have really been making as significant progress as those persons wanted, and a genuine pupil of Ammon from the year 1803 comes to visit you now, do you not want to take communion with him? Further, how does it stand with the rationalists on whose conversion you have been laboring for a long time but who nevertheless are still not converted? Have you already excommunicated them? Or do you stand with them at the communion of the altar while you refuse only the Zwinglians and the Calvinists, who in comparison with them are true heroes in the faith? Nonetheless, I do understand that what you mean is simply or at least chiefly the complete and total communion in faith with respect to what concerns the sacrament of the altar itself. Yet, does this improve matters? Did not Marheinecke,[50] my present colleague in office and your former one, demonstrate how the Fathers held different notions regarding the sacrament? And did any of these Fathers or a pupil of the one or the other mutually exclude one or the other from the communion of the altar? And has it always been the case that controversies about transubstantiation have always and everywhere been settled by resorting to excommunication? Or at that time can everyone who partook of the sacrament together have been strictly of the same mind? And if it were then true that until the year 1549 Calvin was more a Lutheran than a Zwinglian, did he then no longer have communion with them after 1549 as he did before 1549? And if it is beyond doubt that he distinguishes Zwingli's position from his own in the *Institutes*, at that time did not he and his followers have communion with the Zwinglians? Is it not generally known that in the Reformed church both of these positions have stood side by side without upsetting the communion of the altar? And finally, have you been able to refute that among the congregations of the Brethren,[51] with no disorder or friction and without Christendom's being mocked and made to look foolish because of this love and unity, Christians of both

---

50. Ed. note: Philipp Konrad Marheinecke (1780-1846). From 1820 Schleiermacher's Lutheran colleague in ministry at the Church of the Triune God in Berlin, and from 1811 his professorial colleague in the faculty of theology at the recently established University of Berlin.

51. Ed. note: The Moravian Brethren, a pietist community originally established (1722) at Herrnhut under the patronage of Count von Zinzendorf. Schleiermacher received some of his early education at the Brethren college in Niesky (1783-1785) and at their seminary in Barby (1785-1787). It is very likely that the emphasis of the Brethren on community and service rather than on creeds and confessions had an enduring influence on Schleiermacher.

Protestant suasions actually share in communion in the deepest ardor and to the greatest mutual blessing? Surely this was not to be denied, nor could you readily pass over it in silence, but you are an ingenious man always knowing how to take care of yourself.

Yes, you say: "As is to be expected of Christians, the Brethren... indeed do not lack a specific inner attitude... the precious constancy of heart." Still, my Dearest Sir, if this is to be expected of Christians then it is also to be expected of us who wish to be united just as the Brethren are united at this point, and it is my hope and that of many who are of a like mind with me that we shall never lack this inner attitude or this constancy of heart. However, when you, as one in any case might believe, already predict of us the opposite, that is indeed a quite complete and indeed most kindly meant *petitio principii*!

Now, you may also surely have noticed that with this statement not much is said, and for this reason you enlist another artifice to assist you, and, in order to distract the reader's attention from this weak passage, very quietly give the matter another twist, complimenting the Brethren community for their laudable versatility and prudence. Now, I would rather leave this society – highly venerable to me – entirely out of the issue, nor am I especially inclined to congratulate it on this *laudari a laudato viro*.[52] Then, at that point you add this: "You would not have had the slightest reason to think that the Brethren would enter into church union with congregations that are in the process of uniting." As if that was the point at issue! Or as if you yourself could think that that was the point at issue! Are we not then all aware that church union among the Brethren is based upon a polity and a discipline that is unique to them? Thus, what sort of union could we want of them? Can we want them to abandon their polity and discipline? You must see, this is one of those unfounded allusions that can at best lead uninformed readers astray, as though we had had a purpose that we are now most certainly unable to attain. However, if you are of the opinion that in all instances where their ordinances

---

52. Ed. note: Lit: "to be praised by a man who is praised."

permit such a communion and ordering together to occur the congregations of the Brethren will deal with the united congregations should they come into being in any way differently than they deal with orthodox Lutheran or orthodox Reformed congregations, then at this moment I have not the slightest reason to believe that this presumption of yours can be based upon any sound foundation or that time will prove it to be true.

Thus, it is upon this false statement that your reproof of our procedure is based–a statement that if taken quite literally could easily imply the complete dissolution of the communion of the altar – namely, that all along the communion of the altar has been founded on full communion in faith. You state that "people have otherwise always begun initiatives toward union with serious and cautious negotiations over existing differences in doctrine" and that thus we too should have done the same; but in fact you also acknowledge that those initiatives toward union have always failed. Will you not permit us to be wiser than our fathers, to have become wise by virtue of their own example? If the issue is otherwise simply worthwhile, yet starting from one end in view has always brought failure, why should people not just begin from another end in view? Every situation of this kind has its ideal side and its real side, and both are interlocked in such a way that indeed no one can maintain that the one must absolutely and at all times come first, for if you want to affirm this in its total strictness, actually we should not have a Christian church at all, the reason being that doctrine first would have to be entirely settled before the community began. However, it has never been settled, and at no time has there been a general peace treaty in matters of doctrine. Cannot a peace begin with an armistice, just as well as with negotiations during which hostilities are still going on? Without doubt, there are circumstances under which one of these things is better to do and circumstances under which the other is better to do. Cannot a peace be finally concluded and yet certain points left still to be settled by special negotiations and agreements? In our case the one method has never proved successful; why should we not simply proceed to the other and begin with a deed? Nevertheless, I do not have to content myself with saying this, rather, it can indeed be made immediately evident that the other way is impossible.

If those divines from both sides who had come together at the Marburg Colloquy[53] had succeeded in reaching a common persuasion, and thus had been in agreement that such and such and nothing other was what they would teach in their congregations, clearly the union would have been effected, because nothing whatsoever had as yet been settled, nor indeed was there any fixed standard of doctrine. It was rather the case that the congregations were still engaged in the reception of views that were in process of revision, and as far as any of the remaining teachers were concerned, any divergent individual voices would soon have faded away when compared with the great authority of these voices. Yet, as early as ten years later nothing more could have been done by these means, because the church had already taken a more definite and separated form.

For this reason, this kind of effort has always proved futile, and how then, could it be entered upon now? Should we appoint deputies and give them full power of authority to decide upon our convictions? Can the conviction of individual persons really be derived in accordance with these decisions? If we had a Pope or could name one *ad hunc actum*! Yet, Dearest Sir, however much you may doubt whether such a move would be desirable, it simply will not do. Moreover, we must abandon every hope of this kind no matter how much one might be capable of installing such an authority that would be to everyone's satisfaction! Further, even the Pope has indeed never been capable of conjuring up a situation in which everyone really believed the same things.

Consequently, by these means not only would there arise the same situation that you so much detest – a communion of the altar without full communion in faith – but in the negotiations it would also undoubtedly come to light that this situation has always existed and that the notions even of the teachers of the same confession did not at all agree on the obscure formulas that directly pertain to this

---

53. Ed. note: See footnote 24 above.

matter or on doctrines that developed along with it – which as deviations from the simple statements of Scripture already in the year 1816 you yourself held to be dangerous. Moreover, if the deputies then were really in agreement, that is to say, not about the fact that some deviations are of no importance, for this indeed is not your wish, but about establishing a particular way of looking at things, would that not in fact amount to a mass of determinations that we "learned more in school than from life?"

Would you demand that all Evangelical Lutheran or Reformed Christians who have hitherto adhered to the notions of their church with their own consciousness should accept the new ones because this is the way in which the matter has been resolved? Further, if they were to do this either from some form of obedience that does not exist among us or by free consent or even dissent, would you demand that in future these new determinations should always be handed on to all Evangelical Christians and really require and expect this of every pastor in your large diocese? Or afterwards, when these Christians would always be coming to you complaining that catechumens had no desire to adhere to or to understand these determinations, as archdeacon would you yourself not, in turn, have to declare these long-negotiated and disputed determinations to be inessential with respect to genuine and worthy enjoyment of the sacrament?

Thus, why do you want to find fault with us for making a start at the point at which you would necessarily have to conclude? In this perspective, the hasty deed is surely not at all so bad so long as it attains exactly to the same aim at which negotiations must finally arrive, profound and discerning as they may be, apart from whether they should achieve anything else at all! This hasty deed, however, is not at all the same as those hasty brotherly embraces, which indeed could be and had to be only the work of the moment. Even you yourself are not so unacquainted with these matters that you should not know that this deed was not directly preceded by negotiations but by divers impulses, deliberations, investigations and specific actions; and, on the other hand, you are not so all-knowing as to be able to maintain with such certainty that this deed was nevertheless hasty. Rather, this is something about which, like us, you must first be taught by experience as to what was or was not precipitate, and it is at the very least hasty of you to give such a preliminary opinion about it.

Yet how, in fact, do you then characterize this so-called hasty deed? "We excised something from God's manifesto as from a territorial system of law and fashioned a territorial Gospel as we would a territorial militia," for this is what you accuse us of! Or would it have any meaning and purpose for you to say that in cases of former attempts at union religion was still held in too much respect to do this if you did not want it to be understood that it has been done now? You will hardly be able to say that your statements would not warrant these conclusions! Nonetheless, I shall gladly provide you with the demonstration as to where and how we then did accomplish union, if, for the sake of the future – lest it should meet us unawares – you want but to tell me what sort of crime you are then really attempting to define with the help of these peculiarly compounded elaborate ways of speaking.

I truly do not know whether anything has been excised from our territorial system of laws, and I am surprised at you that you can be concerned about such a variety of odd things, small and great – parades, laurel wreaths, secular officials, academics who seldom attend communion, garbled territorial laws – in connection with so many great and important matters! What, in contrast, do you understand by manifestos of God, and how does one eliminate anything from them? Do you mean that because of the union as we view it, it would come to excluding something from the bible? Indeed, I would have no idea how! Or do you call the Augsburg Confession a manifesto of God – you seem to come close enough to suggesting this, though I do not see how both the Reformed and the Catholics can then be found to stand apart at the same distance from the Lutherans! – and mean by this that because of the deed we come to the point of our eliminating *et improbant secus docentes* from the tenth article or of writing *fidelibus* instead of *vescentibus.*[54] More of this later! Your statements here have such a peculiar ring to them, however, that I should believe that this is what you meant; then even the great Melanchthon would indeed have lacked this same respect for religion.

Thus, as I have said, I am completely at a loss here and must ask you for a more detailed explanation, although, I am very afraid that I am prostituting myself. Moreover, if you will say now what you have meant, I will have to beat my breast because I am a simple person who has not immediately understood this subtle way of speaking. I am equally at a loss with the territorial militia. I have some limited experience of how one forms a local militia and I have myself assisted a bit in forming one; but the more I think I know how to do this the less I am able to detect what kind of similarity there can be between a territorial Gospel and a territorial militia and how they respectively come into being, and I would almost like to burst out in similar exclamations about this rhetoric as Festus did about that of Paul – and possibly for the same reason, because the disposition from which yours arises is just as alien to me as Paul's was to Festus.[55]

What, then, is "a territorial Gospel," and have we ever said that we want to create one, or do you have some reason to believe that we would have to create one? If you had said "a territorial confession" that might have some meaning, but a territorial Gospel! In this regard I hope that we are all quite committed to the fact that there is only the one Gospel and that persons can be made righteous through faith in Jesus. Moreover, it is also my hope that we would rebuke not only the person who wanted to impose another Gospel on us. Rather, I hope that we would also rebuke another kind of person who also leaves us with much to be desired, though we would also not want to exclude this person from the communion of the

---

54. Ed. note: The allusion is to those who would alter the Augsburg Confession to make it less objectionable to the Reformed. "They disapprove of those who teach otherwise" is already a softening of the traditional language which is *damnamus* ("we condemn" or "damn"). With regard to the Lord's Supper the substitution of *fidelibus* for *vescentibus* alludes to traditional differences between Lutherans and Reformed regarding the reception of Christ. Thus, Melanchthon proposed (1540) that rather than speaking of *vescentibus* ("to the eaters" or "consumers") at the Lord's Supper, the substitution *fidelibus* ("to the faithful") would be a neutral expression that accepts what Lutherans and Reformed have in common.

55. Ed. note: See Acts 24-26, especially 26:24-25.

altar on this account. I mean the person who observes our faith directly and (*New Summa*, §§ 116 and 117) formulates it so critically that two situations result. First, it is not faith in Christ that initially appears at all but only an external faith, this external faith relies on the divine authority of Christ and gradually is to dissolve into an internal faith that places God before it as an object to be imitated, second, when consequently the matter at issue is faith in God and in his Son, from various grounds that do not at all exhaust and barely touch on the justifying power of faith, rather laboriously and none too precisely, it is concluded that, all things carefully considered, one may say that all wisdom, virtue, and blessedness proceed from a true faith.

As I have stated, we have no desire that the one and long-established Gospel should be taken from us, and we do not want to think of another gospel. Thus, you will also have to explain this way of speaking first, since, as you know very well, we have no intention whatever of setting out to formulate even only a new territorial confession. Nevertheless, the specific reproach that you express is this: that we "have misled the people into an indifferentism toward doctrine." Yes, this in the end is the great offense, that after and as a consequence of the complete collapse of all church discipline, our Christian people are obliged to have communion with the most professed unbelievers and indeed with the most determined despisers of every divine command as often as taking communion occurs to the latter, and that after, as a result of the limited success that the faithful efforts of Evangelical teachers had until now, the situation is still the same, namely, that supernaturalists and rationalists have to have communion with one another, and that everyone would indeed have to view it as questionable if we ourselves wanted to aim at gathering the rationalists into a separate community of the church. So, now we want to ask Lutheran and Reformed supernaturalists whether they too might not just as easily decide to have communion with one another just as indeed everyone has communion with the rationalists of their own confession, and, conversely, ask the Lutheran and Reformed rationalists the same question, to the extent that there are any among us.

Now, in order properly to determine the magnitude of this offense properly, permit us to examine to what extent and in what respects the Reformed and the Lutherans then diverge from one another, that is, toward what kind of doctrines are they then to become indifferent. If, Reverend Sir, given your renowned learning and your well-known knack of descending to the great masses' power of comprehension, you had discussed these points appropriately in your writing, you would indeed have earned no little merit under the present circumstances. However, this you did not choose to do; instead, what is to be discovered in what you have stated about these matters are what appear to me to be misunderstandings, toward the clarification of which I too must now try to make my own contribution as well as I can.

First, with regard to the doctrine of election, which is to some extent a point of controversy between these two confessions.[56] You convert this doctrine, I do not know why, into the doctrine of providence, with which it is clearly connected though not quite identical except when one denies every immediate divine influence and attributes everything to instruction and example, which you nevertheless seem not to do any longer. Yet, as for the doctrine of providence in and of itself, to my knowledge there never has been any difference between these two confessions, so I must wait and see how you can correct my lack of knowledge concerning it. However, if you wish to reduce the matter of election solely to the doctrine of providence, again I do not know from which sources you derive that awful principle attributed to Calvin, namely, "that the good does not have its origin in God's supreme perfection but in God's unconditional discretion."

---

56. Ed. note: It is thus easy to see why Schleiermacher chose to issue a lengthy essay on election in 1819 (included in KGA I/10, 145-222). This was partly as a study preliminary to his own forthcoming dogmatics (1821-22) and at the same time partly to deal with significant resistance to church union. Although all his dogmatic work intentionally bore a Reformed cast, its aim was to serve toward achieving Evangelical unity. Clarifying the doctrine of election he saw to be key to this effort

116

It is a pity that you did not cite the passage in which this is to be found, for again I am uninformed in that I do not know how to locate it in the Calvin I know, as well as presumptuous in that nonetheless I would like to claim that he could not possibly have advanced this opinion in the form in which you present it to us. Indeed, I would like to claim even more than this: that when we descend into the most profound depths of this principle it completely loses its dreadful character and lies in a domain in which there never has been nor can be any controversy between the Lutherans and the Reformed, for it is not at all the domain of the revealed God but is that of the hidden God.[57]

Now, to take the matter further, what does this principle have to do with your footnoted anecdote about Princess Wilhelmina?[58] Is the question of having an English or a German fiancé to be understood as the question of the good and its origins, then? Or, craftily borrowing support from her father, is it that the more or less Reformed principles advanced here by the Princess are those that she wants to vindicate against her Lutheran mother? Patently, this is in no way the case; rather, though in a somewhat unsuitable manner, for which a princess can surely be excused, she is in fact speaking in terms that are certainly derived from the doctrine of election, nevertheless, what she wishes to say could just as well have been stated in the most authentic Lutheran terms. Or, in keeping with the Lutheran doctrine of providence, do you not think that a Lutheran princess could defend herself against the unreasonable demand of taking an oath concerning future actions for which at this present time conscience can as yet produce no bases for decision? In point of fact, I do not understand to what end you have introduced this charming tale, which appears to have nothing in the least in common with Harms's propositions, with church union, or even with the confused language of Babel that at first attracted your indignation. Indeed, if the princess had gone on to respond to her royal mother, saying that it would surely be futile to swear an oath

---

57. Ed. note: For further clarification see Schleiermacher's understanding of the doctrine of the triune God, *Christian Faith*, §§170-172.
58. Ed. note: Daughter of King Friedrich Wilhelm III (1770-1840) who ruled 1786-1840, and Queen Louisa.

on her eternal salvation since this had already been determined by God's absolute eternal decree and that thus the matter could not at all be up to her, then indeed she would have been offending against Calvin's doctrine of election, in a way from which Calvin and his followers had always most definitely distanced themselves; but at that point you would have had an occasion for what it is that you are doing! The only thing that I learn from this story at present, as from the application to which you put it is this: I certainly cannot judge the extent to which it belongs to the matter from a subjective perspective; that for you there is something that you call "the tactics of faith," something about which I would dearly like to be better informed as to what this is, so that if it is something praiseworthy and beneficial I may still obtain it, for hitherto this is something that I have wholly lacked and I have had to make do without it. However, I would really prefer to be informed as to the hidden intention behind your use of that story. Was it simply that you wanted to divert us from the actual point of controversy so that we might not see how trifling it is?

Now, at all events I do not wish to be led far afield, but would ask you whether you are in agreement with me on the following points or want to teach me better. Even having made allowances for the Remonstrants,[59] there is first the fact that in the Reformed church opinions about the doctrine of election are by no means everywhere the same; rather, not only do the various confessional writings of the different churches express themselves differently on the matter, but it is also widely accepted that different opinions have developed among theologians without leading to any schism. Thus, in the Reformed church it has always been the case that the communion of the altar has taken place amidst different opinions on the subject and notwithstanding the fact that some of the Reformed confessional writings, and in particular the Confession of Sigismund,[60] have put their utterances in such a way that all the differences in the ecclesiastical opinion of the Lutheran

---

59. Ed. note: See footnote 28 above.

60. Ed. note: The Confession of Electoral Prince Sigismund (1614). This confession represents the formal introduction of Reformed teaching into Mark Brandenburg. It was to this statement of faith that Schleiermacher subscribed at his ordination in 1794.

church almost completely disappear. Consequently, with regard to this aspect of their church practice the Reformed can find no obstacle to entering into the communion of the altar with the Lutherans.

Second, with at least the same justification as when you state that regarding the doctrine of the Lord's Supper Calvin was for a long time more Lutheran than Zwinglian, I can also state that with respect to the doctrine of election both Luther and Melanchthon for some time shared the opinion of Calvin, and as far as this matter is concerned I can appeal to your own statements. Now, of course, Melanchthon had no hesitation in making quite public the fact that he had changed his mind, but did he or did Luther challenge all those who had formerly agreed with them to change their minds too or otherwise they would refuse them communion of the altar? No such thing is known to me, at least. Thus, I conclude that even adherents of the Augsburg Confession, which on this point of doctrine, to which every Calvinist can subscribe because it completely avoids the point of controversy, have no reason to deny communion of the altar to the Reformed.

Third, that in the *Institutes* as well as in the *Consensus of the Genevan Church*[61] Calvin and all those in the Reformed church who have closely followed him, properly and adequately always secured themselves against all practical consequences that were related to their doctrine, such as the one that if given persons do not know whether they are destined for salvation, they could then presume to accomplish it for themselves and thus that in this regard duty and one's spiritual welfare are not at stake. It is rather the case that the particular version of this doctrine of election expressed in certain Reformed confessional writings and text books bears no other tendency than to put forward a formula whereby, on the one hand, God's omnipotence can be preserved in such a way that one does not have to exclude the divine will as a ground for whatever it is that occurs, and, on the other hand, to preserve the divine justice in such a way that one cannot say a divine injustice is shown in something that occurs insofar as it could not occur

---

61. Ed. note: Frequently referred to as the *Consensus of Geneva* (1552), Calvin produced this treatise mainly in order to defend his teachings on predestination.

without the will of God. Whether this problem can be resolved more by means of one formulation or rather more by means of the other, in this connection going into a detailed discussion can always be left aside. What I do submit to you is simply this: that this doctrine thus undoubtedly belongs more to the academy than to life and controversy has been dragged into life only on account of the premature zeal of those who engage in this; and that, precisely on this account, there is no controversy on this doctrine between Reformed and Lutherans on the level of practical Christianity, and thus, no attention should be paid to this controversy even in matters pertaining to purely ecclesial relationships and arrangements.

Now, in addition to these points, and in case you should want to dispute any of them, I simply present for your consideration in this respect, that, as regards our regions, at which originally we aimed with union, no new danger whatever is arising because of this union. The fact is that it has become a widespread practice for Reformed Christians to attend Lutheran sermons and for Lutheran Christians to attend Reformed sermons. Even with the best will in the world we could not prevent this, and I also doubt whether an anathema from Dresden could prevent it, however powerful it might be. Thus, if dangerous propositions are expounded in the Reformed churches derived from the doctrine of providence or from the doctrine of election, thereby Lutheran Christians are caused just as much or just as little harm with the union or without the union.[62]

Then, second, the doctrine of the Lord's Supper is itself a matter of controversy between Reformed and Lutherans. However, with regard to this point also you have not proved your statement that we should have begun the union with negotiations about dogma, so that on this point too you have shed more darkness than light. What you have to say about this is not to be found in the same place, a practice that is quite natural when one writes with enthusiasm and that can even be quite salutary when one writes with great deliberation. Thus, it would also be difficult to follow you step by step, and here too it seems to me to be more

---

62. *Union.* Ed. note: Usually the term Schleiermacher uses is *Vereinigung. Union* seems to refer more particularly to an official status.

advisable to put before you simply and plainly some points by way of a defense of our proceedings now that the main point at issue is whether or not you are in agreement with them.

First, it is well-known that in the Reformed church there was no insistence that there should be a complete uniformity of notions about the Lord's Supper or indeed that any difference would have disturbed the communion of the altar. This happened as follows. First of all, the somewhat limited and arid Zwinglian doctrine that the sacraments are mere signs that demonstrated to the church the faith of its members more than they evoked or strengthened this faith was never generally accepted, and already prior to Calvin, Bucer had also attributed an internal efficacy to the sacrament. Rather, agreement existed only about what the sacrament was not, namely, in denying the bodily presence of Christ in conjunction with the bread and wine. Now, since from the very beginning Reformed Christians who denied any specific internal efficacy of the sacrament shared communion with those who affirmed it, why should all those who deny the bodily presence not have communion with those who affirm it as long as the action itself is ordered in such a way that they do not appear to be affirming what they deny, whereby an untruth would come into play? Thus, on the part of the Reformed, on this one condition and indeed on the basis of the long-established practice of their church, there can be no obstacle to their entering into the communion of the altar with the Lutherans.

Second, when you nevertheless want to persuade us by citing several passages torn out of context from Calvin's *Institutes*, Book IV. 17: 3, 4, 8, 10 and 24, that on this point union could also be brought about by negotiating about dogma, and indeed in such a way that Calvin is reconciled with the Augsburg Confession in its unaltered form, then I fail to understand how you and your assenting reviewer from Leipzig can maintain this view. You would have to have skipped everything in Book IV.16 on what is said against those "who maintain that the bread of the Supper holds enclosed the body of Christ in and underneath itself who on that account assign to the body of Christ a ubiquity contrary to its nature because they in fact think that they could only have community with Christ if Christ descends into the bread; but they do not understand the manner of descent by which he lifts us up to himself."[63]

You would have to have skipped how in section 19 he expressly stipulates that "the presence of Christ in the Supper would have to be set in such a way that nothing detracts from his heavenly glory, which has to happen when one wanted to fasten him to the element of bread or enclose him in the bread, nor does any contradiction arise with the very being of human nature, which would happen every time the body of Christ is viewed as parceled out to a number of places at once, or is ascribed a boundless magnitude and spread through heaven and earth," and how he goes right on to say that "when these two points have been set aside, I freely want to accept whatever the faithful's genuine partaking of the body and blood of the Lord can bring to light." You see, with this formal protest no linking of Calvin with the unaltered Augsburg Confession is conceivable.

Moreover, everything contained in subsequent sections is so full of this attitude that I fail to understand how you arrived at the final passage that you cite, from section 24, without at least having perused all of it, though it is all expressed in the same good Latin style. Moreover, why did this Latin style not entice you to go beyond section 24 to section 31 for there you would have clearly read: "However, those who accept no presence of Christ's flesh in the Supper unless it lies in the bread are greatly mistaken, for in this way they leave nothing to the concealed working of the Spirit, which unites Christ himself to us. To them Christ does not seem present unless he comes down to us, as though if he lifts us to himself we would not enjoy his presence just as much. The question thus regards solely the manner and means, because they place Christ in the bread, while we do not think it permissible for us to draw him down from heaven." Still, even if you had not read so far as this, by the passage you cite from the 10th section you could not have

---

63. Ed. note: Calvin, *Inst.* IV. XVII, 16.

taken Calvin to mean that the body of Christ can be brought down from heaven by means of the working of the Holy Spirit and be enclosed under the bread, for this would establish too much of a conflict in the relationship of the Son to the Spirit, and it is already stated in this very passage that the concealed power of the Spirit is to raise us up to Christ in heaven. Thus, even if all Reformed Christians were pure Calvinists, as far as this matter is concerned we cannot engage ourselves in bringing Calvin into accord with the unaltered Augsburg Confession. So, on the basis of this point too it is wholly unjustifiable to proceed toward union by beginning with negotiations about dogma.

For my own part – and certainly many people share my thoughts about this – I had no desire for this union to take place if anyone had to abandon some aspect of one's religious notions especially in regard to such a sacred matter as this. It is for this reason that the Reformed among us have not demanded of their Lutheran brethren that they should even in the least depart from the essential content of the Augsburg Confession, and when on page 30, with the statement "but it is self-evident that to this end not the slightest change can be demanded with respect to our first and principal Confession!" you intend to give us to understand that such a demand has been made or will be made, then if you are talking about us in this territory – and indeed you nowhere make any mention of the Nassau Alliance[64] – this is a suggestion without foundation. I do not think that you wanted to make this statement, but this is how your words will be understood by every uninformed reader. Moreover, neither have the Lutherans among us expected that the Reformed brethren should give up their notion on the matter, whether this notion is then more Calvinist or Zwinglian, and conform to the unaltered Augsburg Confession. Rather, the one thing that is self-understood with regard to this matter is that no one who participates in the union should take the *et improbamus secus sentientes*[65] along to the Lord's table even if this position is retained in one's

---

64. Ed. note: The 1817 union established between the Lutheran and Reformed churches in the Dukedom of Nassau was the first such in Germany.

65. Ed. Note: "and we disapprove of those who are otherwise minded."

Dogmatics, and, – like Luther in several letters subsequent to the Marburg Colloquy – can express the heartfelt wish that God might lift any remaining scruples and fully restore to the truth those who have gone astray.

However, by means of negotiations this result would certainly no more have happened today than it did then, for the following reason. Suppose, for instance, that we had also proposed what Calvin himself does in the 16th section of Book IV.17, namely: "If they wished to explain their opinion in saying that in that bread is proffered in the sacrament a proffering of the body is bound to this, because what is essential is also inseparable from its sign, I would not strongly object to this," then, given the justifiable adherence of many Lutherans to the exact letter of this notion as it is laid down in the Augsburg Confession, this would have been of no help either, rather, the differences would have stood out even more strongly. This is so, for since we were so thoroughly justified in presupposing that even if we attempted union without settling matters of dogma, the various opinions on points of controversy would indeed be under consideration and held against each other in a more lively way today than has been the case for a long time, how would matters have originally proceeded in connection with the negotiations themselves! Certainly they would have proceeded no better than at the Marburg Colloquy itself. Moreover, the principal participants at those proceedings, no doubt quite rightly, shared the presentiment that it would not be easy for agreement ever to be reached – not on this basis anyway, for no other means of achieving it occurred to them.

Third, even if one also accepts that Reformed way of conceiving the matter, the actual point of controversy between the two churches that affects the Lutherans most closely is then to be found only in the fact that the one group believes that the mysterious partaking of the body and blood of Christ takes place in that in an incomprehensible way the two are present in the bread and wine, while, in contrast, the other group believes that this mysterious partaking indeed also occurs with the partaking of the bread and wine but by means of the raising of the soul to the ascended Redeemer effected through the power of the Holy Spirit in persons of faith. This was how you should reasonably have conceived the contested standpoint and should not have stopped at the usual condensed phrases, such as these: "Whether Christ gives merely his body, or bread; whether the bread merely signifies the body of Christ," for the essence of the Reformed notion even of the Zwinglians is by no means fully characterized in this way, and "whether he is really present by virtue of the words of institution," for in no respect does this statement definitely express what is distinctive in the Lutheran notion. Rather, the person who would submit only to the article of the Augsburg Confession as abbreviated by Melanchthon could also maintain this, as could the person who would couch one's confession in the passage cited from Calvin.

Now, on the basis of any correct reading of the point in dispute, what immediately follows is this: that according to the one opinion, in the sacramental partaking of the body and blood of Christ unbelievers[66] share no part even if they partake of the same bread and the same wine, because the Holy Spirit does not raise up their souls, and according to the other opinion, they do share in that partaking, because on account of the bodily presence the Holy Spirit is inseparably connected with the partaking of the bread and wine.

Now, if these two are the only points in dispute, might I ask you if it is right and proper for the communion of the altar among those who are otherwise in agreement to be prevented because of this difference? Do you think that at this sacred action any devout Christians could be disturbed by the belief that while they are themselves convinced that they partake of the body and blood of Christ with the bread and wine, their neighbors believe that they can participate in this partaking only by means of their souls being lifted up to heaven? or must they themselves not reasonably be raised up in this sacred moment in such a way that they believe themselves to be in heaven with the bread and wine and that the very thought of the issue would simply be an interruption of their devotion? Indeed, this

---

66. *Ungläubigen.*

is surely how even the erudite theologian should be grasped in this moment, and thus for the theologian too the question should be of interest only as a matter of speculation on the subject – that is to say, in that the theologian is working for the academy but not in that the theologian is serving the church, while for this same reason this question has no interest whatever for a layperson. Or should and can any believing Christian take an interest in whether unbelievers also partake of the body and blood of Christ such that on this account one should refuse communion of the altar to one's believing brethren? If no unbelievers are present at the altar itself, this question is of no interest whatsoever except as a scholastic one, and actually no unbelievers should be present, for it is surely a casual and inappropriate thought of yours that Calvin and the Moravian Brethren are in particular agreement about one thing, that Christ instituted the Lord's Supper only for believers. This is rather a doctrine of the Lutheran church, including your own, and it embarrasses me to have to demonstrate this to you. To put it very briefly, it arises from that practice of your church which requires that confession – especially private confession, which you indeed very much prefer – and absolution should precede any partaking of the Lord's Supper, for does one not presuppose that the person who makes confession gives oneself to be known as one is, and should your ministers perchance give absolution to unbelievers if they are not convinced of the person's contrite return to belief? Thus, it is by means of this practice that you actually exclude unbelievers, and if Christ had instituted the Lord's Supper for them too, this is something that you must not do.

The same consequence also follows from your maintaining that unbelievers also partake of the body and blood of the Lord when they partake of the bread and wine but that they indeed clearly do so to their judgment, at least as this is indicated in the second main confession to which you subscribe.[67] However, Christ cannot in fact have ordered them to their judgment; you must then have combined the Lutheran doctrine of the Lord's Supper with the Calvinist doctrine of

---

67. The KGA I/10 editors note that the reference here is to *Apologia Augustanae Confessionis Latine et Germanice*, ed. F. Lücke, Berlin, 1817, p. 272.

predestination in a most peculiar and harsh way. Now, given this disposition of the point in dispute, I for my part find it very natural that even many members of the Lutheran church, with our ministers who head them, have had no reservations about joining with their Reformed brethren in communion. Moreover, when you state that this is "presently more a communion of devout feelings than of clear and precise belief," then if I had been passionately engaged in the controversy and thus had wished its success at any price, from that remark I would call to mind one of your old complaints to the effect that the concept of twilight usually gains the victory, for our union would then be a twilight affair.

However, it is of course not so. Rather, all involved in the dispute have their clear and also very distinct beliefs, except that they hold that this belief does not have to be defined in a completely equal way on every point for everyone. Moreover, are you then earnestly of the opinion that as regards any complete and equal exactitude in everything the Augsburg Confession even in its unaltered form would be sufficient and would guarantee this? Is it perhaps the case, not only in that Confession but also in the Apology, and indeed I may say in any of your creedal symbols, that the distinction between the Lutheran and the Catholic way of conceiving things has not emerged so clearly and definitely, in positive and not merely negative formulas, that it would not be possible to make certain modifications to it without violating the symbolic formulas? Is it not the case that in your church itself the great Melanchthon has frequently been defended for having undertaken his well-known change not so much to draw closer to the Swiss as to distance himself more definitively from the Roman theory? And did he at least not also believe that on this point faith was indeed not yet sufficiently clear and definite?

Now, likewise neither does our present community lack a definite creedal symbol. It is the 14th of the Marburg Articles,[68] and what we are about is wholly and simply this, that we give a different turn to the 15th article, stating that

---

68. Ed. note: See footnote 24 above.

because we see that the matter on which we are unable to come to an agreement settles nothing with regard to the main point at issue, namely, the spiritual efficacy of the body and blood of Christ, as brethren we wish to celebrate the Supper of the Lord together and thereby refrain from raising the point of controversy while furthermore asking God to establish us ever more in the right understanding. Furthermore, if someone at that time had said to me that you would not have approved of this I would not have believed it.

I would have said that anyone who wishes "to be openly delivered from the symbololatry that has in any case already declined,"[69] cannot reproach us when on this one point we revert from the year 1530 to the year 1529. I would have said that anyone who "has no sense of any calling to pursue further the unfortunate controversy over the symbols that has so greatly renounced the religion of love or the question of the bodily presence in this action, since we are in full agreement ... about its spiritual purpose,"[70] must rejoice to see this controversy set aside in such a way. Moreover, all the more must this person rejoice, since the person who[71] considers a moderate union that brings together the separated brethren into one family of God without depriving them of their individuality, even between Catholics and Protestants, to be indeed difficult yet desirable and possible nevertheless – an opinion by the way that I do not share[72] – this must be such a union of Protestants among themselves. Nonetheless, all of this still comes from Erlangen, though I would also have thought that in spite of the footnote in your new *Summa* that is addressed even to unbelievers, stating that the body of Christ is present to them in the partaking, no one who still confesses that Lutheran church doctrine has been formed in such a way as to evoke pious sensations, even if these do not always result in clear concepts, would reproach those of us who are

---

69. Ed. note: Here Schleiermacher cites Ammon's *Ausführlicher Unterricht in der christlichen Glaubenslehre*, Vol. 1/2, Nürnberg/Altdorf, 1808, 490.

70. Ed. note: Here Schleiermacher cites Ammon's *Biblische Theologie*, 2nd Ed., Vol. 3, Erlangen, 1802, 135.

71. Ed. note: Here Schleiermacher cites *Ausführlicher Unterricht*, 490-491.

72. Ed. note: See e.g., *Christian Faith*, §§19, 24-25.

committed to union precisely from the perspective that we lack a clear and definite belief. Anyone who states so definitely that all the ends toward which the Holy Supper is directed are united in a spiritual union of hearts and minds with Christ must also indeed grant to the Reformed that these same ends can be attained in their communion. Moreover, why should not both Reformed and Lutheran attain these ends together, given that each does so of itself, to the effect that a rite is found that disturbs neither the one nor the other? Now, "in spite of the fact that our Lord's Supper is more ecclesiastical than biblical," the person who nevertheless so earnestly counsels those in authority in the church "to do everything to recommend anew to our contemporaries that this sacrament be acknowledged," would, I should think, readily grant to our people that we too should attempt this as long as it was made clear to such a person that when many families and persons in close relation to each other are separated at the sacrament because of some difference between the confessions, such a union would in fact make the sacrament much more immediately effective in life and so commends it from the best point of view.

Yet, all these remarks will now sink into insignificance for you in the light of your absolute commitment to the Augsburg Confession, and you will not care to share the perplexity that we will have to run into when sooner or later we are asked to which church we belong. This is so, for then indeed either even the Lutherans among us would have to desert the Augsburg Confession or even the Reformed among us would have to confess to it, though at that point they could of course prefer to do this right then, without being asked. However, coming to this pass, my dear man, is not at all what they wish, because they cannot, and perhaps they wish it all the less since they have not yet forgotten what has otherwise been stated often enough, namely, that it is just as certain that many teachers in the Lutheran church tended toward the Reformed notion of the Lord's Supper as that many teachers in the Reformed church tended toward the Lutheran view of election.

Accordingly, we shall indeed have to concern ourselves with how things will fare when such a question is put to us. For the time being we shall have to twist and turn so that one person will say: I subscribe to the Helvetic Confession[73] but I support those congregations in which Christians of both confessions have communion together; and the other person will say: I subscribe to the Augsburg Confession but I do exactly the same. Moreover, under all the temporary arrangements that have existed for a long time this will be by far the least harmful and the most unconstraining. Indeed, I hope that we shall consider ourselves sufficiently satisfied with this arrangement when we have first really come to the point at that stage – it is important to note that presently only the first seed is in evidence – that when we are asked: But do you not rather wish to establish a new, third church so that you can finally stand forth clearly for yourselves, we shall always persistently answer, No.

Yet, who is it that actually can and should put this captious question to us? Some other Protestant church? In what ways, then, does each have dealings with the other, and to which of these churches, and to what purpose, would we then be bound to be answerable, or which one would then have a right to interfere in any way in the affairs of our Protestant church in the State of Prussia? Of course, you will say that these questions betray more a feeling of power than a feeling of law; they demonstrate much more that we would have really broken away, each part from the great corporate body of the people with which it was hitherto united as religious brethren, hence the reproach that you direct at me "that without having the benefit of a conscience communally bound by God's Word, we have altered names, customs and principles, as we pleased." Moreover, as you understand it, this is surely all the less worthwhile since it is simply an external association with both parties holding mutual inward reservations and against which the protest of any one Lutheran or Reformed person would probably suffice, for you have now indeed reiterated one of Harms's theses to this effect in his own words.

---

73. Ed. Note: See footnote 31 above.

Nor should I wonder! Allow me to begin my explanation with this last point: We readily and freely admit that the protest of even one Lutheran or Reformed person against our union would be sufficient, but only for that person. The reason is that, as we have surely made sufficiently clear, we have no wish to persuade or certainly to compel anyone, and if such a person were unable to find a second person with whom to celebrate communion in the fashion long-established, then, in order that it should be a communion, the person's father confessor would be the second person. However, if one is perchance able to protest on behalf of all, because this person has alone kept the faith of the church while all the others have departed from it, for you have also reiterated Mr. Harms's 77th thesis, I do not understand how you could have stated this since you had our declaration in full view, one that Mr. Harms could not yet have seen, in which it is so clearly stated that no one needs to depart from one's belief on account of this union.

How can you honestly state on page 30, and render it dubious, that perhaps it was our wish to avoid any debates about dogma, since we explicitly acknowledge diversity as to dogma? Or do you want to maintain that the *improbamus secus sentientes*[74] and what has resulted from this belongs just as essentially to doctrine as does everything else and that it must also just as essentially manifest itself in connection with the separation of community among churches? Now, certainly in this case and in this one alone you would be right! Yet, what an enormous horror must the expression "to depart from the faith of the church" have aroused in you if you had lost the connection of this assertion with your former views and remarks! Or do you want perhaps to descend into even more profound depths – for there one will have to be bold and get to the point just to seize hold of you at some point – and say that even though all who partake do not need to share the same notion among themselves, each partaker must nevertheless share the same notion as that of the one administering communion? Indeed not, for in this depth nothing is concealed, even if according to the opinion of the participant the celebrating

---

74. Ed. note: See footnote 54 above.

minister has a more meager view of the sacrament, on this account the minister would be unworthy at best. Moreover, since the power of the sacrament is dependent not upon what the minister does but upon the power of its institution, no necessity arises from the fact that community among churches would have to remain separated. This is the one principle that we have set forth, and only insofar as you can say that this principle stands in contradiction to all previous principles may you say that we have altered any principles.

Let us then ask why it was, however, that in Marburg Luther and Melanchthon then so stubbornly declined to accept communion among churches? It was because they understood that the Swiss would then have to allow the Wittenberg doctrine to be taught in Switzerland as well, and because they themselves would have had to allow the Swiss and the Strasbourg doctrine also to be taught in Saxony. They dared not hope for the former according to what had been reported to them about Zwingli's hard[75] statements, and they do not seem to have wanted the latter very much because it would then have appeared that they had otherwise proceeded much too impetuously and unfairly against Karlstadt,[76] at least as far as this point is concerned. It has always seemed to me that in general the Marburg Colloquy would have taken a different turn if the Saxons had not begun with the notion that the Swiss wanted to come directly to Karlstadt's assistance. Still, be that as it may, we who seek to be united do not share this hesitation. We grant each other permission to expound the Lutheran and Reformed doctrines according to the conviction of each whenever it is necessary to deal with this matter, provided that the principle itself as it is realized in practice is also declared along with them. Now, if we reconcile in such a well-considered and prudent fashion, and not, as you misrepresent it, by means of some premature action – how a detrimental circumstance has caused sin – will we forfeit our forbearers and our faith on this

---

75. *Hart.*
76. Ed. note: Karlstadt (Andreas Bodenstein) (1480-1541.) From 1505-1523 he taught theology at the University of Wittenberg as a colleague of Luther. Karlstadt espoused a more radical program of reform than Luther, consequently, the two frequently came into conflict. He resigned his academic position in 1523.

account? However, a person who would deny that time too has broken down this dividing wall between the two confessions and that on these points different opinions can be held without the closeness of community among churches suffering thereby, may at least wait until that person can appeal to its success.

Further, allow me simply to ask this: How is it, then, that you can say that our religious authorities disregarded every type of doctrine, since changes were not made in this regard, but in regard to ritual only, which in the new *Summa* is for you also certainly something quite different from a type of doctrine and stands behind that? Yet, a second question is: How, almost in the same breath, can you say that we had altered principles and that our union would be merely an external one? Surely, only one of these two statements can be true. Consider a person who at some point changes principle on a subject so as to be joined to another and who arranges the connection in such a way that it remains merely external. Surely that person would have had to set about this in a very clumsy manner and would undoubtedly have held in reserve some other internal relationship. Indeed, this person would have had to begin quite ineptly and then in sensing this ineptitude would surely feel that he would have done better if he had called for assistance from elsewhere!

Permit me to ask a third set of questions: Do you think it is really true that the union of like-minded people who are in each other's company so as to share in the same spiritual partaking is merely an external one? Does this union consist in mere fraternization among people distant from one another, who in a religious and social respect are not in each other's company with equal standing? Do they do this to hold the same notion regarding the manner and means by which the connection between external and sacramental partaking, including that of unbelievers, becomes internalized? I think not! Moreover, you cannot believe this unless you retract what you have otherwise stated: "that all the ends of this sacred action converge in the union of hearts and minds with Christ, this more than any need for a more exact definition of the presence of Christ in the Lord's Supper as belonging to the essence of the action." Thus, according to this, the difference between the Reformed and the Lutherans is unessential to you yourself; and if you do retract this position, on this account you have no question to put to us. You also state elsewhere that "Jesus would not have reserved it for his disciples, and that a heartfelt and impartial presentation of the religious purposes of this venerable meal is more powerful and efficacious than any mysterious development of empty dogmas; that the sacred obscurity of this solemn religious action should be honored by means of the creedal symbolic statements of your church, an obscurity that should perhaps not ever be wholly removed from such statements if they are to work upon the hearts of the people and to arouse them to pious feelings."

How all of this fails to correspond with your present statement about our union is, on the one hand, sufficiently clear; on the other hand, I would prefer to defer offering proof of it until you demand one and now rather move on to the other point that "without consultation we have altered names and morals just as we pleased."[77] Morals? If morals and practices are for you one and the same thing, you should not rail so much over the difference between internal and external union, for at least as far as I am concerned morals are something internal and practices something external. Morals in this sense we have not changed, only practices, but in the Reformed church even practices have never been the same everywhere, and they are different in the Lutheran church too, though to a lesser extent. This difference has developed apart from any particular consultation, just as a new difference has developed among us without any specific and general consultation.

However, if these changes were the result of our doing "just as we pleased," I can admit to this claim only in a very limited sense. Attempts to find a form under which Reformed and Lutherans could unite to partake of the Lord's Supper have arisen of themselves in such a short time and in so many places that one can hardly say any more that this is a matter of doing what one pleases. One rather has to

---

77. *Aus eigener Willkühr*, Ed. note: below "arbitrariness" also translates *Willkühr*.

134

believe that it has an internal and natural basis in the progress of religious development. That the task was differently fulfilled in one place or another, that, if you will, is doing what one pleased, but it is certainly not an arbitrariness without consultation, for indeed nowhere have things become the way they are simply on the basis of a someone's gesture and command, just as without voluntary consent in such matters nothing would be accomplished. What our king has done[78] – for why should I hesitate to speak of that? – with his declaration amounts to nothing other than simply wanting to let the need for union bear influence freely wherever it arises. What he has otherwise contributed to this effort he has done in part as a respected member of certain congregations and in part he has advised it, and only those with whom he has taken counsel would be to blame if they did not made their full conviction heard, cautioning him against any arbitrariness that would prevent that internal and natural basis from freely developing in its own way.

Only an arbitrariness such as this would be determinate and worthy of censure, but it would also scarcely be able to assert itself. Thus, one cannot say that what has really taken place and continues to happen in this matter has arisen purely out of our simply doing what we please. Rather, the situation in each place has become what it now is through the concurring view of those who took most interest in the matter. To be sure, it is difficult to offer as a sufficient reason as to why there should be a given outcome in one place and a different outcome in another, but to do so is also not at all necessary, because everyone certainly agrees in declaring the external form to be less essential. Thus, this ambiguity present in our new first fruits is but a very insignificant one. Eventually, it will indeed become strong and hallowed, and every appearance of arbitrariness will vanish, if we simply continue in the right sense and in the right manner.

We have changed names. However insignificant this matter seems to me, let us not hesitate to say a few words on the subject so that it can be thoroughly

---

78. Ed. note: The reference is to Friedrich Wilhelm III's request to officials of the Lutheran and Reformed churches that a suitable order of worship be developed for a joint service of Holy Communion and that the two churches should celebrate the sacrament together on Reformation Sunday, 30 October 1817.

discussed. Incidentally, I do not think that it is the name "Protestant" that you have in mind. Mr. Harms indeed made a sympathetic reference to this, as though it would be forbidden to us here. It is simply a pity that in this very passage he adopts the unhistorical bias that claims that the name would generally have come from "to protest against."[79] Nevertheless, you see that this name is not disallowed us. We live toward our superiors, thanks be to God, in a very liberal relationship, and when they give us advice we make use of it according to our conviction and with this they are satisfied, though I do not think that this is what you mean. Thus, among us the one church is called the Evangelical Lutheran, the other is called Evangelical Reformed. The term "evangelical" is for both equally long-established – or do you venture to count up the ancestors, and does anything depend on this? Yet, is it also equally true for each church that the name is very much the main thing? It could well be that for you it could seem to be the less essential thing because you do believe that your church stands at the same distance apart from the Reformed church as it does from the Catholic church, for in this way the ascription "Lutheran" whereby your church differs from the Reformed church must be just as important to you as the "evangelical" ascription whereby both differ from the Catholic church. I certainly do not think that this is the general view but would rather surmise that it is the opposite.

Yet, for both groups the other name used is also certainly of value and importance. It is so for the Lutherans, because it indicates their relationship to a great man whom we Reformed also acknowledge as a rare, chosen instrument of God–and, incidentally, do not casually dismiss as a mere *vir egregius.* We too have never shrunk from joining in the glorification of his memory, even though this could mean that our Zwingli and Calvin are more overshadowed than they deserve. As for the Reformed, on the other hand, their name is of value, because even in a second position it shows that they do not yet want to name the church after a

---

79. Ed. note: Schleiermacher is recalling the original meaning of the word, namely, Lat. *protestari*, to be a witness, make a solemn declaration.

particular person, though they know very well that this would not have been done on purpose but has resulted from the way in which their church has arisen of itself.

Now, as to these surnames – and what else are we intending to do by their use? – they must surely be applied retrospectively as a way of signifying those respects in which we are not yet wholly one for the present, for indeed, if you then ask a certain person among us: What, then, is your understanding of the Lord's Supper? this person will still respond: the Lutheran, while some other person will answer: the Reformed. However, to the extent that we have become one, and if we want to signify this unity, both of these surnames will surely have to disappear. The Reformed will then console themselves in its now no longer appearing, in spite of some small differences, as if they had honored the great man less after whom only their brethren hitherto called themselves. The Lutherans will console themselves in its no longer appearing as if they placed less emphasis on "boasting of no person."[80] Hence, as far as this usage is concerned, "evangelical" is all that is left to us. However what do you then think regarding this statement: that "the Lutheran church has no need of any new title as evangelical, because it was evangelical from the outset, continued to be so, and will remain so?" Is the Reformed church evangelical of less long standing? No. When "Lutheran" and "Reformed" disappear, is the "evangelical" that remains to us something different from the "evangelical of long standing?" No. Here can it at all possibly be an issue of proffering titles and stamping them out? No. Here too I do not understand whether it is the entirely unfounded notion of a new territorial Gospel that the enemy has sown among the wheat that leads you astray or whether it is the general bad temper that those friends found in your writing, the reason for which I do not at present care to fathom.

Meanwhile, should perhaps the reason for this coming into my hands without me deliberately seeking it and should it be none other than that we have not only generally changed names, morals and principles but that "we have made changes

---

80. Ed. note: II Cor. 10:17-18.

without having consulted with the great community of the people?" On this matter, however, I have to appeal to what has been stated above, even if I thought to believe that a consultation about names and practices can produce a more satisfactory result more readily than a consultation about dogmas, I would find that the former was just as little possible as the latter. Of course, we would certainly have been able to take counsel with your Reverence, for Dresden is close enough, and perhaps if we had discussed these matters together you would have seen some things differently from what you do now, and then in the name of the church of Saxony you surely could also join us in our venture. Still, would we not also have had to negotiate with Copenhagen and Stockholm, with Hamburg and Tübingen and Heidelberg, with Bremen, Strassburg, Zürich and Bern, and, in addition, with so many others that I have omitted that I think not all of them would think ill of me? Moreover, with that arrangement how far would we likely have advanced?

The main point, however, is that in these matters too, consultation provides no genuine surety, for can the clergy hold sway over the consciences of their congregations? In the Lutheran church, however magnificently extended – for it is indeed about this church in particular that you speak – are the congregations organized in such a way that they can be consulted, or is it not rather the case that in most areas one is still striving toward such an organization? It is precisely for this reason that we have not engaged in consultation but have taken an initiative, and we quite calmly await the extent to which the need that has been stimulated will be given an airing and taken up elsewhere. However, it is precisely for this reason that we have also positioned ourselves in such a way that we for our part shall not be forced apart.

However, whether it is then because of this lack of consultation or for some other reason, you are so displeased that you neither give any consideration whatsoever to this declaration[81] of ours nor demonstrate to us its inadmissibility,

---

81. Ed. note: Schleiermacher is referring to his *Amtliche Erklärung der Berlinischen Synode über die am 30. Oktober von ihr zu haltende Abendmahlsfeier,* 1817, an English translation of which is also included in this volume.

and that is neither kind nor conscientious. Instead, your displeasure is such that in a somewhat rude tone you also bid us to spare you our contract in faith, which in your view has no basis or covenant, and our communion as brethren, which you take to be rootless, and that you predict of us that we will not be acknowledged but will be viewed with suspicion, and indeed that soon "among our very selves we shall be calling each other matriciders and falsifiers of the faith." Now, as far as the maligned community of brethren is concerned, I would certainly like to ask you whether you are authorized to make this declaration, which according to the context in which it is actually placed, is made in the name of the entire Lutheran church, or whether you are sure that people from outside it would agree with you, in which case we too may have some friends! Still, that is your concern, not ours. As swiftly as you were writing you may well not have had this surety, but you will undoubtedly not delay in acquiring it as soon as possible. We shall wait this process out, and we can do so quite calmly, for if first among us who live in the State of Prussia union has gained ground where it is deemed needful, it could certainly do harm to us when a Protestant church outside our own area refuses the company of brethren[82] because something inimical and disturbing lies in it. However, we are certainly not guilty of having this, and I do not understand what kind of negative consequences this situation could have for us. This is so, for we remain within the territory of Prussia, and here we take care of ourselves, and here we are always acknowledged even by those who have not yet directly entered into union, which presents no difficulty. As far as other territories are concerned, if we were desirous of calling some capable minister to us from elsewhere, it would then simply depend only on whether he lets himself be alarmed when someone says to him: "You are moving to a congregation with which we keep no company as brethren. Anyone who is not really attracted to us and who lacks the proper courage is indeed not especially welcome among us." The person who lacks neither will indeed then perhaps answer: "Farewell! You are too scrupulous for

---

82. *Brüderschaft.*

me. I am moving to a territory in which there is greater freedom without prejudice to the convictions I have held and continue to hold, and so the detriment to you could perhaps be greater than to us." However, as far as those among us who should perhaps be induced to travel and to move elsewhere, I would really then like to know where even with the best of ill-will, the particular church police who would trace them and deny them worship and sacrament were suppose come from! Nor do I understand how such a resolute ill-will can be borne against the matter other than by individual persons.

Accordingly, we are quite serene about all this, just as we explained before,[83] and I myself too, as you see – should you have found me severe and harsh previously when I spoke about your iridescent opinions and shuffling presentations – have become quite calm and composed now that we have come to this point. We have set forth our covenant, no one can deprive us of our roots, and we can respond quite confidently and calmly: "We are true children of the Reformation and not bastards." However, as far as your prediction is concerned – I have every respect for this gift which is not granted to me – but the prophet is proved true in the fulfillment. Your example of the church Council of Florence[84] is, to be sure, somewhat outdated and since then times have greatly changed. Likewise the predictions that you shore up with specific parallels seem to me not genuine but false. I would really like to set them in contrast with another, better one that would be a comfort to the many who might be alarmed by your statement. Yet, as I have said, I cannot at all prophesy, and so the only thing I can offer is a historical view of the matter, seeing whether the backward-directed prophet can rescue the forward-directed prophet from a bad dream.

The Reformation began at very different points and under very different circumstances all at the same time. Thus, it would have had to proceed with a miracle if despite the Reformation's having everywhere begun in the same spirit

---

83. Ed. note: Another reference to Schleiermacher's *Amtliche Erklärung*. See footnote 81 above.

84. Ed. note: A council (1438-1445) summoned by Pope Eugenius IV, the chief aim of which was to seek reunion with the Greek Church.

140

and having been based upon one and the same foundation, they would have been formed the same everywhere with regard to particular doctrine and morals. The more there were of such efficacious points, the more easily it could have happened that reform would have penetrated the entire church. Since this did not occur, but a separation resulted instead, it would have been natural for the new formation to have united in one whole. However, in that the same principle declined into a turbulent, unruly emotion, in various places it generated a quickly passing phase that destroyed itself and some of the conditions that surrounded it, and in that it passed through narrow-minded, unrefined minds and hearts, it produced carica- tures and errors rather than truth. Yet, this phase also occurred in that varied formations of what was good and true came to be allied with one or another of the sides that were taken, and on account of their sharing similar abortive and distorted notions and practices, they were prevented from fully acknowledging one another.

The striving for concord never ceased, but because of that separatist tendency it was prevented in its complete effect.[85] Had there been no enthusiasts, no turbulent Anabaptists, and no foes of order, Luther with his followers would not have inveighed against the Swiss regarding their sacramental views. If there were no false brethren and no half-hearted souls, the Swiss would not have been nervous about the Saxons, who still looked too Roman to them. By such means the Lutheran and the Reformed churches were retained in their separation. No one will fail to recognize that even this separation had some beneficial results and hindered the general diffusion of certain biases that took possession now of the one church and now the other. Yet, when such biases abruptly come into prominence their ability to hold sway gradually decreases, and we may hope that the time will now soon be over for such a power to be exercised generally. At all events, already the separation between the two churches is much too loose for it to be able to have

---

85. Ed. note: on "division," "separatism," and "schisms," always key concerns for Schleiermacher, see *Brief Outline*, §§54-62 and §234, also *Christian Faith*, §§87:3, 108:5, 121:1 and 126:1.

any effect in this regard, and the more the two churches have come into calm contact, the more the causes for misjudging each other have disappeared, the more generally it is acknowledged that in Protestantism the relationship between the freedom of the individual and the binding power of the whole must be held in tension, and finally the more it must be granted, on more lofty grounds, how closely that art belongs to the church too, all the more must the relationship between the striving for separation and the striving for union have changed.

Nevertheless, since victory of the uniting forces has not been fully complete while their whole mass was still in flux and in the process of formation, the separatist tendency has certainly settled itself in firmly established structures and the uniting tendency has been able to renew itself from time to time only by fits and starts. Does this mean, however, that it has now become a dangerous tendency, because formerly it was too weak? Do we have to consider history closed? Moreover, does anyone have the right to say that things should remain as they are now? On the contrary, it seems to me that this striving for unity is one that will legitimately continue to operate effectively. Furthermore, if it can be said that the relationship between the two opposing forces has greatly changed, then the reverse is possible too: the striving toward union can assume predominance, Protestantism as a whole can become one, and the striving toward separation can simply serve to settle the smaller differences that should no longer interfere with the unity of the whole. If it can be brought to a clear understanding that greater differences exist within each church quite without detriment to their unity than that which divides the two, then it also follows that the separation no longer has any internal power, that it exists only as a consequence of habit and in a mechanical fashion, and that the forces that seek union will be victorious over it.

However, this victory cannot arise on the basis of mere understanding, and the forces that strive for union thus can also manifest themselves only where a special need for union is at work among us and propels us; wherever there is no sense of this need it can always still be driven back. In our actions we in whom this need is

142

at work have also to be conscious of it in a quite simple and childlike way. On that account we also must by no means want more than what this need requires, and hence we also would not act in the way that you demand. On all matters that range outside this domain we can only express our view. Now, the extent to which our action will become a means toward effecting something general and inclusive, or the extent to which the resisting activity in different points will still prevail – an activity that we must also acknowledge to be a quite natural and irreproachable phenomenon as long as it stays within its proper limits – is something I am unable to calculate and thus also cannot predict. What I do hope is, of course, that this time around something of benefit will already have arisen for us, because something has happened that can no longer totally retreat. Moreover, I have thought it necessary to express my view as to what remains, occasioned as it is by your remarks.

Allow me, Reverend Sir, once again to return to your communication to me, and naturally, at this conclusion of mine to your conclusion, in which, even if I might chastise you when and where I will, you nonetheless expressed your wish for my continuing personal well-being. I rejoice in this wish, and in your granting it to me, and even supposing that you might want to retract it after this outpouring of the heart its fulfillment is sufficiently secure for you. It is so, for it lies in my nature ever to have a particular weakness for those in whom I have caused pain in the belief that they have a love of truth and who I have no reason to believe are incurable. No one can wish more eagerly than I that you might succeed in completely vindicating yourself against all the rebukes that I have directed to you; and if you are able to do this, you must also thank me for having given you the opportunity to do so, and the bond of goodwill is then tied on both sides. At that point, I for my part shall need no further apology or justification and in advance shall renounce all claim is any other than what is already contained in this document itself. If you succeed in making it clear to us that your theological statements are internally consistent and that you do not contradict yourself either consciously or unconsciously, then you will indeed have to grant me that appearances were nonetheless very much against you. For my own part, I have formed no definite judgment concerning these appearances, as in general it is not my style to find fault with individual persons as such, and in this context this would hold true not only for the theologian but also for the person without the most exact knowledge.

However, so that you are able to be cleared of everything, it would not have been honorable of me if I had not also stated even the most serious judgment that at a number of moments I could be inclined to issue and that others have no doubt also been tempted to utter. Furthermore, so that I hand you yet another advantage and you can clearly see the extent to which you are involved with me, I consider myself still so free to tell you quite openly how I debated with myself after I once again read through what I had written, material that in part already lay before me in print, that is to say, I conversed with myself, saying: But think about what you are doing! Is it, after all, your duty to be involved in this matter? Was it you who began or initiated the union? Is it you who are attacked in Ammon's document? Can you not be content and bring to completion what you have already owed for such a long time? Will you not gain the reputation of being a quarrelsome person? And I answered: Yes, that is correct; I have no immediate duty whatever to defend the union. On the contrary, attacked as it is here, as if it were the spiritual welfare of the Lutheran church that is at stake, in some respects others would have been closer to it than I, namely, those men whom the king has especially commissioned to make this matter their business,[86] and also those elsewhere who have initiated this enterprise. However, would it be a good thing in any gathering of persons if no one spoke and acted other than the person who by virtue of one's office has reason and authority to do so? If indeed two of my younger friends have already

---

86. Ed. note: Schleiermacher was pointedly excluded from this commission.

spoken well and vigorously in its favor,[87] why should not I as well? If it is not my duty I still have the right, and if an inner motive is added to this right, some act will result, come what may. If I had been the object of a personal attack, however, it is indeed to be hoped that I would not have written, for as yet I have not carried on any personal feud, and I have no intention of doing so. Moreover, as long as I remain true to this principle I cannot in any case justifiably gain the reputation of being a quarrelsome person. Indeed, as yet I have done nothing else of this sort other than to defend in accordance with my conviction some good thing that had come under attack, and whatever has been said after this about myself personally I have let be.

However, still conversing with myself I continue: Cannot everyone see that this document is a very personal attack? If your intention was only to defend the union, what have the changes and inconsistencies in Mr. Ammon's system to do with you? You have cast insinuations toward him; can he not say that you have also brought some forward against him? Have you not wantonly stirred up a nasty business for yourself? After all, when your opponent has played tit for tat, beginning perchance with your discourses on religion and your soliloquies, and then reviews your sermons, hunting for inconsistencies, do you not think of these old discussions of yours on God and immortality and on repentance and conscience? Moreover, if your dogmatics were already available, as it should have been long ago, and your Christian ethics, would you not have a fine piece of work to do then?

Nonsense, I replied, do not vex me with such needless torments! I already had the wish to have such a task accrue to me, for I certainly know how all of this is in accord within me and how I have become none other than I am without my taking notice of it and I do never pretend to be anyone other than I am. Now, if anyone were really to force me, it would be a good thing to show how conscientiousness

---

87. Ed. note: Schleiermacher is referring to Karl Heinrich Sack's *Vereinigung* (see footnote 2 above), and to Ludwig Gottfried Blanc's *An meine Mitbürger über die Vereinigung der beyden, bis jetzt getrennten protestantischen Kirchen-Partheyen*, Halle, 1818.

about theology and about philosophy stand in a reciprocal relationship to each other and how dialectical rigor and pious confidence are compatible with each other. Meanwhile, I hardly think that the challenge would become so urgent that I should not wait until everything is resolved of itself in an orderly fashion. Still, I have cast no insinuations against Mr. Ammon; but rather have stated clearly enough my wish that he should explain to us all those points on which I seek clarification. Given that I am faced with unspecific charges that could leave him in doubt as to whether he should defend himself or not because I could indeed say later that this is not at all what I meant, I have wisely guarded myself against them. Yet, however I may have considered the matter, I could not get around saying what I said.

Why, I asked, has Mr. Ammon woven his text so ingeniously that one does not know whether his main intention is to defame the union, believing that for the purpose he has suddenly to be supported on the strictest of symbolic grounds? Or was it his main intention to declare that this was the direction in which his investigations had gradually led him, the result of which was also his aversion to the union? Ultimately, however, I observed that the matter was not settled in this way; rather, he still owes us a properly comprehensive explanation. If he is suddenly going to adopt the strictest positive concepts, he also has to demonstrate to us the use to which he puts them in his doctrinal system and not merely their function when it comes to bragging and dispute. I have wished, I noted to myself, only to give him the occasion to let us wash down the bad taste of what we had previously heard with a potable discourse, and the better it then tastes to all of us the more thanks I shall have earned, and the simpler it will be the better will it taste.

Good, I said, but now I would like you to consider yet one more thing. You speak rather boldly about the union, as though one could rely on the fact that it will inevitably take root and come to pass among us. What burden are you taking upon yourself with this way of speaking? Are you not aware that the matter still

146

stands on rather shaky footing? Are not all kinds of voices beginning to be raised against it? Has not the person from Leipzig who reviewed Harms's *Theses* already called it a nuisance with such surety, as though that were the general opinion? In the same journal does not the reviewer of Ammon's *Bitter Medicine*[88] agree, taking the same tone? Are you sure that those who are friends of union will not easily be made laughable which can harm the cause even by means of superficiality, hastiness or pettiness? Moreover, does it not almost look as though you were then committing yourself to stepping into the breach and defending it? What kind of clumsy words are these that at long last you are uttering here, I answered. Can anyone in fact say that I had ever defended anything if it did not please me? Of course not! The matter is dear and valuable to me, and I also believe that it will prevail over many an attack and over many of its own mistakes. Yet, anyone who makes false moves will do so at one's own risk. Moreover, what of this talk of yours about the newspapers! In the end, these are surely inconsequential enough for you to remain silent regarding them.

Thus, once again I have given everything my consideration, and having discussed it thoroughly I no longer have any hesitation in sending you my letter as it stands. May you simply accept it as it is intended, and may it be as evident to you as it is to me that in mutual confidence with regard to this matter, there was nothing more that either of us could have done.
Berlin, 7th February, 1818.

Schleiermacher

---

88. Ed. note: The persons who reviewed both chose to remain anonymous.

V

Supplement

to my Letter to Mr. Ammon[*]

1818

Mr. Ammon's response to my letter arrived so quickly that I cannot feel called upon to discuss it in detail. I also think that he would have taken longer to answer if he had wished something by way of a rejoinder, for being so quick to respond in this way implies two things. First, his response abounds in confusions and mistakes that would be so laborious and time-consuming for me to disentangle that I must leave this task to the readers themselves. However, for their guidance and caution I shall select a few examples.

On page 43 of my letter I state that it would have been worthy of Mr. Ammon to warn us about church union if he really took it to be so dangerous and so spiritually destructive. Indeed, this was a quite natural expectation, for if the union becomes more generally accepted among us, then sooner or later the Lutheran Christians of our former Saxon territories will also be woven into it. Moreover, the more painful his separation from them has to have been the more I credited him with so much attachment to them that he would indeed have wanted to risk a word

---

[*] *Zugabe zu meinem Schreiben an Herrn Ammon* (Berlin: Realschulbuchhandlung, 1818); SW I.5, 408-422; KGA I/10, 93-116.

of caution so as to protect them from such spiritual ruin. However, I could justifiably assume that even before any decisive step had been taken in the process of church union Mr. Ammon must have been informed about it since it has been sufficiently discussed in public. Moreover, I did not need to appeal to the fact that I had heard tell of letters that Mr. Ammon was supposed to have written on the subject, in which he had treated it not at all as dismissively as he did afterwards in the *Examination*. It is also doubly gratifying for me that I could make this assumption without having to make such an appeal, for with respect to these letters I must indeed have been falsely informed, since Mr. Ammon now states that he has had no correspondent in Berlin other than myself.

This, then, was what I had stated about church union. However, on pages 8-10 in his response Mr. Ammon so presents the matter as though in that passage in my letter the question under discussion was not church union but the celebration of Holy Communion at the Reformation jubilee and as though I had expected him to have warned us about this celebration. Moreover, he does this by citing statements in quotation marks that nowhere in my letter have anything to do with the subject. This is the case, for on page 43, where I speak about being "well-informed," there has as yet been no discussion about the celebration of Holy Communion. Hence, on this account I return the entire discourse that Mr. Ammon holds to be mine as though I had not received it, and throw the misquotation into the bargain.

Of course, this is a mistake, a minor accident, but just as minor accidents often redound to the benefit of human beings the same is true here. That is to say, following this fortunate mistake Mr. Ammon could in his hastiness all the more easily skip the passage on pages 45 and 46 where I really do reproach him for the way in which he speaks about our celebration of Holy Communion, about our embraces among brethren, and about our sacred meal, which could just as well have been a common one. If it was because he had some regrets about his highly inapt expressions that he did not especially mention this passage, well and good; but if these too are to be excused along with Löscher and Cyprian, then let Mr. Ammon continue to stroll about in Löscher's footsteps, and I certainly do not want to disturb him again by casting in his way a piece of granite that he might mistake for a lump of sand and want to trample it down.

The second example is this: On page 25 of his *Bitter Medicine* Mr. Ammon ascribes to Calvin the principle that the good is rooted not in the highest perfection of God but in God's unconditional choice.[1] Nowhere can I find this principle in my Calvin. Rather, as I consider the matter more closely, on the basis of my modest acquaintance with Calvin, I find sufficient grounds to assert that he could not have written this. Then, on pages 42 and 43 of his response Mr. Ammon wants to demonstrate to me that Calvin did write what I have denied he wrote. So what then did Calvin write? "That God's will is the supreme standard of God's justice, so that we must reckon everything that God wills to be just because God wills it."[2] Yes, I had known this for a long time! However, could I believe that this is the passage that Mr. Ammon had in mind? Is it here a matter of "unconditional choice?" Is it here a matter of "the roots of the good?" Could anyone who has even haltingly produced a *Dogmatics* let oneself imagine such a mistake! Who would not have to understand Mr. Ammon to mean that Calvin said that the good and not the bad is good, that this is grounded in the unconditional choice of God and that Calvin sets this unconditional choice in opposition to the highest perfection in God. Thus, I expected that he would point out something like this. Then, with the help of this note (from Book III of the *Institutes* – I believed the vindication would come from who knows which seldom-read commentary of Calvin!) – Mr. Ammon believes that he has at least not diminished the abundance of my knowledge. No indeed! He has even increased it, that is to say, with regard to my knowledge of Mr. Ammon's precise way of expressing himself and of the definitiveness of his concepts. Now

---

1. *Unbedingten Willkühr.* Ed. note: See Schleiermacher's reference to this in his *To Ammon,* p. 99 above.

2. Ed. note: Calvin, *Inst.* III, xxii, 2. F.L.Battles' translation reads: "For God's will is so much the highest rule of righteousness that whatever he wills, by the very fact that he wills it, must be considered righteous." Library of Christian Classics, Vol. XXI, (Philadelphia: The Westminster Press, 1960).

that he is no longer an academic teacher either he must have significantly altered his disposition, or these are then the two passages in which Mr. Ammon appears most visibly as the victor over me. One sees the kind of mistakes on which they are based, and if readers who are warned by this example also look closely at other passages they will not fail to discover mistakes of a similar kind throughout. However, I excuse these mistakes and the haste as well, and simply for this reason I pass over them in silence.

Now, on account of this same haste a second thing has also arisen, namely, that Mr. Ammon has not at all, or as good as not at all, or at least not at all thoroughly, dealt with what are really the main points in my letter. When he responded I thought either that I would have to be instructed as to where I went astray – but just as with that passage from Calvin this enjoyment has been spoiled throughout – or that I would at least have to be offered the opportunity to make some scholarly contribution to the debate that would have lent some interest to the controversy and would have advanced the issue itself. For my own part, I have contributed what I could. On the basis of the partly incorrect and partly ambiguous remarks of Mr. Harms and other commentary that Mr. Ammon has poured over them and that is rather inadequate with regard to those substantial points, I took the opportunity to define the points of controversy between the two Protestant confessions more clearly, not just as to what I took them to be but as they are generally deemed to be. Further, I took the opportunity especially to bring the actual task that is to be accomplished in connection with the doctrine of election to a simple formula that can provide better guidance than the customary phrases, which have only continually complicated the matter. If Mr. Ammon had followed this path, a new way of dealing with this subject could have developed among us, and then one would have seen whether the victory in these quarrels is as beyond question as Mr. Ammon thinks, or whether these quarrels had just never been properly fought out. Instead of this, on page 41, Mr. Ammon prefers to have passed over the matter in silence rather than to have brought it to light and boasts of his non-polemical disposition, though indeed without polemical considerations no dogmatics and no single topic within it can be put in order. Moreover, in the same moment when he brags about his non-polemical disposition he again commits an error when he has me state that the doctrine of election and the doctrine of providence have nothing in common, whereas on page 57 I have expressly stated that both doctrines are indeed interconnected but are not quite one and the same. However, on page 58, the invitation to remedy my lack of knowledge that Mr. Ammon relates to this subject is to be found in reference to something quite different. That is, it seemed to me to be quite odd that Mr. Ammon had wholly abandoned the usual designation of this point of controversy and reduced it to a more general dogma. For uninformed readers, the thought could easily arise that it is as if the Reformed had quite different notions about providence in general than the Lutheran church had. I had good reasons to explain clearly that as regards the doctrine of providence in and of itself there is no confessional difference between the two churches, and so that people might believe this – in spite of Mr. Ammon's having seemed to insinuate the opposite – I knew of no quicker way than to call upon Mr. Ammon to charge me with ignorance on account of this assertion, if it were false. Now, here again Mr. Ammon has also switched things so prettily and has so confused matters that anyone without my document in hand must think that I have produced nonsense. Then, on account of this, he certainly robs me of the pleasure of doing dogmatics with him, for when confronted with such dexterities I cannot hold my own and indeed cannot even bring myself to exposing all of them.

The same has happened with regard to the second point about the doctrine of the Lord's Supper. Here too I thought that this should produce some scholarly advance, for apart from this aim I would have no inclination whatever to carry on any controversy about such matters. Now, it was for this reason that I also sought to group in the most precise way the actual points of controversy that continue to exist between the two churches in regard to the doctrine of the sacrament, gathering together everything that is actually symbolic and disregarding the statements of

152

individuals. On page 68 I then put the question to Mr. Ammon that if the two points that I had raised were the only differences in the doctrine of the sacrament, would it be right for these differences to hinder communion of the altar among those who were otherwise in agreement? I can find no answer whatever to this question, and so I also do not see how we could advance any further. Instead of answering the question and in order to demonstrate to me that in the Reformed church the most intimate association of Word and Sacrament is really hindered or denied and that I must thus become Lutheran, Mr. Ammon at one place cites two passages. One passage is from Zwingli,[3] and he also might have expected me to know it, since surely he knows as well as I do that Zwingli is not the Reformed church. Then there is a passage from Calvin[4] (page 29), where he again meets with misfortune when he emphasizes statements as being directly contrary to the Lutheran doctrine of the sacrament when in fact they are in complete agreement with it. This is the case, for the fact that faith is advanced only when the Spirit is added to the sacrament is a point that the Lutheran church has always maintained just as much as Calvin did. Moreover, it has never maintained that in themselves – and here this clearly means apart from the Spirit – the sacraments possess a hidden power to strengthen faith, even in unbelievers too, and once again I must call on Mr. Ammon to charge me with lack of knowledge about this matter as well. Thus, it is with regret that I again have to say that a more exact explanation of the expression "communion of Word and Sacrament" that would best lend support to the whole discussion is absent, and for this reason I cannot deal with the matter.

Elsewhere, on pages 45-46, he also quotes a passage from Luther. It was easy to see that this was the one that I too had in mind in connection with what is stated in my letter on pages 68 and 70. Rather than simply quoting Luther to me, here Mr. Ammon thus had to refute my refutation of Luther. Just as little has Mr. Am-

---

3. Ed. note: Ammon had quoted from Zwingli's *Fidei Ratio*, (1530). An English translation of Zwingli's statement of faith is included in *Zwingli: On Providence and Other Essays*, Eds. S.M.Jackson and W.J.Hinke (Durham, N.C.: The Labyrinth Press, 1983), especially 46-56.
4. Ed. note: Ammon had cited the catena of statements referred to here from Calvin, *Inst.* IV. XIV, 1-9.

mon dealt with the argument based on several points and put forward in various passages of my letter, that given the present situation of the Protestant church no union between the two confessions can be achieved at all by modifying a creedal symbol but that, in spite of these differences, the unity of the two will be a real unity just as well as the unity that any one party possesses of itself is a real unity. With no regard whatever for this point, Mr. Ammon simply reiterates his assurance that the union that we presently strive to achieve is merely a formal one and can be of no advantage. In this way it becomes clearly impossible to turn a controversy with Mr. Ammon into a vehicle for adjusting different points of view. Thus, disappointed at the outcome of this interchange I am breaking off the controversy. I do so because I may hope that these investigations will be sufficient to demonstrate on which side the sense for truth lies and where the missed notes and false fifths and discordances are to be heard.

However, I can no more express my thanks as regards the dogmatic point, for the enrichment of my knowledge with a passage from Calvin's *Institutes*, than I can as regards the practical point, for the instruction in good sense given to me by Mr. Ammon. Indeed, he is of the opinion that in order to promote the union I should not have cited[5] those passages in which Calvin most definitively states the difference between the Lutheran understanding and his own, and that as moderator of our Synod I also should not have said that I would always be committed to the Reformed school in theology, for this latter remark could also cast suspicion upon the present efforts toward union as if it aimed at the repression of the Lutheran church. Now this is indeed much too nugatory, for in the State of Prussia the Lutheran church is too strong to be repressed, and the Reformed church has certainly never appeared to be at the point of wanting to repress, and it could least be in a position to do so at present, since for the past ten years it has been placed under the same Lutheran head as the Lutheran church. Furthermore, this passage almost

---

5. Ed. note: Schleiermacher's own footnote here reads: "On the basis of this assumption Mr. Ammon could certainly wish to persuade us that Calvin is to be identified with the Augsburg Confession in its unaltered form."

sounds ridiculous to us in the lack of awareness it shows in attributing such an importance to the moderator of the synod of the district of Berlin as though he were the foremost minister in the province when in fact he is simply the elected chairman of a single, purely advisory assembly of which there are hundreds of the same in our country. However, quite apart from this mistake, perhaps the difference between Mr. Ammon and myself can be no better highlighted than when he attributes this cleverness to me and I abjure it. Also, he always wants to pass over things in silence, whereas I always want to speak openly and bring matters into the light. Moreover, this is not only because here we have a different kind of union in mind than he. We want to know that different opinions exist, but we join together in union because we consider the difference to be insignificant. We want to grant that both schools of thought exist side by side in the one church and that each person should express his or her opinion when necessary. Further, since this was also something that I stated clearly on page 76, I certainly do not understand how Mr. Ammon can attribute this principle of cleverness to me as a gift, for I truly do not know what I am to do with the charming present. However, even if I did share his opinion that the dogmatic differences have to be settled prior to the union, certainly as far as my way of doing things is concerned I would not know how I should settle them unless I set them as clearly as possible in the light beforehand so that everyone would then know the most troubling things the other party had ever said about them. In contrast, one can more or less see how Mr. Ammon would set about things if he had to preside over any settlement of dogmatic differences for the benefit of the union.

In his protest against the union, I also expected Mr. Ammon would speak regarding yet another point, but I had deliberately not alluded to it lest everything be repeated twice. The point concerns Luther's letter to Probst,[6] and I had hoped that this should present an opportunity to discuss both the initial characteristic differ-

---

6. Ed. note: The letter to Jakob Prob[p]st is dated 1st June, 1530. It is not included among those translated in *Luther's Works* (American Edition). See however *Luther Werke*, Weimar Ausgabe, *Briefwechsel*, Vol. V, 338-342.

ence between the two starting points of the Reformation and the way in which they have always continued to merge together over the intervals of time. Now, to be sure Mr. Ammon does cite this letter, but here also only to repeat quite bluntly that it is characteristic of the Reformed church to elevate reason above the Word of God, and indeed probably individual human reason as well, which has been fickle from time immemorial. Thus, there is no point of connection in this uninformed and groundless remark either. Moreover, the prospect of certain discussions of an historical nature that could have been of interest to the public has been ruined for me too. It certainly seems that Mr. Ammon has more of a preference for anecdotes than he does for history.

I leave it to the readers themselves to judge how thoroughly Mr. Ammon has treated that part of my letter that deals with his *Dogmatics*. In this respect my only complaint is that he asks too much of me. I am expected to have read everything, every preface, every occasional writing, and even the philosophical journals in which he has been snarled at and the public newspapers in which he has been ridiculed. No. At this price I would rather not have undertaken this little examination of his system that seemed to me to be necessary. Mr. Ammon most obligingly assures me that he has read all my publications, but also that he soon forgot them all. That is indeed also not surprising if he read them all in such a cursory way as he evidently read this one, which was specifically directed to him. Well and good. It only leaves me with the regret that the trouble he has taken has been so arduous and futile. I readily concede that I have not at all read all of his publications, but those that I have read I have kept well in mind, and it is to be hoped that this is demonstrated in my critique. Unfortunately, I have to admit that I do not read these magazines nor am I acquainted with his more recent sermons. However, for the matter that concerned us here I do not think this is necessary.

Instead of all the specific remarks that he quotes here and there, instead of all the appeals to good friends and to all the old and more recent slanders that he has endured on behalf of orthodoxy, Mr. Ammon should rather have engaged in a thorough refutation of the contradictions that were pointed out in my letter, not only the contradictions between the old and the new *Summa* but within the new *Summa* itself and also the contradictions between this and *Bitter Medicine*. This could have led to dogmatic discussions about the doctrine of the Trinity and about the essential points of the order of salvation that perhaps would have become of interest to the entire theological public. However, Mr. Ammon had no time for this because he had to respond so quickly and I have been cheated of this hope too. This is so, for the way in which Mr. Ammon now offers me certain items from his *Summa*, which are supposed to please me, and the way in which he tiptoes around and strikes at certain points in my contributions and not without some refined confusions that could prompt the reader to believe that I had said things that never occurred to me, none of this can summon me to enter into his defense, and for this I hope the entire theological public will absolve me. Indeed, with this inconsistent, superficial to-ing and fro-ing even I can take no satisfaction, either in the concession to the rationalistic tares[7] he mentions or in the not yet completely pure pitch of their monochord on their "harmonica," because even the content of the concession cannot be judged. Moreover, I simply must guard myself against doing this; that is to say, I do not at all want to be obliged to declare everything that Mr. Ammon has declared to be rationalistic tares or suprarationalistic wheat to be that. Even the reference to the twenty-two year old preface, in which Mr. Ammon previously admitted, openly and definitively to a rationalistic supranaturalism, is of little help to me, for I know as good as nothing when someone ever so openly declares oneself for something, whereby even today, as I believe, a person does not know how to think adequately definite thoughts any more today than one did twenty-two years ago.

For my poor part I already become quite uneasy when I hear the peep of "ra," the "irra," and the "supra," attached to words, because it would certainly appear to me as though this terminology leads to ever more tangled confusions. Moreover, I

---

7. Ed. note: See Matt. 13: 24-30.

would be just as glad to free myself from this terminology with a plain and clear presentation, as Mr. Ammon yearns for the peace of the country estate away from the whirlpools of today's shallow philosophy. However, so that the concert might become full-voiced and today's shallow theology might see in what sort of circles it can rotate to its heart's content, I also humbly propose for the irrational and rationalistic supranaturalsim not only a supranaturalistic rationalism and irrationalism but even a naturalistic and unnaturalistic suprarationalism. Moreover, if these mortals – for indeed not all of them can be of a higher origin – will stay where they are, each armed and armored – to the consolation and joy of all those who think that much knowing confuses and who for this reason build their huts with little knowledge but with much of "opining" and "seeming," "but" and "nevertheless" – then I hope that the ancient inclination to kill each other off will come over them.

However, as far as Mr. Ammon's rationalistic supranaturalism is concerned, this is surely something wholly unique about a system that, as on page 32 he himself says, proves its validity by means of its gradually measured repetends rising to a pitch at which it becomes a pure ecclesiastical tone. Nevertheless, if Mr. Ammon would only grant that this raised pitch is not constant and that – for indeed Mr. Ammon does not claim to have spoken in terms that are other than musical – even in his most recent *Summa* it is only the bass octaves that are raised while the treble octaves still retain the old timbre such that for the time being nothing can be purely performed in using them, then I want to set my mind at rest and wait for that "measured repetent," be it in Dresden or at the country estate, when the purity of pitch will be perfected, and I no longer want to hang like a German millstone around any cheerful walker's neck. However, suppose that instead of all this music of monochords and harmonicas, of bowed instruments and the buzzing of insects that he lets us hear in his response and instead of all the stilted expressions and for me to some extent incomprehensible allusions Mr. Ammon already early had wanted to consider me worthy of a thorough defense of the controversial points, before which defense and indeed with all knowledge of human nature and insight

158

he could not assume the role of a persecuted orthodox believer, for he also cannot dispense with theater and a role to play. Then I would readily have picked up the gauntlet he had thrown down, now, however, for reasons that have already been discussed, I rather accept the extended hand as a sign of peace without enquiring whether Frankish honesty is any better than Saxon, in that I do not take the trouble to make any precise distinctions between provincial honesties but prefer to stick simply to the German. Moreover, herewith I wish to consider myself excused for not answering Mr. Ammon's response item by item. It is to be hoped that my principal aim will indeed have been reached, namely, that whatever Mr. Ammon deemed proper to express against what is being proposed about the forthcoming union among us and in other German territories may be neither over – nor underestimated but assessed according to its own merits. I must still prevent two misunderstandings that could creep in and also rectify an error, though these things have no immediate connection with the controversy.

On page 13 of his response Mr. Ammon claims to be angry with me about my wanting to involve him in an open war with our local synod because of the additional weight that my moderatorial vote carries. This sounds almost as though Mr. Ammon thought that he would have half of the local ministers on his side if the question were discussed as to whether his improper statements about our celebration of the Lord's Supper should be praised or not. It sounds this way, for I still think – and he has not defended himself against this – that his remarks regarding embraces among brethren and the Lord's Supper in the place of which a preparation of common bread and wine would have been more appropriate, allude to this religious celebration,[8] and he must first still seek to discover to what old piece of ancient history this can be ascribed. I do not think that Mr. Ammon would carry this half of the votes, not even a fiftieth of them. However, what I really wanted to say is that this could easily prompt the idea that I wanted to come out against him almost as an advocate of the synod, or if things had turned out badly for me then

8. Ed. note: A difficult sentence the meaning of which is not exactly clear.

perhaps I could call upon the synod to assist me in restraining the man's power. Yet, all of this is a misunderstanding. Just as that celebration of the Lord's Supper was agreed upon and observed before my function in the synod began, similarly this time my function in the synod had ended before my controversy with Mr. Ammon began. Hence, this controversy has nothing in the least to do with the synod nor the synod with it.

The second misunderstanding is this: Mr. Ammon states that page 5 of my letter begins with extracts from a rather dated exchange of letters that I myself had initiated, and since Mr. Ammon seems to be uncertain as to whether the statements are quoted correctly, according to his excellent memory – though my own letters are an exception – some readers could be misled as to the whole context of the matter. However, the context is the following: Eight years ago there had been an exchange of some letters between us, and at that time it was I who initiated the exchange. Since that time there has been a complete pause, and the present and latest exchange was initiated by Mr. Ammon, and the statements indeed read just like this and they refer to what is stated about the union in his *Examination*. I comprehend the injustice that I am said to have committed by quoting these statements even less when Mr. Ammon himself declares them to be a mere formula of politeness. Yet, if they were meant to be a temptation to my modesty then I regret that I did not succumb to it. Nor does it strike me as an injustice that I also reminded Mr. Ammon of another passage in his letter, a passage that did not seem to me to be in agreement with his statements in *Bitter Medicine* that at that time had just gone to press, for it happened in such a way that no one who read this could produce the passage from it oneself. This could cause injustice to Mr Ammon only if my suggestion that the two did not agree was unfounded. Then it was up to him to shame me by demanding that I make the passage known so that it could be seen that both statements were in agreement with each other.

I have given notice of one further thing from this exchange of letters and that is that Mr. Ammon has set aside all sorts of remittances to the periodical. However, this in itself seemed to me to be so completely harmless that my conscience gave me no warning when I chose the letter form and put pen to paper. However, when Mr. Ammon acts almost as though I had profaned the sanctity of a properly confidential exchange of letters, readers could easily draw a completely mistaken conclusion from this about the circumstances of this present exchange that was renewed by Mr. Ammon and that consists of two letters, one sent and one received.

However, this observation still leaves the error itself. Mr. Ammon attributes to me a book entitled *On Revelation and Mythology,* one that I have neither written nor as yet even read. Moreover, I almost feel that I should call upon the assistance of the publishers of that book in order to disprove this false rumor, for I have already openly and very strongly protested against this when it was also attached to me in the *Leipziger Literaturzeitung.* In spite of this fact, the mistaken allegation has entered Ersch's writings, and it was probably here that Mr. Ammon found it. Thus, if I may be said to have snapped at him in this letter and if he cites anything else from it, then all of this is something that I must refuse to tolerate. It only strikes me as rather ridiculous, since Mr. Ammon has a particular talent for forgetting all of my publications without exception and yet indeed could recall certain parts from this one, that he would not have had some doubt as to whether this one was in fact mine. Indeed, a friend has already comforted me with the thought that now I can simply relax from defending myself against false authorship by referring people to Mr. Ammon. If he has forgotten the book, then indeed I must bear the responsibility, but if he has remembered it, then I can confidently decline it.

Schleiermacher.

VI

On the Proper Value and Binding Authority
of Symbolic Books[*]

1819

No one should go behind this title in search of some presumption that anything new can be said about this subject. It has been so frequently and widely discussed over such a long time that indeed one cannot believe that any significant point has been left undebated.[1] Even now, as the point of controversy that is so frequently brought up and so constantly smoothed over is receiving a renewed impetus with the jubilee festival of our church renewal,[2] the question for me many pose as to "whether the church itself is secure in its stability and progress," which is conjoined with that other one as to "whether it earnestly and faithfully relies on its confessional writings and duly protects the influences that inherently belong to them,"[3] has not come up as if any new opinion on the subject has been advanced.

---

[*] "Über den eigentümlichen Wert und das bindende Ansehen symbolisher Bücher," *Reformationsalmanach auf das Jahr 1819*, Zweiter Jahrgang, Erfurt; SW I.5, 432-54; KGA I/10, 117-44.

1. Ed. note: See the note referring to this point in KGA I/10 (1990), p.119, where the editors, Hans-Friedrich Traulsen and Martin Ohst, cite works by two earlier writers, Johann Georg Walch (1733) and Heinrich Philipp Konrad Henke (1793), In the rest of this essay they likewise offer very helpful historical references.

2. Ed. note: The occasion referred to here was the celebration of the 300th anniversary of Luther's publication of the *95 Theses* (1817).

3. Ed. note: The same KGA editors suggest a likely source in Friedrich von Bülow (1818).

162

However, something else has come as a surprise to me and certainly to many others, namely, that some behave as though they could treat an entire period of time, one that is familiar to us and of considerable significance, as though it had never been lived through. Moreover, they act as though they could wipe away the characters that it has engraved on the tablet of our history as with a sponge, and then, in a more facile way, as can sometimes happen in dealing with the antiquated features of a *codex rescriptus*, conjure up the script of the seventeenth century and count it as our own.

This approach must be alienating, especially if one recalls the great influence quite recently exercised by so many honorable and memorable men who resisted all the constraints of the symbolic books and who quite publicly departed from them in stating their own views. If this resistance seems to indicate a very rapid reversal of prevailing opinions, we certainly must be very concerned that this judgment could be premature. If, however, we take into consideration that not long ago a great many people did not dare to go public with their higher estimation of the symbolic books, or that now a good many people no longer dare to go public with their divergence from them, this situation too is no less questionable. Such is the case, for even as we now look forward to a more brisk engagement regarding the areas of religion and theology in public life, it is more than ever necessary not only that those who make their appearance in this public life should know where they stand in relation to one another but also that the church community at large should know where it stands in relation to its spokespersons. Furthermore, if views are brought forward and find approval that lead to laws and measures that crucially encroach on that public life, it would be doubly irresponsible if those who cherish an opposite conviction should choose to keep a timid silence. Hence, I too do not wish to remain silent, especially now that I have been called upon from several sides to speak, and on account of this occasion I have wanted to claim some space most preferably in this widely-read journal to contribute what I can so that in this highly important matter nothing will occur to our common disadvantage. What I

shall say will simply record my considered vote regarding all those historical infer-
ences which are variously adduced by both sides, and my aim simply is to set forth
clearly and calmly what by my own conviction can be justified or not on the basis
of general principles, and what in the way things lie currently is or is not com-
mendable.

First, it seems to me that the contrast between these views must be grasped in
the sharpest form in which it has already been presented elsewhere and in which it
now presents itself anew. Here, however, it seems to me that the distinction between the two Protestant confessions matters little, and for the time being at least I
shall wholly disregard it. The pertinent contrast then, seems to me to be this: that
some among us want to retain a binding authority for the church's confessional
writings where it already exists, and to attribute the same such authority to them
where it does not exist. By dint of this approach, their content would become the
norm for public teaching at least in all the activities of divine worship. Opposed to
this view are others who enter the most strenuous objection, which in its strictest
form cannot otherwise be grasped than to say that since these confessional writings
were meant only for their time, they should be viewed simply as memorials of that
time and that no further influence on our endeavors is to be granted them than all
the labors of various other predecessors must have on the efforts of their successors. Those of the one party fear that without this expedient our church will inevitably continue to decay and believe that its critical condition cannot be remedied in
any other way. In contrast, those of the other party fear for the injury and oppres-
sion of individuals on account of this measure and believe that only when every
trace of a binding human authority has disappeared can the freedom of spirit necessary for preserving of a living faith flourish. However, given this dual one-
sidedness it seems to me that both sides are mistaken in what they affirm and that
they are right only in what they deny.

To support the necessity for a binding authority for the church's confessional
writings mainly two points are adduced. First, they would comprise the foundation

for all the public and legal circumstances of our church, so that if we were to depart from them we would thereby establish a claim that would make trouble for us with regard to our ecclesiastical entitlements. Yet this, I believe, is not something that we should concede to anyone who wants to assert it. To be sure, the religious peace has been concluded, and in this connection a position of ecclesiastical entitlement was publicly established, first with the German princes and estates who had presented the Augsburg Confession to the emperor and who had confirmed their commitment to it, then only later and as likewise committed to a particular confession the Reformed were also included in this establishment. However, any person who sees in this situation a necessity that all Protestant congregations must now therefore be bound to every single statement of confessional writings available at that time, in that this person desires to take this view precisely and quite literally, must have completely forgotten about the statement concerning the religious peace.[4] Actually, to the extent that the Augsburg Confession refers to this provision its statements concern their doctrine, religion and faith, church practices, orders and ceremonies as they are established or as they subsequently will be established. Now, how doctrine and order established later might be in agreement with those established earlier is solely our concern and our interest, and we can concede to no one other than ourselves the right to judge this matter. Not to the Catholic church, which could lay claim to our church property and entitlement. Not to the Catholic authorities through whom these claims could be put into effect. Not to the church, because having labored at doctrine since that time with the greatest diligence and zeal, and having devoted ourselves to the understanding of Scripture and to the sources of doctrine, we cannot appoint persons to be our judges who by their virtually total inactivity have sufficiently demonstrated their lack of interest in this matter and so have also exhibited their incapacity to make such judgments. Not to the state, for if under this pretext a Catholic state sought to deprive only its

---

4. Ed. note: The Peace of Augsburg, 1555. The settlement acknowledging the co-existence of Roman Catholicism and Lutheranism in Germany and permitting that in each *Land* citizens should follow the religion of their ruler (*cuius regio eius religio*).

Protestant subjects of rights that already belonged to them, it would seem to me to be acting like a government that at one time had tolerated the Order of Freemasons but then sought to expel it because in their meetings all kinds of things occurred that clashed with the mysteries of that order. This would mean that it would indeed have to admit that as a government it is at all events secular and that in this respect it has no understanding of this subject. But if someone wants to suggest that on this assumption it seems to be quite beside the point even to have mentioned the Augsburg Confession in connection with the religious peace, I would respond that the matter is as follows.

In the confession the reforming teachers sought, on the one hand, to present an account of the kind of changes in the church that should remain unalterable on account of the pressure of their consciences and on the basis of doctrine, but on the other hand, they also sought to distinguish themselves from enthusiasts[5] who had arrived on the scene at that time too, and who along with church abuses also dissolved all civic bonds at that same time, and sought to undermine the authority of the ruling powers. The reformers must have been alarmed at being mistaken for their enthusiast opponents by virtue of such defaming views. Now, in seeking to establish a set of legal arrangements with the Protestants people did not want to favor the enthusiasts at the same time, nor could the protesting princes and estates wish for this either. Hence, the concern was in part to designate those with whom one wanted the religious peace to be established, and in part to retain a free hand against that peaceless principle which was deemed disruptive of the social order.

In both respects, attention was especially directed toward the Augsburg Confession. It was the first public act of the new religious body; it was signed only by public persons who for their part also had to uphold magisterial authority; and it contained articles that were to curb contrary forces on account of the unsettling

5. *Schwärmer.* Ed. note: A term describing those on the more radical "left wing" of the Reformation. See, for example, Luther's *Letter to the Christians at Strassburg in Opposition to the Fanatic Spirit* (1524), and *Against the Heavenly Prophets in the Matter of Images and Sacraments* (1525), in *Luther's Works,* American Edition, Vol. 40, Eds. C. Bergendorf and H.T. Lehmann (Philadelphia: Muhlenberg Press, 1958), 61-223.

166

consequences that the freedom of this opposing doctrine could entail for the commonweal. Thus, the Augsburg Confession was set forth as a sign, in part because of its articles, in part because of its signatories, and in part because it was set down by the new party itself as a protection so that in this way no one would ever need to meddle with it in its inner concerns again. However, the freedom also to depart from the Augsburg Confession in strict points of doctrine was not in any way meant to be taken away from the Protestants by virtue of that statement. Rather, that postscript cannot be understood apart from the fact that this matter was placed entirely in the hands of those princes and authorities whom the confession had designated or who would subsequently subscribe to it. It was made incumbent upon the Protestants that, without disturbing the peace, they should establish new doctrine, orders and practices. Thus, whatever they would arrange regarding doctrine through their church governance, would be declared to be at least compatible with the spirit of their undertaking. How such governance was to be arranged in the various provinces and locales was to be based on the competence of those versed in such matters and this was included in the peace too so that only that which was not acknowledged by everyone but was rejected could lose its claim to the general peace. Only in this way can it be understood that nothing that had no affinity with either of these two religions, either with the old one or with that of the Augsburg Confession, was to be excluded from this peace.

Now surely we should insist on this point, and most readily accept it for our purposes, in that already at that time the Protestant church was declared to be more flexible in legal terms than was the Catholic church, for where its doctrine, order, practices and ceremonies are mentioned there is wholly lacking that characteristic supplement, "as they have been established and subsequently will be established," so that in this respect we find ourselves at a distinct advantage. Thus, when it is placed entirely in our hands as to who shall be allowed to participate in our entitlement and who shall not, what sort of interest could we possibly have in restricting ourselves in our freedom of judgment by laying down the strict letter of a creedal symbol as the norm? Thereby we would at the very least be behaving in a spirit quite different from that of those who first participated in the formation of the Augsburg Confession and who left us their example with their dealings in the Palatinate. This is so, for when there was an attempt to hold something against the Elector of the Palatinate from the imperial side, and the intention was clearly made known that he should be excluded from the religious peace, the Evangelical princes indeed raised the question as to "whether he was therefore sympathetic to the Augsburg Confession, for he seemed to be committed to Calvinism." The Evangelical princes answered: "The Elector indeed departs from the one doctrine of the Lord's Supper in the Augsburg Confession."[6] Nevertheless, they also had to protest against every exclusion from the religious peace, in that particular deviations in doctrine must always be allowed to occur, just as had also occurred even in the Roman church, and in this case they had always thought to dissuade the Elector from his errors by means of repeated discussions and to persuade him of something better. Already at that time, just as there was little intention of making the church's legal situation and its religious peace dependent upon exact correspondence with the letter of the creedal symbol, victory of the true Protestant spirit over the sectarian spirit was proportionately all the greater!

Yet, the circumstances of those dissidents in the Protestant church on whose account it is to be feared that the attempt is now being made to infringe upon our common entitlements are apparently much more favorable. The reason is in part that neither orthodox nor more modern believers have ever been excluded from the church community and in part that we are no longer in any need – in order to prove how hard we strive to lead back those who have gone astray – of any special assemblies or colloquies that can easily be shown to have foundered if they have not immediately produced satisfactory results. It is rather the case that the need to convince continually proceeds by way of written discussion of all contended points. The more alive we ourselves are to persuasion by the leading teachers of

---

6. Ed. note: No source for these statements is cited in KGA I/10.

our church, the more confidently must we indeed live in the hope that our labors over those who have gone astray will not be in vain. Moreover, since not infrequently the experience of this is subsequently confirmed by the most unambiguous examples, what sort of challenge would we be obliged to undertake if by strict exclusion we peremptorily ban any number of people from our community in this way and precisely thereby make their instruction and their return more difficult? Thus, if we simply follow long-established examples and seek to remain true to the charitable disposition of our predecessors in the church, then with respect to our legal and religious entitlement we shall find no grounds whatsoever for establishing so rigorously any symbolic letter such that anyone unable to agree with it cannot remain in our community. Rather, any such arrangement must first be justified on quite different grounds.

Now, the second point that is frequently brought forward is this: that obligation to the creedal symbol is necessary in order to secure Evangelical Christians in whatever belongs to their faith, particularly against the activity of ministers who have renounced all the basic teachings of the church and who under cover of an unlimited freedom to teach disseminate a hollow unbelief. However, just as the wish to tie the bond of the creedal symbol more firmly may seem capable of arising only from a somewhat uninformed anxiety, so it appears to me that if this anxiety is its basis, then it is simply the outbreak of a well-intentioned but ill-considered zeal. The reason is that, the means seem on the one hand, to be inadequate, and on the other, to produce a great many things that were not intended. That is to say, if there are only a few individual ministers of whom one can rightly complain that they are sunk into unbelief, then it would be better to consider some other means that would at once bridle the few without oppressing so many others so severely. Furthermore, it would be difficult to deny that a strict obligation to the creedal symbol would upset a good many ministers – and among them even the most zealous – in the candor and impartiality of their research and deliverances, and it would make their whole situation a source of anxiety, indeed perhaps even make it unbearable.

In contrast, if the danger is pressing, and if it originates with a great many unbelieving ministers, then indeed a principle of exclusion can hardly be applied in this way. This is the case, for a great number of unbelieving ministers is inconceivable apart from an even greater number of unbelieving lay people, most of whom would be from the higher estates, since it would indeed have been along with them and also precisely at the time when receptiveness for such matters became manifest that they and those who would be future ministers were sharing in exactly the same sources and modes of education. If a strict obligation to the creedal symbol were then introduced, a good many of the unbelieving ministers would nevertheless have to come to terms with their consciences by resorting to all sorts of interpretations and reservations. Who then should stand guard over those who are holding their mental reservations? Should perhaps those ministers who are well-disposed – instead of devoting their time to defending disputed teachings in the interest of disseminating more accurate views – be required to spy on their backsliding colleagues in office? Moreover, if they were also to offer themselves for this dismal business, now that unbelief is indeed also so prevalent among lay people, from whence should the right lay people obtain the right position to make any charges against their brothers-in-office effective? Or wherever any examination of ministers was being conducted, would it not be obvious that men would be present who are thoroughly seized by the spirit of the times? The law would indeed stand, but there would be no one who would hold to it, and to many others still, it would be more of a dead letter. If we grant nonetheless that the law would be observed, it would still not be our wish that the defendant should be condemned without a defense, and what would be the situation then in regard to the decision?

As others have already noted, if the Word of the Bible can be distorted by interpretations, can not the words of the creedal symbols also be twisted with the help of the same rules and skills? If it can be proved that these rules are false and that such skills are futile, no obligation whatsoever to symbolic books can be required. Rather, one can deal with them on the basis of the perspective that their position is contrary to Scripture, which Protestant Christians have accepted all along as the norm of faith and which is not despised even by those who readily refuse any obligation to the symbolic books. However, if one is unable to do this, then one has to accord to those rules a relative validity and also to accord to those skills a relative value, and if one complains only about their misuse and misapplication with respect to Scripture, how indeed will one prevent the same misuse and the same excess when those rules are applied to gaining an understanding of the symbolic books? Further, if they cannot immediately be corrected either by replacing them or banning them when it comes to clarifying Scripture, how can one assume this right when it is a matter of clarifying the symbolic books?

Perhaps it can be objected that this apprehension can be allayed by experience: "for the artificial methods that were applied to Scripture were never the same as those that were applied to the symbolic books, and this is quite natural given their different characteristics. Furthermore, the symbolic books are purely didactic treatises that are not admixed with parables and images. They are indeed composed with a certain skill. Their expressions have reference to an educated, scholarly sphere of discourse in which everything is properly explained, and with regard to them all artificial theories of interpretation were deemed to have no further application."[7] In this connection, however, previous experience by itself can prove very little, because as yet we have by no means really had the case that would occur if a strict obligation to the symbolic books were now to be introduced. This is so, for at that earlier time when the symbolic books were objects of great importance, our art of interpretation lay in the cradle, and those higher and complex opinions and insights the misuse of which had produced so much that is perverted were still undetected, hence interpretation of the symbolic books had to keep more to the immediate letter. In contrast, already from the time that those more recent efforts in

---

7. Ed. note: Again, no source cited.

criticism and in the art of interpretation had gained the upper hand, an exact correspondence of religious notions with the symbolic books was no longer taken to have such high value, thus no particular effort was made to refer to them. Although it was granted without hesitation that the reformers had really held those notions, which the impartial reader apprehends from their utterances, the imperfection of these notions was also acknowledged and such as were considered to be better were placed alongside them.

Yet, if a value is now to be assigned to the symbolic books such that everyone must be in exact agreement with them and act as their advocates, to be sure some quite different phenomena can be expected. Moreover, a few brief indications will suffice to show how higher interpretation – which in the first instance seeks to understand an author as well as the author did and then even better – opens up a wide field as applied to the symbolic books. For one thing, it will be a normal and generally accepted maxim that to the extent that statements in the symbolic books might place restrictions on our research and opinions we must conceive them in the least burdensome sense; further, that to the extent that they are the expressions of individuals, they can be properly clarified only in their interconnection with the entire style of thought used and with other statements of the same men; still further, that all the portions that deal with doctrines of faith and ethics – those which are not cited as specific to those symbolic books with which we are concerned here but which are simply taken over from older confessional writings – are simply to be regarded as statements that the reformers themselves had not worked on thoroughly at that time and in the entire course of their education and vocation had found no call to engage in any study of them. Thus, the following maxims also apply: that the expressions of the older confessional writings on these points are confessionally binding upon us only to the extent that they derive from a correct application of principles that the reformers themselves adhered to in other respects, but that until this can be ascertained to people's satisfaction on all sides, any ideas that deviate on those points should be refuted only on the basis of Scripture. Furthermore, these same maxims must apply with respect to all assertions that are necessarily supplementary to the symbolic books on such points, those that since the composition of those books have drawn the attention of researchers and that have been expounded on in various forms but that were neither purposely studied at that time nor appropriated from earlier writings. Finally, when it comes to the interpretation of the symbolic writings all these rules by which certain statements and claims are included in the symbolic books, and also in the sources that they follow, claims that have been derived from Scripture, these must prove their use to us in that the symbolic books are indeed seen to enjoy an authority as authentic interpretations and explications of Scripture.

If any strict adherence to the symbolic books should be introduced and prove sufficient to satisfy those needs of the church, and if there should be little objection to these principles for their interpretation, then it can easily be seen – especially since that authority is one that would certainly not be extended to its epitome and its interpretation and is one that it has hitherto not enjoyed – how little there would be to be gained by such an arrangement for the uniformity and perseverance of theological opinions, how easily all sorts of distortions would attach themselves to the healthy and indispensable use of these rules to which the biblical Word has been subjected, indeed also how little more the most unbelieving person could wish for when one sets about one's work with aptitude and discretion. Thus, presupposing that a preference and predilection for unchristian ideas were to remain widespread, and that this would also insinuate itself widely among the order of the clergy, then, in and of itself alone, an augmented binding authority of the symbolic books not combined with coercive and arbitrary measures – which are always detestable and which besides cannot be applied without going through that intermediate stage – would be as good as useless for remedying the evil. Yet, should we not then have concern, as often happens, that when people have done much and yet not reached their goal, they then exceed all limits, supplementing even an extreme position with one that is utterly extreme? Moreover, should we not also take heed that with this measure we might find ourselves on the direct path to that which is most coercive of all, to that which after its brief dominion returns everything to its former blemished condition?

Of course, some will say that all of this may be quite correct, and that on the basis of this presupposition it may be foolish to employ such a measure; nevertheless, because the presupposition no longer has currency, and because, as with so many other upheavals, the dominance of unbelief too has at least been rendered unsteady, then, by means of a renewed and more vigorous return to the origins of the Protestant church, it is now time to prevent the return of such a period of distracting and disintegrative arbitrariness. It should be simply for this reason, and also because we are disposed to be conjoined with our ancestors in the faith, that we can and must adopt a measure naturally engendered by recollection of the recent past and in this way certainly salutary for the future as well.

All right, on the other hand let us consider what will be the natural consequences of our taking advantage of this tendency in this way. If the binding authority of the symbolic books is to prevent every single minister who is still of an unevangelical mind from spreading his beliefs through the exercise of his office, then once they have insinuated themselves into their office everything will indeed depend upon their hearers' attention to whatever is presented that is in conflict with the symbolic books and will then report it. If they do not do this, the arrangement is, in turn, proved futile with respect to all those who know that they must come to terms with their conscience on account of the oath they are supposed to fulfill and who in spite of their deviant opinions have nevertheless taken up the ministerial office. Yet if, as it were, we were to charge our congregations to exercise such vigilance, as always happens by virtue of such an obligation, if we summon them to pay such attention to the letter of doctrine, which in services of divine worship is for the most part simply a means toward presenting and communicating the living impulses of piety, then we cast a gloom over the whole atmosphere in which they are to be involved, and we divert them from the actual purpose of gathering for worship. This we would do, for whether or not there is anything to criticize, the person who criticizes or scrutinizes whether nothing would be found to criticize is not being edified. Indeed, not only does this occur, but the whole relationship between ministers and their congregations is brought into confusion.

It is bad enough that for a long time, influenced by what has been written on theological subjects in a popular vein and obviously directed deliberately at quite a large public, that our congregations have adopted a rather noisy mode of theological argumentation that cannot in fact be profitable even for those among them who are educated though not really scholarly. Nevertheless, it is by means of these circumstances that this contentious spirit is made legitimate. Wherever obligation to the symbolic books is heightened or is introduced for the very first time, our congregations – many of which and indeed most of which have hitherto been strangers to these books – will not hesitate to get acquainted with them. Indeed, it would really be absurd to lay on ministers an obligation to the symbolic books and not make them available in the congregations as widely as possible. In this respect, there will always be a few who are inclined to compare themselves with the minister and with his deliverances and can make themselves conspicuous in making a hunt out of it. However, we know very well how little can actually lie behind this posturing.

In conformity with our duty, we direct our hearers themselves to the bible, not only to be edified by it but also to heighten their vision both for what is praiseworthy as well as for what is imperfect in the church. However, they cannot achieve the kind of understanding that is needed to form judgments about the letter of doctrine by means of such a use of Scripture. Everyone can and should be sensitive to whatever is said against the needs and the inner certitude of the Christian mind and heart, but if something runs contrary to the symbolic books, that is only for the few to judge. In taking the other path, room is but opened for the curiosity and empty darkness of those who neither wish to edify themselves nor are fit to advance the congregation, and means are delivered into their hands for calling forth bad relationships and for misleading the honest hearts and minds of those who would rather be edified and advanced but lack the requisite confidence. In contrast, for the minister who already has enough to contend with besides this, in attaching still another relationship to it all amounts simply to wantonly placing even more obstacles in his way. This is troublesome, for even though we would have abandoned all priestly presumptions and are quite satisfied only to be servants of the congregation, precisely with our insights we would still seek to serve those who should learn from us and would thus consider it unfitting to let them judge us. All this then has to be borne just as much by the person for whom this measure of belief is unnecessary as by others.

Of course, it will be said that initially these evils are not to be avoided but that they will disappear when the obligation that must be taken up eventually actually debars those from assuming the ministerial office whose ideas fail to conform to those of the symbolic books. My response is simply to ask, will this really happen? We must not deceive ourselves about the position of the ministerial office. Certainly, among those who would willingly devote themselves to it and those in whom the clear inner calling for it is not lacking there will always be some – certainly at least as long as what has been written among us over the last fifty years still continues to have an impact in its historical context – who are indeed afraid that no matter how firmly Christian piety may be rooted in them, once they have been torn loose by our scientific mode of research and related efforts it will not be possible for them to cast all their notions in the molds that over three hundred years ago seemed to the best minds not to leave anything more to be desired. So, from among these men will we now hold back the most noble and conscientious – as long as the sacred Word has not already been besmirched – from the ministerial office? If so, this would surely not be for the great benefit of the church!

Yet, how few of these will there be, and how many will there always be, who though in no way truly in agreement with the symbolic books nevertheless commit themselves to them without being very much at odds with themselves or tormenting themselves with reproaches. In keeping with the example of prominent men, they console themselves with the thought that human perspectives and opinions change, that this indeed makes it tolerable, quite desirable even, that a person should not be bound, indeed should not be prevented, from expressing one's thoughts especially with regard to things sacred. They persuade themselves that they can easily avoid contradicting the symbolic books without its being exactly necessary for them to say anything that explicitly contradicts their conviction. Indeed, as with love in a marriage, they hope that conviction can also be reached while they are in office by means of amiable habituation. Moreover, they can persuade themselves of the former approach and can have hope for the latter approach because they lack any genuine and lively feeling for what conviction and inner truth is. Thoughtless and weak, their hearts will never be steadfast. In spite of the strictest obligation attached thereto, we retain such persons in the ministerial office, though certainly not to the great advantage of the church, for as always they will probably never cease to be moved by every wind of doctrine[8] and, given their sham convictions, changeably to follow some fancy or advantage or shimmer of human wisdom and mode of persuasion. Certainly, however, the happy time may perhaps finally come when no one who can possibly think of devoting himself to the ministerial office will either possess or seek or be capable of holding any other notion in religious matters than those contained in the symbolic books. But when? Only after a long time when nothing would be put forward but what by then would certainly be the dead letter of doctrine in the symbolic books, a few on the basis of conviction, most out of custom or fear, but in a word, by everyone who is involved in public instruction of adults and youth, so that in the religious domain nothing else would be heard any longer. However, such a time certainly cannot come before the best in our theology has gone to ruin because of this measure of conformity of belief and until there is no longer any connection between it and scientific education in general. For this reason, moreover, I can also say only that perhaps this time will

---

8. Ed. note: Eph. 4:14.

come, because I doubt nonetheless whether people will be able to bring the Protestant church to this pass.

In contrast, the best and most characteristic element in our theology is the more excellent form that dogmatics has acquired through the Reformation together with the lively impulse to engage in study of Scripture and about Scripture. Undeniably these are our strengths, for even if the Roman church has to some extent shared in this process, for the most part this has occurred only because of the repercussions of Protestantism upon it, and if among us these matters have occasionally been obscured, this has happened only to the extent that we have not held firmly enough to the contrast between ourselves and the Roman church[9] but have again lost our way in what is traditional. Still, what will become of these strengths if a strict and powerfully backed obligation to the symbolic books were to be established for everyone? For one thing, it is certain that the speculative and the historical spirit will resist and struggle, and theologians will seek in every way to demonstrate how even the very spirit of the symbolic books itself necessarily leads beyond their letter. In the end, however, the more the multitude would submit to the letter, the less would the call for independent research and for reconstruction have arisen, and the more both of these would disappear from our academic chairs and from our world of books. This applies not only to dogmatics but also to interpretation of Scripture, for there would soon cease to be any interest in the latter if it can no longer have any effect on the former.

If everything that is to be found in the symbolic books were deemed equally sacred, thus if the figurative notion of the last judgment were a dogma in exactly the same sense as the doctrine of the Son of God, and if the magical efficacy of the devil upon the soul were seen to occur in the same way the operation of the divine Spirit does through the Word, then for a person engaged in the art of interpretation what would remain in the character of these books would no longer be worth the

---

9. Ed. note: For further discussion of this "contrast" see *Christian Faith*, tr. J.S.Stewart and H.R.Mackintosh (Edinburgh: T. and T. Clark, 1928), §24, 103-108.

trouble. If the scientific form of thinking were to continue to hold sway, there would be nothing left to it other than scholastic precision in dogmatics and completeness of grammatical and lexicographical work in exegesis. Ultimately, there would be no choice for theology other than to become a purely traditional area of study, divorced from the rest of culture, and so to become extinct. However, if speculative interest as well as historical and critical interest cannot be eliminated, then there would be no alternative but for a clandestine teaching to develop either alongside or behind the public one, and this would be the worst that could happen to us until the latter is, in turn, overcome by the former.

All of these consequences are of course based on the presupposition that our creedal symbols themselves cannot be changed and that no new symbols can stand in the place occupied by the old ones. Moreover, I too take this to be the sole presupposition on which we Protestants can proceed here. This is so, for it is evident, and this is something that some people have had in mind, that if, on the one hand, an obligation to symbolic books should exist, yet on the other hand, the existing symbolic books themselves should be revised and altered as required from time to time, then the situation would be quite different. At that juncture, the incentive to influence impending changes to these symbols according to one's conviction would already keep both dogmatic presentation and exegetical and critical research alive. However, this would not work at all, and I cannot comprehend how anyone could think in this way, for how is it possible that precisely the same order of teachers should have an obligation to the symbolic books and at the same time prepare for and implement their improvement, since that obligation can have no other aim than the communication of conviction?

Certainly, as far as the state is concerned, the citizen can be committed to its existing laws and indeed at the same time can prepare for their improvement and implementation, for up to that point one can obey them and yet not be convinced of their salutariness. For the teacher in the church the situation is not the same, however, because this teacher can only be obligated precisely to proclaim the truth of ecclesial doctrine. Moreover, to divide the matter in such a way that somehow the servants of the Word are to be under obligation and that academic teachers rather do preparatory work and are to be under no obligation is something that is also impossible for us. This is the case, for servants of the Word are instructed by academic teachers, and thus they would have to speak contrary to their conviction if they should be persuaded of the appropriateness of some proposed alteration and at the same time hold to their obligation nevertheless. Moreover, once the alteration has been sanctioned how should they suddenly switch from one norm to another without generally betraying an evident lack of conviction? As a result, I find it impossible to imagine that these two things can be compatible, namely, to be under obligation to the symbolic books and at the same time to be committed to a policy that allows them to be changed.

Yet, besides this it also seems to me that the whole idea of making periodic changes in the symbols themselves is completely un-Protestant. The reason is that in our church there is neither one single person to whom we could assign this privilege, nor do we have an available procedure whereby several people could meet together to produce such a result, in that we do not acknowledge a majority with regard to matters of faith to the conclusions of which the minority would have to submit. Hence, we come off much worse – if such a dogmatic norm exists – than does the Roman church, which if by means of a majority of votes in a general council it cannot correct errors and misunderstandings that would have crept in can nevertheless declare them to be such. Now, if this other procedure should not work, all of those conclusions would in fact have legitimacy. Nevertheless, from this consideration it also follows just as incontestably – because the church itself cannot have intended that which must ruin it – that the distinctive value of the symbolic books consists not in the binding authority that some people seek to establish for them, which authority can be so dangerous for our entire church, that before we set up such a norm alongside Scripture we would rather have to risk allowing the church to emerge victorious in the struggle with unbelief ever anew.

180

However, if the victory shifted to our side one day, should there not be some means other than the binding authority of the symbolic books that would enable us to guard against unbelief, or at least to ease it in the future and to make the outcome secure? If we are permeated aright with a feeling for our situation, I think that we will discover that binding authority would not be the first and most natural thought that would occur to us at all. Suppose that unbelief, or at least a sorry, disagreeable and ineffectual view in matters of faith will have gained the upper hand in the church, and suppose that we note that this view is weakening, would this be because here and there that binding authority is still present? Will that have been the stronghold into which the Evangelical spirit had withdrawn and from which it had launched victorious sorties on the enemy, and now, after the latter has pulled back, sallies forth again to pursue that enemy? Certainly not! Or is it because elsewhere something similar to that binding authority has been fashioned? Again, not in the least. This change will rather have occurred only through the efficacy of those who had firmly kept the faith without being bound to such a norm and had been set at greater liberty in their lives as a whole and through the receptivity of those who were still unbiased having been more greatly stimulated. Thus, to ward off a similar power of unbelief in future what plan could be more natural than that of increasing and securing that efficacy by means of a closer union and keeping this receptivity directed to it?

This is also the tendency of the general demand which is expressed in myriad ways. Let us tie the bonds of our ecclesial union more firmly, give our congregations a public voice, not so that individuals should make impertinent judgments about what is orthodox and what is not, but so that the whole community may freely express itself in word and deed whenever its religious sensibility is satisfied and whenever it is offended, and in such a way that inner shame will act as a warning to those who stand at a parting of the ways. This is the right strategy, for what is really at odds with the essential basis of our faith must also somehow manifest itself as injurious to life and not merely in words and doctrinal formulas that are easily misunderstood.

Let everyone who themselves confess that this community has no attraction for them remain as respectably outside it as their character entitles them to be respected. Then, without the yoke of a letter,[10] the Evangelical sensibility and spirit will be sufficiently evident, and our impressionable youth will dwell and flourish in it. By means of a sound Christian education, let us see to it that the number of sacrilegious people will decline so that fewer offenders will insinuate themselves into the teaching office, for these people must always cause damage when they also refrain most conscientiously from all deviations from the doctrine of the church. In contrast, earnest and pious individuals will always bring blessing even if in certain points they depart from the teaching that we hold in common, and under the protection of a better time their efficacy will never prevent a yet more steadfast Evangelical spirit from developing in impressionable young persons than that which they themselves could acquire due to their period of education. Hence, we shall nowhere seek to rely on an oath over which no one is Lord but shall rely on the strength of open arrangements and of a common life, just as any other healthy society does in its own sphere. Then our church will remain the same through the free accord of hearts and minds in faith, it will have a vital awareness of the oneness of its life, and it will feel how every vital striving within it arises from its original principle.

However, if it seems to me that those who find a distinctive merit of the symbolic books in such a binding authority are so very much mistaken, I must indeed consider those no less in error who on this account deny any distinctive authority to them and who seek to classify them in part along with the proceedings of other subordinate discussions of religion or in part along with the dogmatic contributions of other well-disposed and distinguished individuals. It seems to me, at least, that such a verdict betrays a complete lack of historical sensibility, and is an insult to

---

10. Ed. note: The reference here may be to Gal. 5:1.

any healthy common feeling just as anything else would be by which something sacred and highly honored is to be brought down to the level of the commonplace. This is the case, for it is impossible for the immense difference between the first decisive moments of a phenomenon and its subsequent developments to escape historical sensibility. Moreover, it is just as impossible for the difference to escape sound feeling between what even the best of persons – and accordingly this designation also applies to the authors of the symbolic books – says and does as an individual and what one or several persons expressly advance as advocates of a widespread disposition even though these people may be less distinguished. We certainly do feel that no one must advocate the first but that, in turn, everyone who wishes to be part of the whole that is animated by this disposition must advocate and protect it. Incontestably, this is also the truth that underlies the opinion that was criticized above, and the criticism was also leveled solely and strictly against the "how" and the "to what extent" of it. Yet, so that we do not waver indecisively to and fro between two extremes, we must go back step by step and ask: In what sense, then, are those who venerate the symbolic books mistaken and go too far?

If it is not enough to cast the symbolic writings into one same class with others of a similar content, it is too much to place them on the same level with Holy Scripture, and this one can certainly say of those who want to bestow on our confessional writings such a binding authority, for what else can they mean than that the symbolic books should at least stand in relation to the Protestant church as Holy Scripture to Christianity as a whole? What else can they mean, for just as we confess that Holy Scripture must be the norm of faith for each and every Christian, so that nothing should conflict with it but everything should be in agreement with it and can be explicated in terms of it, they also demand that the faith of all Protestants is to consist in nothing other than conformity to the symbolic books and to that which is explicated in terms of these books. Moreover, just as we are unwilling to consider people Christian who not only in our own opinion but also by their own admission, knowingly and willingly consider their position on some matter that refers to God's blessing[11] to be contrary to Scripture, they will not hear of anyone who in exactly the same way considers one's position to be contrary to something or other that is presented in the symbolic books being considered a Protestant. It is precisely this, moreover, that goes too far, for the simple reason that we would then have to hold that within Christianity Protestantism constitutes a new revelation in exactly the same sense that Christianity is a new and original revelation within the entire domain of humanity.

We have never held this position, however, nor shall we ever hold it. In spite of its historical connection with Judaism, Christianity is something quite new and unique, whereas with Protestantism this is not the case, for its emergence from the church that preceded it is something quite different from the emergence of Christianity from Judaism. This is the reason why, by means of interpretation and inference, we try to explicate all Christian doctrine based on Scripture, without reverting to anything earlier or of greater note that could also be considered revelation. Likewise, we cannot explicate everything that is supposed to be Protestant based on the symbolic books. Rather, we can do so only in that we thereby go back to Scripture and supplement from it what the symbolic books themselves still lack in the full content of their doctrines of faith and morals by applying the Protestant principles laid down in them.[12]

Still, four considerations enter in at this point: 1. The symbolic books are not, unlike Scripture, comprised of any originative seed, in that the Spirit that breathes from them and that has brought them forth is not new but has simply become more free, the Christian spirit forming itself into a particular time and into specifically human characteristics. 2. Moreover, it must be granted that this Spirit is not and does not have to be attributed to those who speak in the symbolic books as specifically as it is attributed to the authors of holy Scripture, precisely because the authors of the symbolic books could go back to the earlier Word of the Spirit in

---

11. *Gottseligkeit.*
12. Ed. note: For a more extensive discussion of this matter see *Christian Faith,* §27, 112-18.

the authors of Scripture. 3. Furthermore, for the same reason our symbolic books did not need to be as complete a seed as Scripture had to be, though some things may be taken into the symbolic books that had not yet been greatly affected or fully developed by the Protestant spirit because others animated by the same spirit and in the same measure can and should transform it, whereas if something unchristian were adopted in Scripture there would be no one to whom the right could be assigned to transform and improve it. 4. Finally, it is indeed sufficiently clear from these differences that the symbolic books cannot have the same authority in the Protestant church that holy Scripture must necessarily have in the Christian church in general. In light of these four considerations, there always remains this important and highly significant parallel, that the symbolic books are the first in which the Protestant spirit was expressed in a public and permanent way, just as in Scripture the Christian spirit was first expressed in a public and permanent way, and everything that follows from this fact must be to their advantage.

Another very important difference between these books and Scripture, however, is this: that holy Scripture is directed wholly internally. Everything present there is written, under various circumstances, for Christians; of course, the major portion is written only to some, but precisely to the extent that anything has become a component of holy Scripture it is also written for all. As far as our symbolic books are concerned, the case is quite the opposite. They are entirely externally directed, for they have become symbolic books only to the extent that separation took place in the church, and viewed in terms of this separation they are directed toward members of the Roman church. If a free council had taken place that had brought a settlement between the two parties and had left no rupture, neither the Augsburg Confession nor the Schmalkald Articles[13] would have become symbolic books. It was only because of the rupture that these two writings became symbolic books, the former directed to the Catholic emperors and their nobles, the

---

13. Ed. note: A statement of doctrine composed by Luther in 1537 in response to Pope Paul III's call for a General Council to be held in Mantua in the following year.

latter to councils of the Catholic church. Everywhere in Scripture the main point is the unfolding of the Christian spirit, and the fact that this happens in contrast to Jewish and gentile ways of thinking is simply a matter of ways and means and is wholly subordinate. Everywhere in our symbolic books the main point is the expression of a definite contrast over against the Catholic church, and it was only within and about this contrast that the Protestant spirit could gradually develop.[14]

It is clearly an entirely different matter when it comes to the earlier confessional documents of the church and to the general conclusions reached by the church on the occasion of particular controversies. In contrast, these are directed wholly internally, and they receive their value precisely because no permanent division in the church arose on account of them; rather, in every case they were much more effective in neutralizing any division, if not immediately then certainly in their eventual results. However, it is precisely on this account that they also bear the vague and ambiguous title of "symbolic writings" in a quite different sense than do those in our church. Strictly speaking, one can obviously say only of the Augsburg Confession with its defensive posture and of the various Reformed confessions that they are directed entirely externally. One cannot say the same of Luther's Catechism[15] and the Heidelberg Catechism,[16] and least of all of what was promulgated at the Synod of Dordrecht,[17] and the Formula of Concord,[18] nor would anyone deny the difference between those two sets of documents. What still especially differentiates the catechisms is their popular character, which does not call for the same exact definition of concept as did the symbolic books, which were set forth

---

14. Ed. note: See footnote 9 above.

15. Ed. note: Luther published the Small Catechism and the Large Catechism in 1529. Both are included in the Book of Concord (see note 18 below). The reference here is most probably to the Small Catechism.

16. Ed. note: Published in 1562 and essentially Reformed in its theology, this catechism was accepted as the standard of doctrine in the Palatinate in 1563.

17. Ed. note: The five canons of the Synod of Dordrecht (Dort) 1618-19, assert strongly Calvinist principles against the Arminians (Remonstrants). Among other matters, the decisions of this synod resulted in the dismissal of some 200 Remonstrant ministers.

18. Ed. note: *The Book of Concord* (1580), is the definitive collection of the principal confessional documents of Lutheranism. See the latest English translation (2000).

by experts, and it is on account of this fact that they are not in the same measure appropriate for dogmatic purposes. However, what they do share in common with the Formula of Concord is that they are directed not externally but internally, just as the latter is nevertheless to be differentiated from the symbolic books in that its primary aim is not to instruct but to settle internal disputes.

Nevertheless, I think it is precisely for this reason that the title of symbolic book cannot appropriately be ascribed to the Formula of Concord in the same sense as to those genuine confessional writings. Furthermore, I consider it to be a completely fitting instinct that such a large portion of the Lutheran church did not wish to place it at the same rank, and to my mind the situation is no different with regard to the Reformed church with respect to the Synod of Dordrecht. The reason is that according to genuinely Protestant principles it is not possible for controversies within this church itself – of which one cannot demonstrate that they have overcome the contrast with Catholicism – to be decided other than in a temporary way, or rather, to express the matter quite openly, they can never be decided ecclesiastically but must bleed to death by themselves. The reason for this restriction is that not only do we have no representative structure that could make permanent and binding resolutions, but even if we did have one that we must not have, there would still be no means of deciding which controversies are to be brought to such a resolution and which are not, for everyone surely perceives and feels that not all controversies should be resolved if any trace of Evangelical freedom is to remain. Moreover, just as I consider it to be the right instinct – precisely because from the church's perspective those who met together at that time had no right to decide that something had to be laid down on controversial questions – that such a large portion of the Lutheran church never granted the Formula of Concord the privileged status of a symbolic book, I also consider it to be the right instinct of those who accepted it as a symbolic book to ensure that at least no schism would arise and that others would not be excluded from their church community. With regard to the Synod of Dordrecht, the circumstances were again different, though only apparently so. A schism did arise because of it, but, strictly speaking, it indeed has to be said that it was not recognized as such by the Reformed church as a whole and that those who did not recognize it were just as right in their not disrupting the common community of the church with those who did. Hence, it can be clearly seen that in both cases no decision was made by the church as a whole, and all other similar attempts to be found on a lesser scale also met with even less success.

Now, if we take these two points together – namely, that in the narrower and most generally accepted sense our symbolic books are indeed the first public exposition of the Protestant mode of thinking and teaching, and then also that to this extent they are entirely internally directed, so as to establish our contrast with the Catholic church – then it seems to me that they involve the following considerations. First, these symbolic books contain the points on the basis of which all Protestants must proceed and therefore around which we too must always rally, and we cannot acknowledge anyone who knowingly and willingly departs from them to be a true Protestant. Hence, it also seems to me that every minister should to this extent rightly be urged to make known his assent to these books. In my own opinion, the proper formula for this would be the following: "I declare that I find everything that is taught in our symbolic books against the errors and abuses of the Roman Catholic church, especially in the articles on justification and good works, on the church and ecclesiastical power, on the mass, on the function of the saints, and on vows, to be in complete agreement with Holy Scripture and with the original teaching of the church; and that as long as I am entrusted with the teaching office I shall not cease to expound these teachings and to uphold the orders in the church that are appropriate to them."

That is to say, by no means does this obligation require limitation to the "to what extent," which, converts this very obligation into some idle game. Rather, it is impossible for anyone to want to be a Protestant teacher who is not in agreement with the symbolic books in these matters, for example, the person who does not hold to justification by faith or to the free use of the divine Word, for either that person will be inclined toward the Catholic church or will consider the whole controversy and therefore everything that gave rise to Protestantism to be of trifling importance. However, with this obligation it is not at all implied that the positive formulations of those doctrines should not be open to correction but would always have to be presented in the form of the same letter; rather, this obligation is meant solely to present the Protestant contrast with Roman theory and practice. Now, if someone should say that this obligation then offers no guarantee whatsoever against crossing over to the other side, which is against the deviations of naturalism and free thinking, I would have to admit that it contains no such immediate safeguard. Moreover, in referring to what I have already said about how in my opinion no such guarantee can ever be provided on this path, I offer the following for consideration, namely, that even originally our symbolic books knew of no such thing at all, and thus if we make use of them for this purpose, in so doing we attribute something quite alien to them. Nevertheless, I claim that holding so firmly to our position against the Catholics and continually bringing to mind those doctrines of ours that distinguish us from them has indeed a great deal to do with those orders of the church that alone can gradually bring about a secure protection from both freethinking and any unchristian elements. Also, those who seek and wish only for that which is negative in the church must increasingly come to feel that they have nothing in common with us or we with them.

For this reason, to be sure, and also because in itself it seems to be quite necessary to set in contrast the ever-renewed and perhaps best-intentioned efforts of the opposite side with a clear understanding of the relationship between the two churches – which indeed many of our members from among the people who are not in a Catholic environment are already beginning to lose – I would like to add the second conclusion, namely, that our symbolic books – instead of being pushed aside as objects that have already outlived their purpose and are being preserved only for those who have to take up church history – should rather be put back in the hands of the people and in an appropriate way be made a subject for public instruction. I would consider it a fine and worthy aim if we could succeed in inducing every Evangelical Christian, irrespective of social status or gender, on their reception into the church – in the same sense and scope as I wish of how ministers of the church and with the necessary conviction – to indicate their assent to what our symbolic books set in contrast to the Roman church. Further, in that, on the one hand, this practice has protected our people from the snares of the Catholics, and on the other, it would also certainly keep our church together, at once earnest and strong, and throughout its continuing life in history would preserve it from that vague arbitrariness that in the sphere of religion as well as in the sphere of civic life arises from a loss of historical sensibility.

I advocate this aim so that what some seek to attain by wanting to make the symbolic books something that is different from and beyond their actual intention, thereby attaining for precisely this reason not what they intend but simply much that is alien, disagreeable and confusing. We see this happen, because every enterprise that lacks a foundation destroys itself and at the same time brings its own penalty. So, the goal will be reached much more certainly and without these attendant consequences if we simply acknowledge the true and original dignity of the symbolic books and keep them alive and effective in the church in accordance with their original intention. Now, the attempt to make the symbolic books what they are not has always stirred up confusion and brought utter conflict, whereas everything that occurs in the sense proposed here will certainly be blessed, and it will ever more enjoy the consent of all those who have sincerely taken the true well-being of the church to heart. These people have deviated now on this matter, now on that, only because it is not easy to combine free movement in scriptural study and in the application of Scripture, which is indispensable for our church, with an interest in the church's unity and stability. As long as it was not conceivable that union in the church would be more firmly protected by permanent structures and by an ecclesial polity that would express the shared disposition of the community and make it manifest, there was also in fact nothing left but either a fruitless experiment with some sort of authority attributed to the symbolic books that could not be maintained or an idle and resigned surrender to the sway of circumstances. Only now will it be possible with regard to these venerable writings and the way in which they are continually to intervene in our lives gradually to find the right balance.

May the interest in them that has again arisen, as it rightly should, on account of the jubilee festival of the renewal of our church be joined in this direction. In this way, with the help of the sure and courageous spirit of these books, the new centenary will also be strengthened for attainment of a genuinely Evangelical freedom and steadfastness in faith.

VII

To the Members of the Two Congregations
that Belong to the Church of the Triune God[*]

1820

It is unlikely to come as a surprise to our two dear congregations that after various preliminary approaches we now, with equal cordiality and joy, invite them to be fully merged and united into one Evangelical congregation. Indeed, the fact that several churches in our capital city were founded for both Evangelical confessions meant that such a union was intended for the future, and it is gratefully to be acknowledged that since then less and less value has been placed on this separation among us, and that all factionalism in this matter has more and more disappeared from peoples' hearts and minds. Yet, we have drawn a great deal closer to this union through our indelible memory of the last Reformation Jubilee,[1] at which for the first time members the two congregations together with their respective teachers joined together to celebrate Holy Communion. This was done using a form that had been brought closer to that of the rite's original institution and that did not approximate too closely to any opinion current in one part of the Evangelical church.

[*] *An die Mitglieder beider zur Dreifaltigkeitskirche gehörenden Gemeinen*, Berlin, 1820; SW I.5, 455-462; KGA I/9, 203-210.

1. Ed. note: This jubilee was held on Oct. 31 and Nov. 1, 1817. Schleiermacher's sermon on this occasion is included in the present volume.

Since that time the Reformed congregation and the Lutheran congregation had always been holding Holy Communion alternately according to this same form that unites us. Since then, the Reformed congregation has adopted the Lutherans' altar adornments, which had previously been strange to it. During a vacancy in their pastorate the Lutherans have gladly enjoyed the services of preachers from both confessions and in this way as well have also made known their readiness for union. Thus, nothing further seemed to be lacking other than that they too, following the example of their sister congregation, should observe the Communion rite of union[2] not just alternately but permanently. Then, after this also took place with the tacit assent of the congregation since Dr. Marheinecke's assumption of office[3] we no longer have any apprehensions that there could still be any misgivings in our two congregations about the whole matter of union that we have ardently wanted to bring into being for a long time. Hence, we have delayed no longer in our deliberations about the new ordering of all our relationships, in consultations arranged by the appointed authorities under the leadership of Superintendents Küster and Marot.[4] Having brought these matters to a conclusion, we placed the plan for these new arrangements for our church before the joint cosigning board of the two congregations, and in partnership with these men, who so faithfully attended to the well-being of our congregations, we now want to share with the dear members of

---

2. *Union*. Ed. note: The usual word used here and elsewhere is *Vereinigung*. In the third (1821) edition of Schleiermacher's *On Religion* several long endnotes to the fourth discourse refer to separatism versus the sense for church union and "the true church." See especially endnotes 6-8, 11-13, and 24. In endnotes 6-7 he argues that religious community can be "wholly separated" only by certain "mechanical procedures" some of which, as we can see, have been overcome in the uniting of the two congregations. See also the fifth discourse, endnote 3.

3. Ed. note: Philipp Konrad Marheinecke (1780-1846.) Appointed Professor of Theology at the University of Berlin in 1811, Marheinecke was also Schleiermacher's Lutheran colleague-in-ministry at the Church of the Triune God from 1820. For a valuable account of their respective attitudes and efforts toward union see especially Andreas Reich, *Friedrich Schleiermacher als Pfarrer an der Berliner Dreifaltigkeitskirche 1809-1834*, Schleiermacher Archiv Band 12, (Berlin and New York: Walter de Gruyter, 1992), 145-170.

4. Ed. note: Samuel Christian Gottfried Küster (1762-1838) and Samuel Marot (1770-1865), church superintendents and theological advisors to the government-appointed Consistory of the Province of Brandenberg. Marot was Schleiermacher's Reformed superior from 1816-1830, Küster his Lutheran counterpart.

our congregations all those matters in the document that can directly concern them, so that for our part we might thereupon be convinced of their consent to this work, which is so gratifying and well-pleasing to God. Once this task has been achieved the entire document regarding union can then be placed before our appointed church authorities[5] for approval.

First of all, concerning our service of worship in general, there were so few differences between our former two congregations that even after the union everything can more or less remain as it was before. If as a rule sermons were based on passages prescribed in the former Lutheran congregations but not in the former Reformed congregations, as multifarious divergent practices that exist in other places demonstrated, this practice has no connection with the hitherto existing difference between the confessions, and now as before it is a matter that remains within the freedom of each preacher. The same thing applies to the difference with regard to prayers read aloud, and until a new collection of church formulas appears the former prayers will remain in place for alternate use.

As far as Holy Communion is concerned, in the future members of both former congregations now will be able to participate in every administration of the sacrament without any distinction between them. However, so that our dear members may be assured that they will also receive their edification entirely from the person whom they have especially chosen as pastor when they want to approach the Lord's Table, on each occasion that person will conduct the preparation who is also responsible for the sermon preceding administration of Holy Communion, and this arrangement applies to Preacher Herzberg[6] no less than to the other two pastors. Counting on the trust of our dear congregations we shall come to an agreement about a formula for the preparation for as well as for the administration of Holy Communion itself, one that will be wholly appropriate to the meaning and

---

5. *Behörde*. Ed. note: This term Schleiermacher regularly used for official bodies and persons responsible for church government.

6. Ed. note: David Friedrich Georg Herzberg (1763-1822), for well over a decade second Lutheran minister at the Church of the Triune God.

194

spirit of the union. However, since there have formerly been several differences
with regard to the preparation and the making of confession, we simply make it
known that our intention is that in future we shall always give the preparatory address in front of the altar and grant absolution in the church itself, so that it will no
longer be necessary for communicants – as was formerly the case with the Lutheran communions – to assemble together for absolution in groups within our sacristy, which is at any rate uncomfortable for this purpose. Rather, after the preparatory address has been concluded, communicants will assemble together for
absolution closer to the altar table. Beside the table will also be placed a plate in
which they can place their freewill offerings, as is customary on this occasion.
However, it is self-understood that otherwise all who especially wish to do so are
free to open their hearts to their pastor in the sacristy, and with future arrangements this can certainly take place more easily and more freely.

Our thinking, however, is to administer Holy Communion each Sunday from
now on in effect twice on alternating Sundays, once after the sermon in the main
service and once after the sermon in the early service.[7] In increasing the number of
opportunities for communion in this way, it is indeed also our wish that this practice might induce communicants to distribute themselves in a somewhat more uni-
form way than before. Nevertheless, in the future too, on those holy days on which
the number of communicants tends to be the greatest, communion is to be administered twice, after the early sermon as well as after the main sermon, and preparation for the early communions will then be held before the sermon in the early service.[8] All of these matters, together with what are considered appropriate changes
in the rotation of preachers, will be made clear to our dear members in the sched-
ule for the coming year.

---

7. Ed. note: It was already the practice, when two or more pastors were on staff, for them to
alternate assignments to the early and main services. This practice was then being consolidated
with respect to celebration of communion.
8. Ed. note: Usually this preparation was held on the previous Saturday.

In our city baptisms have never been bound to either parish or confession, so that as far as this matter is concerned nothing will be changed other than that it is our wish that, given the opportunity afforded by union, the ancient Christian practice of the laying on of hands by the godparents, which has been observed until now in the Lutheran congregation, will be made the general practice. In future, baptisms as well as weddings will as a rule be performed by Preacher Herzberg; nevertheless, it is understood that both of the other pastors will also gladly undertake the performance of these official duties as often as they are specifically called upon to do so.

As far as the religious instruction of our youth is concerned, in the future Preacher Herzberg will also take an equal part in this matter; thus, all members of the two former congregations are free to choose to which of the three of us they wish to entrust their children. Schools in the parish will also work in partnership, and in that the hitherto Reformed school is being added to the rest, needy young people who are instructed at the expense of the congregation will also be able to be allotted to each school even more conveniently.

Like us preachers, the other servants of the church have then also come to an amicable agreement about their duties, and the younger and more vigorous man, the hitherto Reformed precentor and verger Mr. Grahl assumes the responsibility for all the duties essential to the verger's offices. Hence, in all matters of this nature our members are to consult with him. Thus, it also rests with him to collect the contributions stipulated for the different duties of office, arrangements about which will remain exactly as they were before with the self-evident exception that the difference in rates between the hitherto Reformed and Lutheran congregations that was introduced at certain points can no longer be continued.[9]

---

9. Ed. note: In part, the reference here is to seat rents. These applied on the main and second floors, while the third floor seats, taken mostly by servants and directly in Schleiermacher's view, were free. Thus, in this round building from his raised pulpit Schleiermacher would have moved his gaze up and down and all around, but he faced those sitting in the free seats head on.

The fact that the church property of the two former congregations is now also wholly merged into one is certainly a reason for everyone to rejoice, and it is something that our church administrators have long desired.

Now, when all of this is put into effect in accordance with our wishes, both of our former congregations will then in fact form the one undivided Evangelical congregation, and those members of the former Reformed congregation who live outside the parish also have the self-same rights in it as do our members who live within the parish, though it is certainly also to be assumed that with regard to the few situations that involve parish duties they will likewise consent to them for the good of the church they adhere to.

Based on these extracts from our union document, our dear members can see sufficiently clearly how the future situation of the congregation and its church life will differ from the previous one. They will also see that no restriction or damage of any kind can arise for them from this union but will see instead how they stand to gain in close connection among themselves and with all their former teachers. However, although we do not expect objections to this work of union from our members, our proposals will not be presented to the appropriate officials until immediately after the end of this year, and we ask that any member of our congregations to whom anything still appears obscure or questionable in this new relationship as we have discussed it here, in the interval will discuss it with either one of the two superintendents so that along with our document they can at the same time make a conscientious report regarding our congregations' consent to it and can demonstrate that in the course of this process everything that is externally appropriate has also been accomplished. We ask this, for we know our dear congregations, and we know that they are not attached to external details but refer all our church arrangements to the advancement of genuinely Evangelical piety. We also know that without regard to former differences they have always been bound together in faith and love. For our part, then, we have no doubt whatever that they will receive this announcement of a complete union with heartfelt joy, that they will be one with us in the pious wish that it will be brought to an early conclusion, and that they, as we, shall expect the rich blessing of God that will arise from this union when we conform to the apostolic principle in a measure even more complete than has occurred here before, namely, that we are to be "eager to maintain the unity of the Spirit in the bond of peace."[10]

Berlin, 6th December, 1820.

---

10. Ed. note: Eph. 4:3. Schleiermacher published a sermon entitled "On Unity in the Spirit" on Eph. 4:1-3 in *Magazin von Fest-, Gelegenheits- und anderen Predigten und Kleineren Amtsreden*, Neue Folge, hg.v. Röhr, Schleiermacher und Schuderoff, Bd 5 (Magdeburg: W. Heinrichshofen, 1827), 234-256; also in SW II. 4 (1835), 636-656, and (1844), 688-706. It could well have been preached earlier, as early as 1821. This sermon certainly makes a fitting accompaniment in proclamation to the efforts described here. See also his 1821 comments on his preparations for church union in endnote 16 to the fourth discourse (cf. endnote 1 to the fifth discourse) in *On Religion*, and endnote 26 for his general call for renewal in the Evangelical church.

VIII

Sermon on Palm Sunday, 31 March 1822
at the Celebration of the Union of the Two Congregations
of the Church of the Triune God[*]

The grace of our Lord and Savior Jesus Christ, the love of God the Father,
and the communion of the Holy Spirit be with us. Amen.

Text: Philippians 2:1-4[1]

So if there is any encouragement in Christ, any incentive of love, any
participation in the Spirit, any affection and sympathy, complete my joy by
being of the same mind, having the same love, being of full accord and of
one mind. Do nothing from selfishness or conceit, but in humility count
others better than yourselves. Let each of you look not only to one's own
interests, but also to the interests of others.[2]

---

[*] "Am Palmsonntage, den 31 März 1822, bei der Feier der Vereinigung der beiden zur Dreifaltigkeitskirche gehörenden Gemeinden." in *Gottesdienstliche Feier bei der am Palmsonntage,
den 31 März vollzogenen Vereinigung der beiden zur Dreifaltigkeitskirche gehörenden Gemeinden*, (Berlin: Th. Chr. F. Enslin, 1822), 13-35; SW II.4 (1835), 236-249, and (1844), 162-175.

1. Ed. note: On Rogation Sunday, May 12, 1822, Schleiermacher preached on the same text
within a series on Philippians but with a different emphasis, later published in SW II.10 (1856),
480-491. Thus the two sermons present an unusual opportunity to compare the two treatments of
the same text and only six weeks apart. (See p. 480.)

2. Ed. note: The significantly different German text (v.s. the RSV above) is translated as follows: "Now, if there exists among you any exhortation (*Ermahnung*) in Christ, any comfort of
love, any communion in the Spirit (*Gemeinschaft des Geistes*), any heartfelt love and compassion
(*herzliche Liebe und Barmherzigkeit*), complete my joy in your being of one mind (*Sinn*), having
the same love, being of one accord and of one voice. Do nothing out of quarrelsomeness (*Zank*),
or vain praise (*eitle Ehre*). Instead, out of humility let each of you regard others as higher (*höher*)

200

My devout friends, how glorious are these words of the apostle, in which he exhorts Christians to that concord which so essentially becomes those who are all members of one body and who through love of one and the same divine Redeemer[3] are also united together in sharing the most sincere love among themselves. Yet, nevertheless, must not the warmth and profundity of the apostle's words – inadequate in themselves yet at the same time surpassing themselves in their mounting emphases – not strike us as unexpected in a letter from that earliest time, when Christians should not have been tempted to fall into discord since they were a little flock that was closely knit already on account of their still being few in number – and even more because of adversities from without? Moreover, should we not almost believe that the apostle had a presentiment that times would come when this very exhortation could not be impressed upon Christians urgently enough? Besides, my good friends, we recall that from the very beginning human weakness was also revealed in various ways amidst stirrings of the divine Spirit, which held sway since the Redeemer's appearance, likewise we discover that in several of the apostle's letters he not only exhorts Christians of different estates and social circumstances to concord and love. Further, quite especially those from among the Jewish people and those from among the Gentiles who had confessed to the truth of the Gospel, were in fact frequently in danger of falling into discord among themselves, so that the apostles and others among Christianity's earliest teachers had to apply all diligence to heal schisms, prevent divisions, and arrange for the kind of common leadership in Christian life that would treat the conscience of one part with consideration and not weigh down that of another part with superfluous burdens. In addition, when we then pursue the history of Christianity further since that time of the apostles we discover the same almost uninterrupted oscillation in the Christian church. At one point we find tendencies toward division or an actual outbreak of it, depending on whether misplaced zeal was successfully

than yourself, and let each of you look not to what pertains to oneself but to what pertains to others."

3. *Göttlichen Erlöser.*

held in check or was the cause of going further astray. At another point we find reunion and calm depending on whether the Spirit of truth was triumphing over error or on whether those who had let the essence of Christianity slip from their inner lives were deceiving themselves and were also outwardly separating themselves from the Christian church.

Yet, if we really want to grasp the power and the innermost meaning of these words of the apostle properly, how can we do otherwise than look also to the future from this scene of abundant change! Oh how glorious it would be if, as the apostle wishes, the "exhortation" and "comfort" that comes from teaching were ever shared among Christians, if in this way, built on the same foundation on which all of us base our salvation, deep "love" would prevail among them, if in this way each person were so animated by the effort to regard the other in "humility" as higher than oneself and to look more "to what pertains to others" than "to what pertains to oneself!" Indeed, if this became everywhere the spirit of the Christian life, as the apostle here entreats, implores and enjoins on Christian hearts, Oh then every dividing[4] wall that separates them would have to vanish away. Then would come that glorious time when the whole of Christendom would be one undivided flock under one shepherd.[5] When this time will come – for it will come as surely as the words are true of him in whom all the promises of God are Yes and Amen[6] – when it will come is not given to us to know but to the Father who has held the time and the hour of this power of the Son in reserve.[7] However, this, my good friends, we can know: that this time of blessing will have to begin when those who are also externally divided yet are least internally separated from one another are again reunited in the exhortation and comfort that come from teaching and in the pure love of brethren for one another. Further, just as the immediate purpose of these words of the apostle was to prevent all divisions among Christians, they also

---

4. Ed. note: Eph. 2:14.
5. Ed. note: Jn. 10:16.
6. Ed. note: II Cor. 1:20.
7. Ed. note: Mk. 13:26, 32.

pronounce his blessing on every reuniting of Christians that has been generated by means of this spirit of love and concord. They also demonstrate to us on what it will depend so that the union that we have established among us and to the inception and solemnization of which this day is devoted, really brings to all of us and to those who will come after us in this Evangelical congregation of the Lord the blessing that is based on obedience to the gentle voice of the divine Word.

With this understanding, my good friends, and with guidance from the words of the apostle, let us now reflect together *on the nature of the union that has been established among us.* First, let us look back at the way in which it has come into being, but then look ahead too, so that we can answer the question as to how we are to live together with each other in accordance with this spirit of union from this present day on – and may it long be blessed by God. This, then, is the subject of our Christian reflection and of our pious meditation today.

[I]

My devout friends, if we desire to recall the origin of this union of the two congregations belonging to hitherto distinct Evangelical confessions, we clearly cannot do this without first considering the division from which we have thereby been set free. When in those eternally memorable and blessed times of the Reformation of the church the light of the Gospel finally broke forth irresistibly and gloriously, after various anticipatory signs and in many repeatedly frustrated efforts – as this is the way in human affairs – and a new day began for the Christian church, the fire lit by the divine Spirit ignited simultaneously in different locales in Christendom but at first especially in the German-speaking countries. Moreover, just as the earliest leaders and initiators were independent of one another and without personal association, it was natural and human that their work also assumed different forms in accordance with differences as to persons and circumstances. From the very beginning and wherever possible, some particularly set about exterminating, roots and all, everything to which the misguided hearts and minds of Christians had attached themselves, and thereby these persons had been diverted from the one thing that is needful.[8] Cautioned by saddening experiences, others made it a law unto themselves to retain as much as possible of that which had persisted in the public worship of the Christian church for many centuries. Moreover, they first wanted to banish only those things that were most objectionable, those that were most clearly marked with the stamp of error and that undoubtedly served only some pernicious superstition so that the piety of the people would not also lose too many of its customary supports or that anxious consciences would not be unnecessarily oppressed or confused because of too many changes.

Now, in conformity with these two different modes of action it was natural and unobjectionable that social orders and worship practices in the new Evangelical church were formed in different ways. Yet, my good friends, this situation was very easy indeed to excuse in a time of such varied and restless movement, but it was still a regrettable misunderstanding having arisen out of human weakness whereby faith and love are unfortunately so often restricted that those who were most earnest about effecting a thorough restoration of an original, pure Christianity could not fully agree concerning those two differences nor concerning far more trifling differences in doctrine. This happened in that the first group feared that the other could all too easily revert to erroneous opinion and superstition and that in a somewhat altered form these could again take possession of peoples' hearts and minds. On the other hand, moreover, the second group was fearful of the first in that the purified Word, now deprived of all ornament, and the purified yet radically reduced orders of worship and of Christian practice might not have sufficient power to support the hearts and minds of people in the same faith and in the same undivided sensibility; rather, the danger was that the more arbitrariness took the upper hand in ways of thinking and in the ordering of the church, the more that which had long been established would be cleared away. Accordingly, it then hap-

---

8. Ed. note: See Lk. 10:42 (Mary and Martha).

pened that no full communion came into being between the two main branches of the Reformation church, rather, not being able to gain agreement with each other with regard to either confession of doctrine or the sacrament of the altar, each party went its own way.

Now, if at certain times this separation was extended and embittered especially because not a little also occurred that was the result of selfishness and conceit,[9] at other times, to the contrary, there was also no lack of heartfelt, mutual exhortation and comfort that come from teaching. Further, often Christians of both parties of the Evangelical church were encouraged and challenged to ponder carefully whether it was still worthwhile giving up this blessing of a larger and more intimate community for the sake of that which divided them. Times did indeed come when it was quite natural and inevitable that many of the better people from both sides in humility counted others better than themselves;[10] when on the one side or the other the light of the divine Word shone more brightly for a time; when on one side or the other a stronger resistance arose against the opponents of some concern held in common; when on the one side or the other the true blessing of a pure Christian piety was to be found at a higher level of fulfillment. In this way, at different times various attempts were then also made to unite the divided congregations and to bind all of them together in one community of love among brethren and in the same consolation of the same divine Word. Yet, the hour of the Lord had not yet come,[11] and even the best-intentioned attempts continually failed, even though they were supported by the authority and the wishes of the great and powerful of the earth, and were brought about and initiated by those who were considered to be the wisest of their time.

Finally, a few years ago[12] – and we all think of this time with heartfelt joy and emotion – when that part of the Evangelical church that had been formed chiefly

---

9. Ed. note: Phil. 2:3a.
10. Ed. note: Phil. 2:3b.
11. Ed. note: Jn. 2:4.
12. Ed. note: The reference here is to the 1817 celebration of the 300th anniversary of Luther's posting of the *95 Theses*.

by the efforts of Luther and his friends was again approaching its centenary memorial festival, it was impossible even for members of the other Evangelical confession not to have shared with their brethren in joy and thanksgiving to God, and only the general desire of all well-intentioned Evangelical Christians was realized in the directive[13] that in our territory the festival of the Reformation of the church should be a common festival for both branches of the Evangelical church. Moreover, as the time then drew nearer the hearts of the ministers of both churches of this our capital city overflowed with joy and love. Furthermore, assured by the approval of the king and wishing to provide an example to their congregations, even before this fine festival, they decided to assemble together to celebrate Holy Communion under a form whereby no one's particular opinion would be offended, and, by sharing together at the Lord's Table, to declare at the same time that they did not consider those matters on which the two churches differed sufficient to divide the church community and to prevent any longer the two churches from becoming and remaining one.

Further, this they indeed did with due deliberation and reflection, without coming to any agreement beforehand, as it were, on this or that controversial opinion. They avoided such a move, in that, in keeping with previous experience, they could only believe that if that which was inexplicable and inconceivable were again to be discussed in detail, and that which was mysterious forced into human words, no such words could be the right ones, and precisely because the right word was lacking simply greater multiplicity of expressions and ways of putting things would always have to appear. On this festive day itself this was the good example that numerous members of the two churches in the congregations of this capital then followed, especially in those congregations belonging to the different branches of the Evangelical church that share one and the same church building who have indicated precisely by means of this common participation at the Lord's Table their feeling of being in agreement about the essential matters of Christian

---

13. Ed. note: See Schleiermacher's address of November 3, 1817, in this volume.

faith, and of how, from their perspective, nothing stood in the way of bringing the former division completely to an end.

So, my good friends, ever since the essentials in this matter had been concluded, and as a consequence thereof in our city we have already witnessed more than one example of congregations that had formerly belonged to one of these confessions – partly of their own choice and partly with the approval of those responsible for leadership in church affairs – retaining teachers who had formerly belonged to the other confession, and it was precisely in this way that the union of the two churches was expressed most effectively.

If we now ask what then remained to be done by way of our preparation for today's special festival, it is indeed only the following few matters whereby what had already generally taken place would be adapted to our special circumstances. That is to say, we, the teachers of the two congregations, cherished the heartfelt wish that at this point we should no longer have divided and limited obligations toward you, dear members of our congregations. Rather, we wanted to be able to belong equally to you all, and now that no one is any longer disturbed by the difference – which to us seemed too trifling for us to set limits to our calling – each can devote himself with all care and love to all those who most would place their trust in him and would desire his services. Those together with whom we had long managed the external affairs of both congregations have wished that the community that already partly existed between the two, and the joint administration of our church possessions might now become a total merger of our holdings, also that the two congregations might cast together everything that serves their Christian worship of God and is there for them, and might stand for one another also with respect to their shared Christian duties to care for the needy and educate young people. Finally, it was certainly everyone's wish that the differences that still remain with regard to worship practices would now also disappear so that the old division would not still appear to adhere to them.

Accordingly, with the assistance and consent of our superiors we have shared in the execution of all these matters without compromising your freedom in your use of our services. We have arranged that the church properties of both parties be held in common without asking how much or how little each party has contributed. Also, for the different worship practices and administration of the holy sacraments of the Christian church we have drafted ways and means common to us all whereby in these matters too all former division is overcome. Moreover, all that was formerly customary in each congregation has so been fused together that alongside one's own each person will discover what was the other's and will have every opportunity in humility to hold it in esteem and to receive it in love. In addition, we hope that by this fusion we have combined the two perspectives in what is essential to our service of worship – which the first reformers of the church thought they could attain only separately – in that, on the one hand we have readily retained everything that gives expression to a genuinely Christian sensibility and can represent a component of Christian faith, but, on the other hand, we have also made a rigorous check to ensure that wherever possible nothing in our service of worship would survive that cannot belong to the worship of God in the Spirit and that has no connection with the essence of Christian piety. This much, my good friends, after all that had taken place earlier, was what still had to be resolved so that we could be wholly united in one Evangelical congregation, and in its historical context this is the significance of the union that we celebrate in this hour which is indeed important and sacred to all of us.

[II]

Second, however, so that this one congregation should also stand the test, let us reflect together on what we shall have to do if we are to honor this union and live together in its spirit in accordance with the guidance provided by the words of our apostle.

If I am to sum up this task briefly, I must remind you that the historical presentation I have just given already makes a distinction with regard to this union between matters that are more internal and spiritual and those that are more external and material, though both appertain to each and are not to be separated from each other. Likewise, if we are to grasp their full meaning, these words of the apostle must also have reference to both. Accordingly, let us now especially direct our attention to each of these factors as well.

First, as concerns the spiritual factor: this aspect of our union would certainly have no value if it did not contribute to the purification and strengthening of our Christianity. Yet, within the whole compass of the Evangelical church there are still a great many well-disposed yet troubled Christians who view with a certain suspicion what has become the intense endeavor among us and in other places in our German fatherland to unite the two separated parties of the Evangelical church. They view this as though it were a work of recklessness and imprudence, and precisely for this reason even as a work of indifference, as if those who favor it most did not have enough to do with the purity of Evangelical doctrine, or as if they had not at least properly reflected on their faith when in regard to church communion they had declared the differences between the two churches to be trifling. Indeed, the apprehension does exist that those who are promoting this union would just as readily revert to being under that yoke of human ordinances that our forebears no longer wanted to tolerate and for the deliverance from which we too still give praise to God with heartfelt thankfulness in our common prayers and entreat God to preserve this freedom. Oh, that we may never give these people any opportunity to have their suspicion justified and to discredit our union. I am certainly not aware, my dear friends, of any reason to be anxious about this. In my own conscience I am firmly convinced that those among us and in the Evangelical church of our fatherland who most earnestly and urgently pursue this union are not persons who out of indifference to all differences in faith would also just as readily form as close a union as ours with all other Christians. Rather, they are precisely those who place a high value on the doctrine of the justification of persons before God through faith in the Redeemer, a doctrine that has been re-established among us, and of their sanctification in communion with him and those who are most sincerely filled with the conviction that no external works or exercises that are alleged to be meritorious and no obedience to human ordinances can ever confer merit on any person before God. Indeed, it must already be clear to everyone that the previously existing separation can be least pleasing only to those who place such a value on that vital main point and on everything that is immediately connected with it that only on this basis would they want to unite and sustain all Evangelical Christians quite strongly. Moreover, just as certainly as I am convinced of this in my conscience, so according to my best knowledge I can but bear witness to our congregations to the fact that this spirit of the Evangelical church rests on these persons and that they have entered into union precisely with this sensibility.

However, we cannot deny nor may we overlook the fact that there are more than enough examples of those who, in order to bring shame on the Evangelical church, again forsake the bosom of the church to subject themselves anew to the yoke of human ordinances in the church that first excluded us on its account. Thus, well should we hear spoken the divine Word of admonition: "Therefore let anyone who thinks he stands take heed lest he fall."[14] And, "watch and pray that you may not enter into temptation."[15] Thus, whether we then view it generally or with regard to our own congregation, only this union can and should but reduce and not increase the temptation to fall back, for the more help that is offered one and the more support one can obtain for oneself, the more everyone will indeed stand secure. Moreover, to what purpose, my good friends, would we indeed have concluded this covenant, to what purpose would we have demolished every previous

---

14. Ed. note: I Cor. 10:12.
15. Ed. note: Mk. 14: 38; Lk. 22:40,46.

210

wall of division[16] if thereby even more spiritual strengths were not to be united in the most heartfelt way, in genuine zeal for the light of knowledge that God has kindled among us? Moreover, the more we take advantage of our union for this purpose, the more we shall do it honor.

Each of us in his or her own way now has a yet greater and more clearly stated right than before to appropriate as one's undisputed possession every instruction that enlightens and every encouragement that strengthens, making no distinction between the two church communities as to which belongs where. Everyone among us to whom God has granted strength and light is now and over a wider compass even more entitled to take steps to strengthen and fortify every weak heart and mind. Everyone now has a yet broader sphere in which one can bear witness to the peace of the soul and to the stability of the heart and mind that arise from our Evangelical faith. May this salutary communion of the Spirit, in which in humility each seeks the good of the other and each edifies and encourages the other, now become ever more sincere in our more extended community. Without selfishness or conceit, may there be much talk among us of that on which the salvation of souls is based, and may those who until now have perhaps still kept themselves more separate also be bound together in this love, and may every individual's meditation as well as all shared scholarship always be conducted and maintained in the true Evangelical spirit through public reflection on the divine Word, a public reflection that at this place of our gatherings will originate from its servants now and in the future.

Moreover, precisely our services of common worship and everything that pertains to their inner content as well as their outer form are then the second matters that I include in the spiritual aspect of our union. Now, in this matter, my good friends, from the beginning it has been the understanding of those whom God has used as God's instruments for the improvement of the church that just as external matters in this connection are of human origin and arose under specific circum-

16. Ed. note: Eph. 2:14.

stances, so too are they accidental and alterable, but essential and not subject to alteration are only those institutions established by our Redeemer himself, who made preparations for baptism and the Lord's Supper and founded proclamation of the divine Word in his church. Everything else in our service of worship is simply to serve to ensure that the Word of the Lord and the blessing of those heavenly possessions that are deposited in the church should enter our souls more readily and more deeply. Accordingly, as soon as something has lost this power it may no longer continue to be part of the worship services among Christians so that what no longer has meaning would not be taken to have any. Now, just as the present form of our common worship service is conceived and practiced in this sense as well, so we will give honor to our union only if we hold fast to these principles. May the Lord grant that not only we for as long as we shall live but also our children after us will discover truly Christian edification precisely in this form of our service of worship, which in its essence each of our previous congregations has taken on from our forefathers and faithfully preserved for us and which we have now brought together from both congregations into one. Still, by no means did we intend to place a value on this letter, which however dear to us it is – nonetheless still is only human – or on any other patrimony as though there were something divine about them and that they should be clung to forever! Rather, with us it is this that we want to resolve in advance, namely, that when the Lord reveals to us something better we want to receive it with joyful and thankful hearts, not snatching at what is new when we have grown weary of what is long-established, but holding firmly to what we have as long as it proves to be a blessing to us; not honoring that which is long-established because it is long-established, so that when what has died away remains mingled with things that are alive, it will not weaken their vigorous power or defile their beauty. Let us hold to this standard, and as far as it depends on us our Evangelical church will never age, but will always be rejuvenated in itself through the power of light and truth. If the different perspectives that are now united among us to form one living community always continue to work together in this spirit, at no time will we lack the opportunity to organize our Christian assemblies in such a way that everyone who feels the need for genuinely Christian, shared devotion, who, filled with the desire to worship God in spirit and in truth,[17] will find their satisfaction there.

Now, however, in regard to the second matter that concerns external and material things in our union, with the obligation of both congregations to provide for the support of their needy members and for the upbringing of their abandoned young people, we have also brought together all the means of assistance of both into one. Thus, may an undivided Christian benevolence now be practiced among all members of the united congregation, and an undivided zeal for the whole among all people who have our mutual concerns at heart. How could the merger of two congregations into one then be better glorified than when our life together in the church would then blossom more vigorously and also prove itself to be active in every expression of Christian benevolence and compassion! Thus, in this respect our wish and our entreaty to our congregations is that the consciousness of belonging to a greater whole that has been formed through heartfelt love might encourage each person to take its cares more vigorously and joyfully upon oneself and to bear its burdens. With respect to Christian charity within the congregation I can also express this wish without even appearing to give the impression that it bears within it a silent reproach. This can be so, for from that time when the hardships of war had caused damage to our place of worship, but especially since the time that some members of the congregation shared with us in the care of what we hold in common, we have received the most excellent demonstrations of the lively way in which our worthy congregations participated in the improvement and embellishment of our service of worship and in all things that must be matters of mutual care and obligation for Christians bound together in this way. Yet, may all who are now united in love among brethren ever be and remain mindful that everything that is to remain worthy and dear to us must also continually remain the ob-

---

17. Ed. note: Jn. 4:23.

ject of our ardent care and lively endeavors. Then, on every occasion in the future too, we shall have equally gratifying demonstrations of the ardent common spirit[18] and fervent love that exists among the members of our congregation. Furthermore, let us by no means forget that if they are merely prompted by the prevailing circumstances of individuals, even charity and generosity neither are so honorable nor partake of the same level of Christian godliness as when they are simply the natural expressions of a genuine common spirit.

For that reason, our final wish then remains, that with the help of our improved polity – which in accordance with the gracious promises of our king the Evangelical church of our territory has looked forward to for a long time – individual congregations including our own might very soon be given the opportunity to be satisfied not only with what love, benevolence, perseverance in what is good, and patient forbearance can accomplish within the life of individuals, but also to show even more vigorously by means of increased participation and manifold service that will be called for, whenever, with the help of a well-ordered polity, a Christian congregation can truly and wholly present itself as such a congregation, how in earnest it is that each individual should look more to others' interests than to one's own and how a love among brethren in which in humility each regards the other as higher than oneself holds sway in all.

These, my good friends, are the gladdening prospects with which we embark on this new situation in our church community! Through the power of the divine Word and with the help of the divine Spirit may all these promises be fulfilled to us. On that account, however, let us now entreat God together in a fervent prayer.

Gracious Father in heaven, who according to your goodwill has prepared for us this day of joyous celebration of brotherly concord: Oh let that which is begun with earnestness and in love also remain ever a blessing among us with the help of your Spirit. Keep us all most closely united in the one thing that is necessary,[19] so that in

---

18. *Gemeingeist.* Ed. note: For Schleiermacher, God in Christ entering the community of faith is the Holy Spirit.
19. Ed. note: see footnote 8 above.

one common confession of him whom you have sent to be our Redeemer, and not forgetting our corruption and impotence we experience the salvation that is prepared for those who through faith in your Son are ever more purified from all vice. To this end, may the common reflection on your Word and the blessed partaking of your holy sacraments strengthen us in our new union now as before. May this congregation never lack faithful teachers who truly proclaim your Word, and in souls in need of salvation never let the thirst be quenched for the water from the spring of eternal life[20] that your Son has opened for all of us and that according to your gracious compassion might never again be cut off from us or contaminated. Strengthen among us the spirit of true concord and love among brethren so that esteeming lightly that which is small we shall strive after that which is great, and in referring all that is earthly to that which is eternal simply possess and use it as a means to ensure that what each has at heart is the well-being of all and what all have at heart is the well-being of each and that together we work out our salvation in truth and love.[21] According to your grace, grant that among us nothing will be lost of the light and of the freedom of conscience that belongs to the Evangelical church, and let this union also be blessed to the end that with increased strength we shall ever more perfectly fulfill these sacred obligations with which we are bound to you and the future generation now that we have been united as a greater whole. Let your blessing rest on the new yet little altered form of our service of worship and from this place in the future as well create a rich fullness of Christian edification for all those who in fear of you and in faith in our Redeemer will seek it here. Preserve in this congregation the fine sense of Christian benevolence and charity so that among us there may never be any lack even of external resources to spread further the blessing of your Word and to guide the light of truth into souls.

Above all, from thankful hearts may we commend to you our gracious king, who takes such a faithful part in this work of Christian union and who as far as the

---

20. Ed. note: Jn. 4:14.
21. Ed. note: Phil. 2:12.

powers of human authority reach in this matter seeks to encourage it in the whole extent of his kingdom. Bless him and his whole family that among us they will continue to be an example of Christian godliness and honor them with true health and happiness according to your grace. Bless the king's government, and as today with all our fellow-citizens we give thanks to you for that glorious victory that crowned the martial deeds of the king and his peoples, so we entreat you that the king may yet further prosper in that which he undertakes in the illumination of the light of your Spirit for the well-being of the peoples that you have entrusted to him. Surround him with judicious and conscientious ministers who will assist him in discerning and implementing that which is right and pleasing to you. In the entire extent of his realm keep his subjects loyal and obedient so that in peace and concord and under his protection we all may lead lives that are well-pleasing to you and worthy of our name. Bless, gracious God, each one among us in the circle of our several callings, and let the parts we play in the public good flourish well. Fill us with the joyful conviction that we are all laborers in your vineyard[22] and that it is demanded of us all that we should build and advance your kingdom, but receive especially all those everywhere and those among us who in the adversities and afflictions of life seek their refuge in you. Revive them with your comfort, and as your grace is shown to be strong in those who are weak,[23] so also may the faith in all of us be ever more strengthened so that among those who love you all things will work together for good.[24] Amen.

---

22. Ed. note: Mt. 20:1.
23. Ed. note: II Cor. 12:9.
24. Ed. note: Rom. 8:28.

IX

To Doctors D. von Cölln and D. Schultz:
An Open Letter from Dr. Fr. Schleiermacher[*]

1831

My most honorable colleagues in office and friends, when you receive this open letter you will immediately presume that it is in connection with your jointly-written *Open Declaration and Preliminary Caution*.[1] However, you will scarcely think that I could be in disagreement with you about this matter, and yet it is not otherwise! I received your article from a traveler prior to your being good enough to forward it to me, yet soon enough before the festival[2] that we have since celebrated for me to enter my protest with you in regard to the same matter. However, as I am a bad letter-writer and a slow writer in any case, I have missed this deadline, and since that time so much has in turn been published on the subject that is the primary focus of your article too that I must almost feel afraid that in this ever-increasing flood of voices, some with names and some anonymous, some famous

---

[*] "An die Herren D. D. D. von Cölln und D. Schulz (1831)," *Theologische Studien und Kritiken,* Jahrgang 1831, Erstes Heft; SW I.5, 667-702; KGA I/10, 395-426.

1. Ed. note: Daniel von Cölln and David Schulz, *Über theologische Lehrfreiheit auf den evangelischen Universitäten und deren Beschränkung durch symbolische Bücher. Eine offene Erklärung und vorläufige Verwahrung,* Breslau, 1830.

2. Ed. note: The reference is to the tercentennial celebrations marking the handing over of the Augsburg Confession held throughout the entire country on 25 June 1830.

218

and some obscure, my words will pass completely unnoticed. Unfortunately, however, along with being slow I have also retained the gift for this tenacity that does not readily permit me to let go whenever I have laid hold of a thought with a certain determination. Hence, what should have come into your hands much earlier and more recently, you now receive as a delayed supplement. Now, if to the objections that originally prompted me certain other matters adhere that I would particularly like to discuss with you, accept the assurance that I knew of no more appropriate way to express my thanks to you for having made this powerful joint statement in connection with the important concerns of our church.

Now with regard to the festival, I readily grant you that under the present circumstances I too did not look forward to it with any particular joy. Considering everything that would be said and written, I was deeply anxious that much might be done to embitter the contesting parties toward each other even more and to incite each other toward even fiercer struggles, which from a human point of view would inevitably have to bring our concerns to the height of confusion. Yet, I could not share the concern that you seem to have entertained that this festival, the arrangements for which had not been made at the time when you wrote, might be made use of as a means of introducing among us a new obligation to the Augsburg Confession. Meanwhile, the day itself very much allayed even my fears. As far as Berlin is concerned, the great participation in this festival pleasantly surprised me; it was so emphatic that indeed there was no church before which crowds of people would not have had to turn away. In an old Evangelical town such as my own beloved native city,[3] which has always maintained an excellent commitment to the church, this is self-understood, and since it has such fertile ground for Evangelical teachers in your faculty now, surely it has never appeared in such churchly glory as at this festival and must have afforded a gratifying sight of dignified celebration. Moreover, as far as this day's addresses from pulpit and podium were concerned, I myself was too much occupied with the former to have been able to attend any ad-

3. Ed. note: Schleiermacher was born in Breslau on November 21, 1768.

dresses from the podium, but as far as I understand from what has been said here I could only take delight in all of them. This is the case, for no one among us appears to have departed from the king's fine statement that we should heartily conform to the spirit of this confessional writing, and those who would readily have us again swear to the normative doctrine of a letter found no interpreter on this day among the Evangelical ministers of our city. Although I have still not received more detailed news about the day, it will certainly have been the same with you as well, and I hope that each of you, having had to be assured beforehand that it was not at all a question of accepting any obligation, will have taken a joyful and serene part in this festival. What has emanated from your faculty as well as from those at other universities and what has been intimated from the podium is now just beginning to be made public in the newspapers and in friendly communications. Yet, I have seen very little of this, and that only fleetingly, but from all sides I expect nothing other than that the two things that you could present as intolerable – though only in a fit prompted by anxious concern – will have been combined, namely, the acknowledgment of the fact in all its importance, and the healthiest aversion to any submission to the letter of the document that was set forth at that earlier time.

Now, it was exactly this that first of all prompted me to think that I should direct this letter to you. I am your colleague in office on the podium, but you are not mine in the pulpit. Moreover, if we men of the pulpit are indeed to receive our instructions chiefly from the podium, then I thought it was incumbent upon me to justify myself to you that I did not give these instructions even to myself and that although I am as far as anyone else from wanting to subscribe to any obligation to that confession or to any other, and in fact–so that I do not appear to misunderstand you – just as I was as far from consenting to or unconditionally agreeing with that confession in all its parts when I appeared before the congregation on that festive day I was indeed by no means anxious that I was being guilty of hypocrisy or of involving myself in a contradiction. I think that on that festive day a minister could also state with confidence from the pulpit that the document that was handed over in 1530 should not be measured according to the criteria of our time and that in many of its sections it has to be judged with forbearance. Indeed, it has been sufficiently made known that the author himself[4] was unable to give it his undivided approval and that he not only made improvements on it in specific points as soon as he could, so that it is still not clear as to which text was the one that was really handed over; rather, Melanchthon afterwards found it indeed advisable to revise it completely in his *Confession for the Saxon Congregations,*[5] calling this confession a revision of the Augsburg Confession. In this process, moreover, he was by no means guided only by the thought that the matter had to be or could be organized differently for the Diet than for the emperor and the princes; rather, it was the fact that inwardly he was so constantly moved by the matter that this forced him to develop a new and different version of it. Now, if the alterations also do not precisely affect the dogmatic content or the exegetical virtuosity, then of course it is natural that if this important matter has always vitally occupied the hearts and minds of people among us since that time, his first version can be a less appropriate and valid statement as far as we are concerned, and the form that we would have to give to such a confession would have to be different to an even greater extent than would be the difference in situation between twenty and three hundred years.

How, already at that earlier time should it have been possible to have examined and tested everything that had been somehow affected by corruptions in church doctrine combated by the reformers and determined in this way and that! Indeed, any layperson with any knowledge at all about what is going on around oneself must realize this – and in fact I would say any not altogether neglected catechumen

---

4. Ed. note: The Augsburg Confession was composed by Philip Melanchthon, (1497-1560), for presentation to the Emperor Charles V at the Diet of Augsburg in 1530.

5. Ed. note: The reference is to Melanchthon's *Confessio Saxonica* (1551), a clarification of the teachings of the Augsburg Confession of 1530 and a refutation of mistaken interpretations of Evangelical doctrines. Text in *Melanchthons Werke in Auswahl*, Vol. VI, ed., R. Stupperich (Gütersloh: C. Bertelsmann Verlag, 1955), 80-167.

from our educated estates. Yet, even if it is entirely and generally granted and we acknowledge with gratitude that over three hundred years our church has not stood still in the matter of purifying Christian doctrine by means of research into scripture, our festival could have caused no detriment to this process. Rather, every Evangelical minister could play his part in this festival in the most dignified manner without committing himself to the detailed contents of this confessional document, and thus equally so no matter how differently he might have thought about specific points or indeed about the appropriateness of this document for our time and for times to come. He could do this, for indeed it is not the document that is signified by the celebration or the fact that it was composed and so has become what it is, but the fact that it was handed over. It is not the document that is celebrated but the deed.[6] If we proceed from this point of view, then as far as even the content is concerned we can take as essential only those testimonies directed against the abuses and errors of the Roman Catholic church and the expressed resolve to want to accept instruction and refutation only from scripture. From this day on the fresh and daring stepping forth with these testimonies has forged a common bond for those who were like-minded, for it was only from this point that they now had something in common to advocate and so stood together all the more steadfastly in every contestation. At the same time, however, with this latter resolve they set us and all their successors free from any bondage to the letter in that with the good will accompanying that resolve they gave us the right to correct any specific items in the confession if we should find them to be in disagreement with scripture. In my view, all of us together have great reason to extol such a deed, and we do well to hand on our consent to this deed to our successors. This intention was also expressed in the selection of texts that the church authorities passed on to preachers, and no one will have failed to note this intention.

Now, however, if we belong to the Evangelical church precisely by our standing in opposition to the Catholic church in this way and by our establishing our-

---

6. Ed. note: See Sermon II in *Reformed but ever Reforming* , trans. Iain Nicol (1997), 35-46.

selves on scripture in this way, shaping it and helping to preserve it, are you in fact correct when you regard our present condition as an internal disintegration of the unity of the church? In this matter, my worthy friends, I am unable to agree with you. I could find such a disintegration, an absence of common understanding and common spirit only where indifference had entered in toward the religious condition of our church colleagues, where lukewarmness had replaced the love that encourages, where predominant alien interests had displaced research into scripture in the daily agenda, or where frivolity had brought the Christian life to ruin. How much more freely did these evils hover around at the end of the last century, so that piety almost went into hiding! In contrast, how openly does piety confront us now, almost at every turn! Among how many public-spirited and charitable associations is active faith the guiding principle, so that I find that the church's common spirit is only increasing. To be sure, in the area of theology the situation is disorderly enough, given so many opinions and so many ways of pursuing it. All things are not always in harmony, and not everything fits smoothly and neatly together. Yet, in fact all of this represents simply the free cooperation that is directed toward the progressive correction of Christian understanding, and it is always founded upon research into scripture. Moreover, the lively interest that each person takes in those whose understanding and ways are not in conformity with one's own is still indeed loving, even though it may express itself from time to time in rough and unruly ways! Further, all the best people even from the parties that are opposed to each other certainly want to hold firmly to the freedom from human authority that was proclaimed in and through our Reformation; no one has the intention of reverting to the former condition of bondage in dead works and dead letters.

Hence, amid all our differences, what I now see is anything but disintegration. On the contrary, these differences are the fermentation of the wine from which alone the genuine refinement will arise. The process moves somewhat slowly, for it is already three hundred years since it began, but it was certainly when the process seemed to be interrupted that the church found itself in its worst situations. It will continue to retain this character as long as we preserve the understanding that as all differences arise they be kept together within the compass of our community so that they can be worked through in controversy and love. In the Roman church differences in doctrine can produce partial disintegrations, because in that context excommunication and the charge of heresy are matters of law, and in my view we have no reason to envy that church on this account. In England and in North America as well such disintegrations can occur, because there is such unrestricted ease about uniting and dividing that even quite trivial divergences readily engender communities that permit of exclusion. However, there, and exactly for this reason, there is so little advance in comprehension because the separated groups become indifferent toward each other, whereas with us controversy and love take nourishment from each other. Indeed, I think I can assert without hesitation that apart from the zeal of the parties involved in controversy we would not have thrived so as to have reached such an increase in theological understanding in all disciplines and that each party has to thank the other – and hence all of us have to thank both parties – more than is usually realized. Just as little, moreover, do I hesitate to think of the old saying as well, that there is little to be gained by an increase in knowledge if it should involve a decrease in customs, for in this respect I too have nothing to complain about as long as there is undisturbed cooperation between the two parts, just as this is what we everywhere encounter in all relationships in the church, in our bible societies, and in missionary associations. Thus, if we simply stick to this path, and if love is preserved in the midst of controversy, then the number of those who are prepared to recognize that the striving for Christian truth also exists on the part of their opponents will continue to increase and from this perspective the condition of our church will become even more prosperous. To be sure, I cannot but grant you this, that in our church individual voices can be heard on some points that if they could carry them through could easily bring forth a disintegration. Moreover, for the important statement that you have made about this matter I would like to convey my thanks to you especially by discussing a bit further, and according to my understanding of the church, a point that you could touch upon only briefly and that our friend Ullmann[7] has merely hinted at.

In this respect I am thinking first of all of those who cherish the lively wish that our so-called rationalists should voluntarily separate themselves from the Evangelical church community. As far as I am acquainted with the matter, Dr. Hahn[8] was recently the first to express this wish; the same aim is at the basis of several more passionate statements and efforts in Denmark, and those who have made themselves known in our *Evangelische Kirchenzeitung* would indeed be satisfied with such a departure. Yet, before I continue, may I insert a small protest with you that concerns myself? You have also reckoned my presentation in *Christian Faith* among those that are rationalistic, and I think incorrectly even in the sense that you stipulate on page 13, namely, as though I sought out a further foundation for the faith-content of holy scripture in the human capacity for religious cognition. I register this protest, for I am aware that I have always simply attributed the faith-content of Christianity to the essential fact on which it is based and to the internal experience of this fact. Nowhere, even in the doctrines presented in the First Part of my presentation, have I attempted to establish such a basis as the one you have in mind, and indeed I know that even the expression "capacity for religious cognition" has no proper place in my presentation. I raise this matter here, honored sirs, not on your account, but simply to document my candor in matters related to that wish, for I am convinced that however much exception has been taken to my faith from that direction, until now I have not been included among those from whom it is wished that they should depart. Indeed, it is my opinion that those who express this wish are not always very clear as to how this wish should be achieved. I do not say this readily, because it is always an individual matter to express earnestly and

---

7. Ed. note: The KGA I/10 editors note that the reference is to Karl Ullmann's *Theologisches Bedenken aus Veranlassung des Angriffs der evangelischen Kirchenzeitung auf den Hallischen Rationalismus*, Halle, 1830.

8. Ed. note: August Hahn (1792-1863).

urgently a wish with which matters stand as they do in this case. At least this is how it seems to me. One cannot turn this question of separation into a matter of conscience for the rationalists, as the outcome clearly shows. Your own essay is also a recent demonstration of this fact, but it also could be very readily foreseen.

Everyone from this side has concepts about the boundaries of our church community, different from those that their opponents hold before them. You too have firmly and bravely affirmed these more extensive boundaries, and it is hardly likely that the one side will be able to make its convictions about this matter acceptable to the other. Already for this reason such a wish could not be sustained with me, in spite of the fact that I readily grant how I do not think that the spread of certain forms of rationalism can in and for itself be very beneficial for our church.

Would there then be still some means of making the separation acceptable to these men? But how? They are in no respect friends of small associations. They would certainly not rejoice about them, no matter how easy it might be to bring about and establish a small community among themselves and from there to direct their controversies outwards, and this I can only praise. I know of no one among them who would not be for the union, that is to say, for such an extension of the church community, and you have had some excellent discussions about the fact that the concept of the church community posited by the other side is incompatible with the rationalist viewpoint. Thus, the promise of complete freedom of teaching, but only outside our church, is indeed a very meager bait. If it is chiefly academic teachers that are intended by this, where outside the church are they then to set up their chairs, and what sort of students are they to expect? Are there so many young men who would be in a position to occupy themselves exclusively with these things without making any practical use of them, if subsequently one wanted to turn them away with the response that they had imbibed merely an extra-ecclesial wisdom and doctrine? In effect, the freedom of teaching would thus be limited to a mere freedom to write. Moreover, should men be willingly content with this arrangement, whose conviction is worthy and who by means of living discourse would be in a position to commend it to a great many youth? This strikes me as the oddest presumption! Nor would it be of any help. This is so, for if all of them were removed from their chairs today, how many young university lecturers would not become rationalistic on account of their studies, for indeed, this is the way in which the majority of them have become so! Moreover, this strange, unreasonable demand that they should be removed because they leave no breathing-space for others is one that would have to be renewed continually, and continually it would be to no avail. However, if this offer applies not only to academic teachers but to ministers as well, and as is then self-evident to that number of people among our congregations who adhere to their teachings, then everything would again collapse at the first obstacle that they would have no desire to separate, because it would not be at all difficult for them to breathe in this communal air. Moreover, out of politeness at best they thus would say: "Dear friends, if it is so important to you to separate from us, then at least take the trouble to arrange the matter; present us with a sound plan for separation, one that we can be satisfied with, then we shall think the matter over." Do you really think that any one of the gentlemen who has expressed this wish has thought the matter through so thoroughly as to have done with his proposal? I would wager everything against this, and not only this, but also that none of them would ever bring such a plan into being. Thus, of what help is it to print documents and agitate hearts and minds to no purpose?

I have recently come across some who are especially cunning with their discovery that they can shift the responsibility for this burden to their opponents by calling on the assistance of the liturgy. That is to say, they give it to be understood that any rationalists who have accepted the liturgy have then given themselves up, for the liturgy is so anti-rationalistic that by having done so they could not possibly persevere, rather, either they would have to convert openly or resign an office, whereby they would have imposed upon themselves the necessity of having ever to repeat something in regard to which they will have to say: "This is what you are reading now, but you are thinking the opposite." At one time I was very surprised at this solution, but indeed more recently the liturgy is intended to be so much and to accomplish so much that has nothing to do with its intention, matters about which it itself has never made any claim, that now I cannot be surprised by this thought either. Yet, it is certainly difficult to imagine anything more unfounded and impractical! In what sense? Is it not the case that for all the supernaturalistic expressions that occur in our liturgy there are rationalistic explanations for them in all the textbooks produced by this school? When the minister reads them in the liturgy is it conceivable that it should become more difficult or more authentic for him to think the same as he has always thought as he does so? Indeed, this is especially the case when he is convinced that as a result of his instruction and teaching the majority of the assembly also thinks nothing other than he does in the process? Moreover, how is it that this public reading should affect him in such a particular way, since great concentration and for many surely great effort is needed so that with the so frequent repetition it does not become something mechanical and allows their thoughts to run totally free? This is the case especially when we are always having to read certain things in regard to which one can think nothing definite at all! Does anyone have any definite thoughts in connection with "conceived by the Holy Spirit?" The two New Testament passages do not combine these two expressions together; even the oldest copies of the symbol do not know this phrase, and it is only because this objectionable combination has been effected in a later and most widely circulated redaction that we have remained condemned until now to repeat every time the confession of faith is presented. There is no difference when it comes to "descended into hell," a phrase that is no more genuine than it is comprehensible. Does the minister then have to say: "This is what you are reading, but indeed you do not understand what you are reading?" How greatly difficult would it be for him also to say: "You are reading this, but because you have always been unable to grasp what one should be thinking about it, you must simply think your own thoughts about the matter?"

Moreover, I do not rightly understand how anyone should want to call this a lack of loyalty or of faith or a *reservatio mentalis*, since by this means it is only the minister's own devotion that he encourages by transferring what has been read into his own way of looking at things, but this has nothing whatever to do with the way in which he performs his official functions. This is so, for indeed it is self-understood that no one wants to advocate what he reads; in this matter the agent is not the minister; rather, those who determine the liturgy are the agent. Otherwise, one would also have to assume that when we read from the Gospels and Epistles in public, we are advocating the possibly incorrect translations and thereby testifying to our belief in their correctness. Thus, how can anyone seriously expect that for a rationalist, and one who wishes to remain such, the public reading of the liturgy would be something intolerable and would make him think of resigning his office? Hence, I think that those who are so very intent upon this distinction between orthodoxy and rationalism and view the two as representing an antithesis between faith and unbelief have simply ordered this wish on ahead to reconnoiter the country like a spy, and that both of you, my honored friends, are not wrong to fear that these zealous men would be all too seriously inclined to persuade any Evangelical reigning prince to reintroduce an obligation to the symbolic books.

However, I am again out of step with you when it comes to another matter. That is to say, you express the concern that in such a case the church would be deprived of a good number of its teachers, and from your statements it almost sounds to me as if in your opinion many would rather resign from their office than subscribe to a symbol. In contrast, I live with the firm hope that not a single person would do this. The person who conscientiously conducts one's office according to one's best convictions, whether this conviction is a rationalistic one or a supernatu-ralistic one, is certainly aware of the fact that one's office, even though it has been received from human hands, has nevertheless been entrusted to one by God and that it is God to whom an account will have to be given. Thus, one cannot volun-tarily resign from it simply in order to be agreeable and pleasing to others. Rather, in such a case, if the person is not oneself internally motivated, one may only yield to power when it takes one's office away from oneself. Moreover, by this I mean not only those teachers who have never or only conditionally subscribed to a symbolic book, but also all those who did subscribe when they assumed office. I include the latter, for will they not all be able to show that among the subscribers themselves there were those who acknowledge no symbolic authority, that already long before them many such people made the same subscription, assumed their office and quietly carried it out in spite of the fact that they made no secrecy of their disagreement with the symbolic books and without anyone's enquiring about how they conducted the practice of their office in this respect? To put it briefly, should they not all be able to show that by means of the deed it was accepted by both sides that this obligation was then demanded and fulfilled merely as a formality, because no one considered it necessary to abolish it expressly? Under such circumstances, as if conscious of his guilt, can any teacher feel compelled to resign his office in order not to be dismissed? Does he not have the same right and even the same duty as the person who placed himself under no obligation whatever to say: I shall not resign my office nor shall I now assume any obligation that was not in effect when I received it? Thus, in this case as in the former, such an administration would have to decide in favor of dismissing the teachers. Should any Evangelical sovereign – not at all to speak of our own, for this would be unthinkable – readily agree to this? Will not the very fact that he would have to determine this without being able to review beforehand on how many teachers this hard decision would have to be carried out deter from such a step any sovereign who does not deal with the affairs of the church from an entirely alien point of view?

However, because this is in fact possible, let us assume that a sovereign had reached the conclusion that some measure of doctrinal uniformity and of a certain kind of doctrine would be exclusively salutary toward promoting an attachment to existing conditions and maintaining loyalty and obedience. Let us assume further that the symbolic doctrines in fact supplied such and that obligation to the symbols could be the sole guarantee of this doctrinal uniformity thus granting that he decided to introduce such an obligation and summoned up the courage to dismiss, in accordance with his power, people who did not want to conform, then I would certainly think that for the sake of his own purposes we would have to advise him to exempt those of us who are academic teachers from this obligation, and indeed that he should leave our faculties just as they are. If he would not want to put his province under lock and key so that no one can get out, of what help would it be to him to dismiss people? Those who had been dismissed would appear as martyrs, and assuming also that no one would press his confidence in academic rights and freedoms even to the extent of being dismissed and then re-emerging as a university lecturer, this same thing would happen elsewhere. Moreover, since nothing stirs up more approval and admiration than martyrdom, according to their ability the youth would strive to make good the harshness of the sovereign. Indeed, still more, would any faculty ever voluntarily let itself be moved to be particular about strict conformity to the symbolic books with regard to its examinations for academic degrees? No, honored friends, I would think that we might rather state this quite straightforwardly, that we regard the authors of our church confessions simply as of our own kind. Like us, they were theologians, and we have the same calling as they did to be reformers whenever and as far as it is necessary, and whenever and as far as we make ourselves felt. Accordingly, we place their works on the same level as our own. In turn, we surrender our works to our successors, so that they may freely make use of them and freely judge them, and this is what we too seek to do with the works of our predecessors. If these works are exegetical in nature, we do not acknowledge any interpretation to be strictly authentic. Instead, we interpret scripture in accordance with our own investigations with God's help and with the guidance of the Holy Spirit, who indeed since that time has not become extinct; these investigations are diligent and painstaking and are supported by a great wealth of resources. If these works are dogmatic in nature, we do not recognize any settled and established formulas, because after a series of generations the same letter no longer means the same thing, and because it would be a dead work to seek to present the Christian faith apart from any connection with what is being thought about it from within and without, just as our symbolic statements themselves arose only from such considerations. Or should such an article for us and in our subject area obtain a different character when it is signed by the princes or accepted by the emperor? These follies have long since been sufficiently refuted, and even given the present occasion this has happened on so many sides that I shall add nothing more about it.

Hence, no corporate body of Evangelical theologians would ever voluntarily accept such a measure. We cannot be dependent upon any symbolic book; rather the opposite, a symbolic book will continue to be of value because and to the extent that we confirm it anew through our teaching and convince our youth of this. However, so that those to whom we grant academic rights may do the same, everyone has to be informed that they are free to teach according to their convictions, for it is only by means of freely formed convictions that convictions can be evoked in turn. Thus, as long as the rights of our faculties are not suspended we shall continue to impart academic degrees according to our conviction, but of course not only those concerning theological learning but also those concerning Evangelical disposition and the zeal of the aspirants for the church, without assessing this zeal according to a letter, however. Accordingly, these degrees and the rights that belong to them will always be available to rationalistic men too. Now, would it then be in the interest of any sovereign who wanted to strive after doctrinal uniformity and the symbolic nature of doctrine to disturb us in this matter and to compel us to make our graduates undertake an obligation to the symbolic books? Obviously not, for with their doctrine they would then find no faith, because the doctrine would be made to order. Moreover, either they would surely find some means of combining the delivery of their own divergent opinion with the performance of this duty, or young people would all the more zealously seek out rationalistic nourishment of their spirits precisely because this is supposed to be made inaccessible to them.

Thus, as I also consider the matter what I always discover is that Evangelical governments, no matter how much value they may place on unanimity of doctrine and no matter how highly they may rate their duty to care for the well-being of the church even in this respect, when it comes to academic teachers they can in fact do nothing other than leave the situation as it is. Otherwise, they would have to overturn the entire university system and organize it differently, and under the present circumstances this is something that I would more fear than desire. If in times when there are opposing views such as at present the government takes an interest in the one side, then in the selection of those whom it especially privileges and pays to be public teachers – given that it has sufficient means to assist in redressing the balance to its side and given that its side was perhaps repressed – it would be an irreproachable action to do this, for what standard is it to follow in its appointments besides that of its own conviction? Halle[9] provides the best example of how this state of affairs must be dealt with. It has to be admitted that for a time it was the rationalists who were in the ascendancy there, but this did not prevent antirationalist young men from graduating with doctorates or from being recognized as university lecturers. Now, alongside those teachers the government has appointed another one who indeed is of like opinion, scholarly and gifted, and thereby it has wholly fulfilled its duty toward and interest in the well-being of the church. Even though he possesses the most brilliant talents, no person who, like this scholar, has started with a professorial chair will lay claim to surpassing in a few years those who in addition to their gifts for teaching have long proved useful to a long tradition; rather, this person will be satisfied with the hope that with effort and perseverance he will gradually reach the same level as they. With well-intentioned zeal his less competent friends may have dreamed of instantaneous success, and when they find themselves disappointed may they be sorry for every youthful soul who then also wants to flow with the current as it has hitherto

---

9. Ed. note: Schleiermacher is referring here to the so-called *Halleschen Theologenstreit*. For some basic details of this episode see *Reformed but ever Reforming* (1997), Editor's Introduction, vii-xii.

flowed without being diverted into a newly opened channel. This is natural! However, if they now urge that the teachers on the other side should be removed, then their friend, if he is wise, will not reach out his hand toward such a forbidden fruit in impatience; rather, by way of calming them this person will portray his disposition to them as that is expressed in the 467th hymn of our new hymnbook.[10] Moreover, this disposition is obviously quite appropriate to a theological way of thinking that so openly asserts its close connection to a truly pious disposition. Likewise, even if the government should cherish the same wishes, it will not yield to pressures of this sort, inspired by some turbulent zeal, because it well knows that thereby it would only invite defeats on the very side that it itself wants to favor, partly from the side of other governments and governments that think differently, partly – and much more likely – from the side of public opinion that relentlessly turns aside from those who seek to oppress at such a point and who by improper means seek to achieve absolute power in the church but who precisely in this way betray a huge lack of trust in the power of their own cause.

Moreover, now that I have attempted to take care of our academic sphere of activity so that the way in which we fulfill our calling should not be surrendered to complete precariousness, let us now see how the situation would be if a government did not violate the shrine of academia but permitted itself to be moved to impose upon ministers an obligation to symbolic books. As we have already stated, even they would not submit voluntarily, and those who did not want to subscribe would be dismissed. Yet, what would their congregations do? I am indeed well aware that congregations are not always very responsive to the prospect of change. Yet, just as they sometimes do more than is to be praised to acquire a minister whom normally they do not yet know particularly well, so from time to time there are also congregations that make the effort to remain in contact with a minister whom they have known and loved for many years, and many rationalistic minis-

---

10. Ed. note: *Gesangbuch zum gottesdienstlichen Gebrauch für evangelische Gemeinen,* Berlin, 1829. Schleiermacher did the major work on this greatly revised hymnal.

ters are held in great affection by their congregations. However, what can be expected is that their attachment will be roused if the minister is not transferred in order to improve himself, but dismissed, and indeed dismissed on account of his teaching by means of which they find themselves edified, which perhaps the minister already instilled in them in their youth, and in which he now instructs their children, particularly since they all have reason to expect from another minister who has subscribed to the confession a different method in delivering teaching, in administering the sacraments, and in instructing youth. Now, if they declare that they want to retain their ministers who refuse to subscribe, should such congregations not also be entitled to freedom of conscience outside the church? Surely, any government that would encounter this arrangement would rather also have to countenance this, for what would be the point in dismissing the ministers if rationalistic congregations were to continue and in this way young people would continue to be inculcated with rationalism? However, if congregations then separate, of course they will take their church property with them! I know well that in theory even this is a controversial question, but in practice it is quite impossible that the situation could be otherwise. To absorb the church property of congregations or even only parts of a congregation to the advantage of the part that subscribes, or even to hold them responsible for assessments and tithing and to compel them to provide for their new ministers in some other way are hardships that are scarcely compatible with the best understood interest of any state. Thus, if this were to be the way of things, schism would really develop. Yet, which of the two communities would then be the one that is long established and the one that is new? From an external point of view, if an order were to go out from the church authorities to subscribe, those who subscribe would appear to be the ones who are long established, for it is they who would have remained in continuity with their prior form of church government. However, viewed from within, the non-subscribers would be the long established ones, for they would have remained true to prior practice, whereas the former admit to the need for renewal. Meanwhile, in our case the sovereign and the authorities would patently adopt the first point of view and thus would say to those committed to separating: "It is not enough for you to refuse to subscribe; rather, in that you now want to form a new community you compel yourselves to do what you sought to avoid, for now you must establish a new confession so that people will be informed about the principles of community. This outcome which is highly singular in the given case is based in our legislation."

Now, if I ask myself how this situation would turn out if all such congregations were unable to consult with one another beforehand, I should not in the least be alarmed that we should see coming to light excessive, bluntly naturalistic confessions polemically directed against the public teaching of the church. There is no significant activity coming from the professorial chair or from any important publication in our literature that points to this outcome, and indeed if something like this were to emerge, it could only come from some disciple of ultra-rationalism – if I may coin a term – who has been driven into some sort of corner. What is to be anticipated instead is that those who have hesitations about subscribing to the Augsburg Confession would not at all be inclined to commit themselves to another one and even less to adopt any individual opinions that it contains. This is the case, for this is precisely how a sect originates, and a sectarian mind does not exist on this basis. On the contrary, such a person always does as little as possible of what one must do against one's will, and for this reason we would retain only brief, generally accepted formulas that could easily be brought into harmony with each other. Sooner or later, unless the most decisive and pointless severity were exercised it would be impossible to prevent those who confessed similar formulas of this kind from forming a church community. Indeed, I would like to say more. If only when drafting these formulas people would proceed with as little exclusiveness as possible, so that for the most part only the obligation to some merely human letter would be specifically excluded, then indeed as long as they still had sufficient influence many teachers who were not at all rationalistic would rather side with the new community and its congregations than remain with one that made a

236

clear declaration only of its intention to establish the authority of a human letter, nothing more.

It was with the greatest astonishment that I recently read in an article by an academic theologian[11] that it is the fundamental character of Protestantism to base itself upon unalterable written foundations and especially to place its ministers under an inviolable constitutional charter. Indeed, I began to feel as if I were suddenly surrounded by darkness and had to grope my way toward the door so that I could again emerge into the free light of day. Moreover, this is certainly how many people would feel who are as little rationalistic as I am. If that principle should gain currency instead of the noble principle of freedom that no assembly has the right to establish articles of faith, I at least would prefer to be part of a church that permits free research and peaceful controversy along with all those rationalists who allow only a confession of Christ and who out of conviction continue to call themselves Christians – and that includes those rationalists against whose mode of teaching I have most definitively declared myself. That would be better than being locked up with the others in an entrenchment that is constituted by an inflexible letter. Now, if this sort of attitude were to occur even half as frequently as I think it does, what kind of vast community would eventually develop outside our hitherto existing church! However, one does not even need to estimate the extent of this attitude to have no doubt about the result of such separation. Yet, it is precisely on this point that these excellent men who labor toward creating such separation do not seem to be altogether clear. At times they talk about rationalism almost as though it were already a dried up and withered wound that could easily be excised, yet elsewhere statements crop up among them that lead to quite different conclusions. I shall simply mention one allegation that has been advanced from that side, one that you will certainly be able to recall. It is said, namely, that the reason

---

11. Ed. note: The reference is to Sartorius' article, "Die Augsburgische Confession 1530 und 1830" in the *Evangelische Kirchenzeitung*, 1830, 385.

for the very great difference in attendance at Tholuck's[12] and Wegscheider's[13] lectures is to be found above all in the rationalistic disposition of fathers who instruct their sons about those public teachers to whom their sons should chiefly commit themselves. Hence, all of these fathers are taken to be zealous rationalists. Yet, is it to be supposed that all zealous rationalists encourage their sons to study theology? Surely the opposite is much more likely! Thus, how many more zealous rationalists are there precisely in those areas from which academic youth throng in such frequent succession, and for every zealous student how many fewer zealous ones are there who become zealous as soon as some challenge arises? In contrast, among those who give their sons such specific advice when they allow them to study theology there are certainly a good number who are themselves ministers or schoolteachers and who precisely in this spirit then have an effective influence on their congregations and on the young people who are entrusted to them. In fact there are ever so many ministers who have been in office for a long period of years, who have undergone their studies wholly in this spirit, and who have also remained faithful to that office.

So, just look around! How are these rationalists to reproduce themselves on every side? It would seem to me that in many a smaller state the non-subscribers would make up the entire established church in such a case, and in larger ones the same situation would obtain in at least some entire provinces. Moreover, what particular reputation would then be gained for the matter if the demand to subscribe were issued from church authorities and in general or at least from a provincial point of view these authorities were to find themselves in a conspicuous minority? What an embarrassment it would then turn out to be for the government on account of this move by the church administration! I have no wish to trouble you by discussing this with you or by drawing your attention to the great inconveniences

---

12. Ed. note: Friedrich August Gottreu Tholuck (1799-1877), a neo-pietist theologian.
13. Ed. note: Julius August Ludwig Wegscheider (1771-1847). Committed to the rationalist school, Wegscheider taught at the University of Halle from 1786 to 1842. See also footnote 9 above.

that would have to arise with any such expedient. To speak frankly, only one other expedient would remain, that is, under such circumstances the government would abandon the given church leadership altogether and would content itself with general control alone. However, it is precisely for this reason that I am also convinced that no Evangelical government in Germany would commit to any step that would bring about the most onerous schism.

However, if this attempt continually proves unsuccessful everywhere I certainly cannot guarantee that some particularly ardent spirits, who are committed to that divisive way of thinking and are impatient in their endeavor to set themselves free from community with what is alien to them, would not prefer to seize the initiative themselves to separate themselves on their part from the greater church and constitute a new community. Indeed, here and there among them there are still some very strict Lutherans who make use of the union as a pretext and want to base themselves on the unaltered Augsburg Confession and the unalloyed Wittenberg liturgy. Indeed, some things that recently occurred in this area can lead one to suspect that soon any almost trivial occasion could be used to make a start in forming such a closed community of those who are like-minded. Moreover, I have no doubt whatever that such an initial beginning would also find its followers. In almost all of the capital cities within our monarchy there are Christian associations of this kind that maintain the bond of community with our church in its present situation only with some resistance. Likewise, in many areas of the country a piety has been awakened that unfortunately is unable to find any satisfaction in the public life of the church. Hence, what would be more natural than that those of this persuasion also think that their cause would best be advanced by complete separation from the church's public life and by an all the more close and extensive connection with those who share their way of thinking. Yet, if we look ahead just a little further, I would indeed have to think that this community, even if it should very soon embrace all these circles, would not remain united for very long. I would have to think this, for once Christians of this disposition engage in inquiries about doctrine instead of striving toward a more mature and undisturbed Christian life and a more inward sharing of Christian experience they tend not to be able tolerate much difference at all. Consequently, any unity among them based upon agreement about doctrine also cannot last for long, because in this area differences always do develop. No matter under which confession they would originally have united, in a short time a separate appendix to it will spring up here and another there, and no assembly will want to remain in community with any group that does not consider this appendix to be just as valuable as the original confession. Just as the rationalists in a similar situation would coalesce more closely, so the splitting among these Christians would ever continue, as experience teaches with the Methodists, the Baptists and all like communities. Now, how would these small communities, in relation to which the established church is not altogether rationalistic but indeed appears to them to be so – in that they all distance themselves from it and even distance themselves more strictly from each other – want to acquire academically educated teachers? Naturally, they would have to abandon this practice, since the actual reason for the whole division was to enable them to keep alien teaching at a distance. Their younger ministers would be given private instruction by the older ones or would be educated in seminaries organized in a narrow-minded way. They would soon find themselves in a condition of having such a lack of theological education as has been true of our German congregations in America, which to a large extent would also be true of the dissenting congregations in England were it not for the fact that there public education is organized quite differently. Now, it is certainly the case that a true, practical Christianity can hold its own admirably even with this lack, for as we all know the movement of the Spirit is not dependent upon such arrangements. However, they would also not have their own secondary schools[14] either and they would avoid the public ones, and rightly so if their young people are not to imbibe different religious notions. Hence, they would also lag behind in general education, with the result that they would be less effective and

---

14. *Gymnasien.*

energetic citizens. Now, I firmly believe that fearing all these consequences and the confusions preceding them, all Evangelical governments that administer our German church will be extremely careful in this direction as well and will not hastily favor any premature tendencies to establish separate communities. Rather, they will make use of their church agencies to bring those who are intent on separating in this way to a full and clear understanding of how their own structure should be formed and what sort of means are at their disposal to establish and maintain it in such a way that it corresponds to their purposes and at the same time also satisfies their duties toward the community at large.

To be sure, a great many of those who urge that we should adhere to a confession do not see that this would have to cause a division, and they do not want one. As far as our Evangelical congregations are concerned, they simply mean well and would like to provide a bulwark for themselves against their ministers so that they cannot preach whatever they may want. You too have drawn attention to the fact that this bulwark is by no means sufficient, simply for the reason that whenever one puts one's trust in it this has to yield some disadvantage. The question arises, without in the least violating his obligation could not any minister alternate between sermons consisting of domestic and moral platitudes on the one hand, and sentimental nature-sermons on the other, all the year through? Would the obligation prevent ministers from spending their week on agriculture, hunting and gaming, and then reading aloud from an old sermon on Sunday? Surely these are things that people think about on their own, but with emotions that make the heart of any true Christian bleed. I wish that your fine country, my own beloved fatherland, were wholly free from them! Unfortunately, however, in our area and in others too they occur all too often. Thus of what help is it to bind a minister to the most excellent letter when he lacks the spirit? It is indeed my belief that the majority of such sinners now come from certain rationalistic schools in which almost nothing is pursued other than polemics against those symbolic notions that are considered to be false and detrimental. However, it is not in this way that the seed of Christian faith will develop, not even in the form that those teachers acknowledge. Young people do not learn to understand their own inner life in this way; they become incapable – and here I deliberately employ a quite all-encompassing expression – of comprehending a single religious thought let alone of developing and shaping it on their own. Yet, the reason for this incapacity does not lie with this style of reasoning in itself but in part with that false method of teaching and in part with deficiencies in personal existence.

Friedrich Heinrich Jacobi[15] was certainly a rationalist, but if he could only have been a professor of theology he would surely have understood this skill and would not have drawn out barren souls who simply fall to the lowest level because in an office such as the ministerial one these souls tend to become bored, in that they have learned only to pull down – even within themselves – and not to build up. I say this quite deliberately: Such are those who presently come from the rationalistic schools. They could just as well come from orthodox schools that we have known to be just as dully submerged in the dead letter, though at present people such as these are less easily to be found. However, if academic teachers were seriously required to adopt an obligation to the confession, we would have them soon enough and this move would effect no improvement whatsoever.

Yet, however much I might agonize over this evil and however clearly I might perceive that this defense against it would come to nothing at all, still I cannot agree with the statement that our congregations are in need of a defense against their ministers. It brings every relationship into such confusion that I hardly know how to deal with the matter, but it involves such a glaring reproach that I can imagine none more severe. Moreover, whom would it affect next? Clearly, it would affect our church authorities. For this reason, my honored sirs, since you both also belong to a church board, I was surprised that you did not take the opportunity also to stress this side of the matter, especially since this view was ex-

---

15. Ed. note: Friedrich Heinrich Jacobi (1743-1819), a philosopher, critical of Kant's system, sometimes referred to as a forerunner of existentialism.

pressed clearly enough in the articles to which you refer. The doctors, members of a united faculty, have spoken well and bravely against these agitated people who are so dedicated to the creedal symbols, but I would wish that the church councils had not remained silent. Or is the situation with our authorities supposed to be such that congregations would lack any defense? Suppose that a congregation complains that in the way in which it was instructed and was introduced to an understanding of scripture it can find no source of edification in what is presented to it by the preacher who has been allotted to it; rather it can only take offense at his style of teaching and can entrust its young people to his hands only with anxiety. Is it then to be summarily dismissed with the response: Nothing can be done to assist you, the man has the freedom to teach what he wants, for he is not under obligation to any confession, and there is nothing left for you to do but to get used to his teaching? It is certainly to be hoped that such a thing would never happen – and I would think it impossible especially in your province, where reasonableness is acknowledged and where mediation or redress would be provided to the best extent possible! Or are we unconditionally to accept what is often enough stated, that these tensions do not come to expression simply because a given congregation has not complained, and it has not complained simply because it knows that it would be of no help? What a strange situation this would have to be if the authorities and the ministers stood entirely on the one side and the congregations on the other! Clearly, it is completely contrary to the nature of things, for from whence do ministers and members of the authorities come if not from the congregations in turn? Thus, would these ministers come – if you would allow me to put it this way – from purely unbelieving congregations that on the basis of unbelief allow their sons to be educated for ministry by rationalistic professors? In contrast, would the orthodox congregations that really have need of defense have so little common spirit, with all their understanding of the Gospel, that they prefer not to decide to let their children who grew up with this understanding become ministers, since they could indeed work to counteract the corruption? Thus, surely this cannot be the way the matter stands. Nevertheless, if the congregations are of so many minds, and the pulpits and professorial chairs are given to so many different fashions, naturally the authorities will share many different principles, so that if it is not simply a matter of lacking a defense or of lacking the proper care that makes defense unnecessary, it will take much wisdom and an abundance of the Spirit to apportion things rightly. By this I mean that things will be rightly apportioned when ministers and congregations fit together as they are matched, and when by means of a common apportioning there will be protection against partialities becoming even more strained and confusion mounting yet higher. Such wisdom is difficult to acquire, and it is no wonder that it cannot always be exhibited in the ways in which our authorities handle their affairs, for to a large extent their incapacity for this wisdom is due to their lack of the one essential thing, namely, community. If there were conferences where representatives of the congregations and ministers advised each other about the concerns of the church, then there would be a means of becoming acquainted with the nature of the congregations. If future ministers lived in and with the congregations and served and assisted in them, there would be a way of getting to know who is a child of the Spirit and how each one is to be used.

Whether we have an obligation to the symbolic books or not will always be a matter of no concern whatever for this purpose. Indeed, in order not to overlook something that just as surely as we continue to be human beings certainly could also happen if such an obligation were to be introduced, that is, that many a minister who was by no means in agreement with the confession would have no scruples about subscribing to it yet would make no further changes whatever in his teaching so that his signature would be simply like a blank page in his life. Would you consider that it would be very much up to you to cast the first stone at such a person? For my own part, I would be very much on my guard against this, especially since he, like every person among us who stands alone, is unable to consider the extent of the influence of his action. Should I condemn a moderate man who would say to himself: "The action that you are taking when you refuse to subscribe has no relationship whatever to the purpose of instruction. Everyone well knows, and thus this includes the legislators of our church as well, that as far as any two human beings are concerned the one does not think the same as the other, and even those who were the first to subscribe to this confession in part did not do it with the same specific degree of conviction and in part did not share the same thoughts when they did so. Thus, it always simply depends on whether there is more agreement or less. Now, if I thought that my divergence was so great and of such a kind that those whom I instruct and stimulate according to my conviction could not belong to the community of the church that was formed on the basis of this confession in contrast to the Roman church, then there would be sufficient grounds not to avoid the sensation that would be caused by a refusal to subscribe. However, this is not the case, and with my signature I indeed confess to nothing but my inner conviction about this."

Untruth is a big word, but of course it is simply an abstract one, and each time it can be applied only according to the nature of the matter. Anyone who wanted to discern here nothing more than a *reservatio mentalis* would have to insist that in the case of such an order, negotiations would be entered into with each individual, negotiations that would possibly never end, and precious little of a communal nature would remain. Moreover, supposing that some such blunder were made in some instance. Would not this calm expedient, which says nothing but for this reason also destroys nothing, be the one that all of us would prefer, so that anyone who is not engaged in an open polemic against the spirit of our confession would quite calmly append his signature? This is preferable to the division we noted and is preferable to these individual compromises, in that it is on account of both of these things that a number of good Evangelical Christians who, however, do not view life from an historical perspective and who usually do not especially concern themselves with the situation of the church can all too easily be led astray when it once confronts them in this form! You will surely share my opinion all the more, as in your area too you certainly do not fail to notice with what attention the Roman church attends to agitations that exist within our own church, and how it knows both how to take advantage of any uncertainty and confusion of any individual among our partners in faith and how to develop then the hidden Catholicism that exists in each person who has not advanced to independence.

Now, my honored friends, if in these respects nothing whatever can emerge that could advance our church if we revert to an obligatory confession, there is still one final thing against you that I have on my mind, and I shall not hold it back. You pursue the point that the Augsburg Confession no longer corresponds with the convictions that prevail in our church. I would wish to maintain the same, but perhaps in a different connection than the one you have in mind. You assert that views are almost too widely divergent to replace that symbol with another one, and in this respect no one will easily contradict you. However, you also point to a future, a better one, when differences will have been settled, backsliders swept along with us, scholastic confusion completely cleared away, the more correct insights made widespread, and then it will be possible to establish a new confession. Yet, what would be the point, and what good could be expected from that confession? Why, indeed, do you too support this prejudice, for I cannot call it anything else, which supposes that the present situation, in which we have no generally acknowledged confession, were for this reason incomplete, thus as if we would be in need of a confession? Even when there was the departure from the Roman church, considered in and of itself a confession would not have been really necessary. The confession was brought about simply by the calumny, the false gossip that in fact was not confirmed by the endeavors that came to light, and by the need of great men to have everything composed in as brief a compass as possible whenever they might want to orient themselves on some matter. With regard to the emperor, the princes, and everyone outside our church, there was rejoicing over the fine work they had accomplished under the circumstances. However, it never occurred to anyone that this activity was supposed to have accomplished something great for our church itself or was supposed to have assuaged some desire that the church had long cherished. Least of all did it occur to anyone that thereby members of the church themselves would first have learned there what they actually believed or should believe, for in all of Luther's writings and in those of his followers that were indeed most widely circulated they found that expressed more animatedly, more powerfully, and more in accord with their point of view. In contrast, the scholasticising formulas and historical references of the confession had to remain ever strange to them.

Thus, what purpose should a confessional document serve for us at some future time? To me, such a document seems simply to be a matter for that era, and only if a schism really occurred among us and a worldly power would have to take note of the principles of the new community in process of being organized, could a confession again become necessary. However, inwardly it would have no great efficacy and it would have a distinctive efficacy least of all precisely because it could again be only a brief summary formulated only with reference to some worldly power and to some external public. However, this is not the assumption from which you proceeded, and you are indeed pleased to look forward to a time when the church would be in a situation to establish a common confession and when it would also do that. In contrast, this is something that I would like to oppose with all my strength, and I would suspect that such a process would only result in corruption if the church were ever to do this of its own accord, for such a document could never be something either desirable or a good thing for the church itself but would always be simply a matter of external necessity. Moreover, for the church's internal use such a brief summary is not needed for adults, and for the instruction of youth strictly defined formulas that give consideration to other opinions are not useful. The catechism calls for a different tone. A good confession is a bad catechism, and a good catechism is a bad confession.

Thus, what is the confession supposed to be? Is it supposed to preserve conformity in the congregation with respect to doctrine, thereby preventing new opinions? If the Augsburg Confession which arose at a time when few individuals rose very much above the general community was unable to do this, how shall a later one be able to achieve it at a time when equality is even more the rule? Or is it supposed to preserve this conformity through the fact that one can exclude all the more easily those who are not in agreement? Now, I have already explained my position on this point and here simply repeat once again that we should not even wish to be able to do that. Moreover, a use other than that related to doctrinal conformity certainly cannot be conceived. Every empty thought is always filled with various unwholesome things. Let us be wary of fostering trust in something that is nothing and precisely for that reason can so easily become an idol. In a community like ours in which free research into scripture applies and must apply, controversies are unavoidable and, depending on the point of view attached to our criticism and on our mode of interpretation, they will be unavoidable for a long time to come. However, controversies assume a quite different form when they move in this domain without further consideration than when an externally acknowledged symbol is established and everyone lies in wait to see whether one's opponent attacks this symbol. In this way, controversies become unpleasant, malicious, and less beneficial to the whole by far.

This fact will prove itself to anyone who considers our history since the Reformation; indeed, even our present moment demonstrates this fact already, since it is only now that these strivings arise to reestablish the creedal symbol. Moreover, I shall not mention how many petty passions otherwise still find support in such a letter or how much verbiage is produced thereby. What would a confessional document have to achieve in order to make this evil good? Further, if we hope for a time when there will be more agreement in our church, are we then to want to revive this evil for the sake of the controversies that may yet come, and should we establish a creedal symbol precisely when it is least necessary? To be sure, it is easier to do this precisely when agreement is broader, but when one considers the value of a creedal symbol for the church itself, this is the situation in any case.

When it can be readily achieved, it is least necessary, and when it is most necessary it cannot be accomplished.

However, if we have been able to establish the union in our province without a creedal symbol – and it has indeed been essentially established even if here and there has wisely been no great hurry to be concerned about the external signs that are of no importance to it – for what purpose should we need a new creedal symbol? It is improper for us to want to be edified on the basis of any human word,[16] for this would give human beings a right over us that we must not concede to anyone.[17] If we simply believe strongly enough that the light of truth that shines among us must ever more illumine everything that lies in darkness,[18] that to seek the truth in love must also really lead to truth,[19] and if we simply believe that everyone who calls Jesus Lord does so through the same Spirit,[20] which also continues to glorify what the Spirit receives from Christ[21] and which in each person applies every gift for the common good,[22] Only if we have fully achieved this, with firmer steps we come closer to the condition that I consider to be the actual goal of our German Evangelical church, namely, as a counterpart to the many divisions that are characteristic of England and America, to live in a community that is wholly free and that in contrast to Catholic constraint is simply bound together by Evangelical freedom. Much has already taken place in that the union links all of us just as much with the Lutheran church that is not united as well as with the Reformed church of Germany and of allied countries that is not united. Thus, through us and in us these churches are united whether they then may know it and want it or not. They will soon take notice of it and will also want it this way at least until the matter comes closer to them.

---

16. Ed. note: I Cor. 2:5.
17. Ed. note: I Cor. 7:23.
18. Ed. note: Jn. 1:6-9.
19. Ed. note: Eph. 4:15.
20. Ed. note: I Cor. 12:3.
21. Ed. note: Jn. 16:14.
22. Ed. note: I Cor. 12:7.

Yet, much more can still happen. If there are some Christians whose conscience forbids them to swear an oath, why should we not represent them before
the state and ask it to deal with any Evangelical Christian who feels similarly bound
by conscience in this respect as it deals with the Mennonites? We should do that,
for why, on this account, should such Christians be required to separate and incor-
porate themselves in some small community? If there are others who do not want
their children to be baptized until they are instructed and are able to make their
own confession, let us do exactly the same thing, for infant baptism is not an essential matter. If some want to exclude the Apocrypha from the bible and yet for
their part tolerate the fact that others conform to this usage, what should we have
against this, since the church indeed has no ecclesiastical use for these books. You
may add to this list what you will. Indeed, even if a congregation wanted to celebrate Holy Communion in the evening because it is so instituted, or to arrange the
liturgy in such a way as to include something otherwise unusual, as long as all
things are attributed to Christ, as long as everyone stands equally firm against human ordinances, I shall rejoice the more freedom is advanced thereby. Everything
will be tolerated, but everything will also be disputed, but only in the sense that
when things become heated, everyone will be aware and take note that brethren
are quarreling with each other. If in this way we will have overcome the power of
the creedal symbol to ban in general, only then will everyone with proper joy – just
as now only a few do – be able to extol that confessional document as a fine work
of its time and the act as well as a successful act of faith, and no one will have any
reason to protest against this festival, because, on the other hand, no one will be
present who can base any unmerited claims on it.

Yet, in that I have returned in this way to the point at which I began, I see that
you have surely retracted your protest now that you are able to read that this is the
only thing about which one of the contributors to the *Evangelische Kirchenzeitung*
is in agreement with you. However, what I have written, I have written, and on the

whole I think I can be assured of your mutual consent that it is only in this way and no other that we can come into the open with the concerns of our church.

Bibliography

Ammon, Christoph Friedrich. *Ausführlicher Unterricht in der christlichen Glaubenslehre für Freunde der evangelischen Wahrheit nach Gründsätzen*, in 2 parts. Nürnberg/Altdorf, 1808.

_____. *Biblische Theologie*, 2nd ed., Vol. 1-3. Erlangen, 1801-1802.

_____. *Bittere Arznei für die Glaubensschwäche der Zeit. Verordnet von Herrn Claus Harms, Archidiaconus an der Nicolaikirche in Kiel, und geprüft von dem Herausgeber des Magazins für christliche Prediger*. Hannover/Leipzig, 1817. [This text is included in KGA I.10, 429-443.]

_____. *Entwurf einer reinen biblischen Theologie*. Erlangen, 1792.

_____. *Inbegriff der evangelischen Glaubenslehre*. Göttingen, 1805.

_____. *Summa theologiae christianae*. Göttingen, 1803.

_____. *Vollständiges Lehrbuch der christlich-religiösen Moral*. Göttingen, 1806.

Blanc, Ludwig Gottfried. *An meine Mitbürger über die Vereinigung der beyden, bis jetzt getrennten protestantischen Kirchen-Partheyen*. Halle, 1818.

Calvin, John. *Institutes of the Christian Religion*, tr. Ford Lewis Battles, in Library of Christian Classics, Vol. XXI. Philadelphia: Westminster Press, 1960.

Cochrane, Arthur C.. *Reformed Confessions of the Sixteenth Century*. Philadelphia: Westminster Press, 1961.

De Vries, Dawn. tr., Friedrich Schleiermacher, *Servant of the Word*. Philadelphia: Fortress Press, 1987.

Gesangbuch zum gottesdienstlichen Gebrauch für evangelische Gemeinen. Berlin, 1829.

Harms, Claus. *Das sind die 95 theses oder Streitsätze Dr. Luthers, theuren An- denkens. Zum besondern Abdruck besorgt und mit andern 95 Sätzen als mit einer Uebersetzung aus Ao. 1517 in 1817 begleitet.* Kiel, 1817.

Kantzenbach, Friedrich Wilhelm. *Schleiermacher.* Hamburg: Rowohlt Verlag, 1967.

Lücke, F. *Apologia Augustanae Confessionis Latine et Germanice.* Berlin, 1817.

Luther Werke, Weimar Ausgabe, *Briefwechsel*, Band V.

Luther, Martin. *Against the Heavenly Prophets in the Matter of Images and Sacraments* (1525). In *Luther's Works*, American Edition, Vol. 40, eds. C. Bergendorf and H.T. Lehmann. Philadelphia: Muhlenberg Press, 1958.

_____. *Letter to the Christians at Strassburg in Opposition to the Fanatic Spirit* (1524). In *Luther's Works*, American Edition, Vol. 40, eds. C. Bergendorf and H.T. Lehmann. Philadelphia: Muhlenberg Press, 1958.

McIntyre, John "Confessions in Historical and Contemporary Setting," in *The Presumption of Presence*, Essays in Honor of D.W.D. Shaw, eds. Peter McEnhill and G.B. Hall. Edinburgh: Scottish Academic Press, 1996.

Melanchthons Werke in Auswahl, Vol. VI, ed. R. Stupperich. Gütersloh: C. Bertelsmann Verlag, 1955, 80-167.

Nicol, Iain. *Reformed But Ever Reforming: Sermons in Relation to the Celebration of the Handing Over of the Augsburg Confession (1830).* Schleiermacher: Studies and Translations, vol. 8. Lewiston, NY: Edwin Mellen Press, 1997.

Redeker, Martin. *Schleiermacher: Life and Thought*, tr. John Wallhausser. Philadelphia: Fortress Press, 1973.

Reich, Andreas. *Friedrich Schleiermacher als Pfarrer an der Berliner Dreifaltigkeitskirche 1809-1834.* Schleiermacher Archiv, Band 12. Berlin and New York: Walter de Gruyter, 1992.

Sack, Karl Heinrich. *Für die Vereinigung der lutherischen und der reformierten Kirche. Wider die 21 letzten der 95 Sätze von Claus Harms.* Berlin, 1817.

Sartorius, Ernst Wilhelm. *Die Augsburgische Confession 1530 und 1830.* In *Evangelische Kirchenzeitung*, 1830.

Schleiermacher, Friedrich. "Am Palmsonntage, den 31 März 1822, bei der Feier der Vereinigung der beiden zur Dreifaltigkeitskirch gehörenden Gemeinden." In *Gottesdienstliche Feier bei der am Palmsonntage, den 31 März vollzogenen Vereinigung der beiden zur Dreifaltigkeitskirche gehörenden Gemeinden.* Berlin: Th.Chr.F.Enslin, 1822.

—————————. *Amtliche Erklärung der Berlinischen Synode über die am 30. October von ihr zu haltende Abendmahlsfeier.* Berlin, 1817.

—————————. "An die Herren D. D. D. von Cölln und D. Schulz (1831)." *Theologische Studien und Kritiken*, Jahrgang 1831, Erstes Heft.

—————————. *An die Mitglieder beider zur Dreifaltigkeitskirche gehörenden Gemeinen.* Berlin, 1820.

—————————. *An Herrn Oberhofprediger D. Ammon über seine Prüfung der Harmsischen Sätze.* Berlin: Realbuchhandlung, 1818.

—————————. *Der christliche Glaube, nach den Grundsätzen der evangelischen Kirch in Zusammenhang dargestellt, 2.A.*, 2 Bde. Berlin: Reimer, 1830-1831. ET: *Christian Faith*, tr. H.R. Mackintosh, J.S. Stewart, et al. Edinburgh: T.&T.Clark, 1928.

—————————. *Kirchenpolitische Schriften*, hrsg. Günter Meckenstock unter Mitwirkung von Hans-Friedrich Traulsen, *Kritische Gesamtausgabe* I/9, hrsg. Hermann Fischer et al. Berlin/New York: Walter de Gruyter, 2000.

—————————. *Kürze Darstellung des theologischen Studiums.* Berlin, 1811, 2.A., 1830. ET: *Brief Outline on the Study of Theology* [1830]. tr. Terrence N. Tice. Atlanta: John Knox Press, 1967. [Revised edition: *Brief Outline on Theology as a Field of Study.* Lewiston, NY: Edwin Mellen Press, 1990; tr. of 1811 and 1830 editions.]

254

_____. *Oratio in sollemnibus ecclesiae per Lutherum emendatae saecularibus tertiis in Universitate litterarum Berolinensi die III. Novembris A. MDCCCXVII habita.* Berlin: Unger, 1817.

_____. *Predigt am zweiten Tage des Reformations-Jubelfestes in der Dreifaltigkeitskirche gesprochen.* Berlin: Reimer, 1818. [Also in SW II. 4. Berlin: Reimer, 1835, 67-76, and 1844, 98-109.]

_____. *Sämmtliche Werke* I.5. Berlin: Reimer, 1846.

_____. *Sämmtliche Werke* II.4. Berlin: Reimer, 1835 and 1844.

_____. *Sämmtliche Werke* II.10. Sydow, ed.. Berlin: Reimer, 1856.

_____. *Theologisch-dogmatische Abhandlungen und Gelegenheitsschriften,* hrsg. Hans-Friedrich Traulsen and Martin Ohst, *Kritische Gesammtausgabe* I/10, hrsg. Hans-Joachim Birkner et al. Berlin/New York: de Gruyter, 1990.

_____. "Über den eigentümlichen Wert und das bindende Ansehen symbolisher Bücher." *Reformationsalmanach auf das Jahr 1819,* Zeiter Jahrgang. Erfurt, 1819.

_____. "Über die Einigheit im Geiste." In *Magazin von Fest-, Gelegenheits- und anderen Predigten und Kleineren Amtsreden,* Neue Folge, hg.v. Röhr, Schleiermacher und Schuderoff, Bd 5. Magdeburg: W. Heinrichshofen, 1827, 234-256.

_____. *Über die Religion: Reden an die Gebildeten unter ihren Verächtern* 3.A.. Berlin, 1821. ET: *On Religion: Addresses in Response to Its Cultured Critics.* tr. Terrence N. Tice. Richmond, VA: Jon Knox Press, 1969.

_____. *Zugabe zu meinem Schreiben an Herrn Ammon.* Berlin: Realschulbuchhandlung, 1818.

Traulsen, Hans-Friedrich. *Schleiermacher und Claus Harms.* Schleiermacher-Archiv, Band 7. Berlin and New York: Walter de Gruyter, 1989.

Ullmann, Karl. *Theologisches Bedenken aus Veranlassung des Angriffs der evangelischen Kirchenzeitung auf den Hallischen Rationalismus.* Halle, 1830.

Zwingli, Huldreich. *De vera et falsa religione commentarius.* Zürich, 1525.

_____. *On Providence and Other Essays,* eds. S.M.Jackson and W.J.Hinke. Durham, N.C.: The Labyrinth Press, 1983.

Indexes

Subjects and Concepts

Academic freedom of teaching and learning, 3, 58-60, 228ff

Apocrypha, 249

Augsburg Confession, 1, 3, 15, 49n, 99-100, 112, 113n, 118, 121-124, 126, 128-129, 153n, 164-167, 184-185, 217n, 218, 220, 235, 238, 245-246

Altona Bible, 85n, 90

Antichrist, 69

Baptism(s), 195, 211, 249

Baptists, 239

Basel Confession (1534), 47n

Book of Concord (1580), 185-186

Brethren (Moravian), 107-109, 125

Church of the Triune God (*Dreifaltigkeitskirche*), Ch.VII, 107n, 192n, 199; church property of, 196

Church Union, a theme addressed in virtually every chapter, but see especially, 101ff, Ch.VIII, 208ff

Common Spirit (*Gemeingeist*), 213n, 222

Communion of the Altar (see also Holy Communion, Lord's Supper), 106-112, 125-128, 151-152

Confession/Absolution, 125-126, 193-194

Confessio Hafnica, adopted by Danish Lutheran Church (1537), 49n

Confession Saxonica (1531), 220n

Confession of Sigusmund (1614), 117

Consensus of Geneva (1552), 118

Curia, 67n

Devil, 87, 177

Differences (alleged) between Lutheran, Reformed and Roman Catholic Churches, 74-82

Doctrine, (in general), 55-60

Dort, Synod of (1618-1619), 83n, 186

Ecumenical Movement, 3

Election, doctrine of, 115-119, 151f

Enthusiasts (*Schwärmer*), 165n

Excommunication, 106-107

Feeling and intellect, relationship between, 79f

First Helvetic Confession (1536), 47n, 84n, 129n

Florence, Council of, 139n

Freemasons, Order of, 165

Halleschen Theologenstreit, 232n

Heidelberg Catechism (1562), 185

Heresy(ies), 101

Holy Communion (see also Lord's Supper), Ch.I, 86, 121-122, 147-148, 192-193, 205, 211

Holy Spirit, 89-91, 121-122, 124, 152

Justification by faith, 32, 38-41, 77, 114, 187, 209

Liturgy, 226-228

Lord's Supper (see also Holy Communion and Communion of the Altar), Ch.I, 46n, 81n, 104-105, 113n, 120-134, 136, 151f, 159, 167

Mennonites, 249

Methodists, 239

Nassau Alliance, 122

Orthodoxy/heterodoxy, 98n

Peace of Augsburg (1555), 165-168

Polemics, 12

Practical Theology, 52-54

Presence of Christ, sacramental doctrine of, 119-128

Predestination, doctrine of, 125-126

Providence, doctrine of, 115-119, 150-151

Rationalism (ist), 94-100, 114-115, 156f, 224-228, 234

Reason, 69-71

Remonstrants, Remonstrant Articles, 83n, 117, 185n

Roman Catholic Church/ Protestant Church, contrast between, 177n, 184-185, 187-189

Schism (Separatist tendency), 140-141, 187, 192n, 200f, 234-235, 238f

Schmalkald Articles (1537), 184

Second Helvetic Confession (1566), 47n

Small/ Large Catechisms of Luther (1529), 185n

Symbolic Books, 71-72, 91, 96-97, 99, Ch.VIII; status in relation to scripture, 182-185; as externally directed, 184-186; subscription to, 228ff

synods, synodal polity, 17-18, 52, 153, 158

Sociality (*Geselligkeit*), 54

Supernaturalism (ist), 94-100, 114-115, 156f

SCHLEIERMACHER: STUDIES AND TRANSLATIONS

1. Friedrich Schleiermacher, **Brief Outline of Theology as a Field of Study**, Terrence N. Tice (trans.)
2. Friedrich Schleiermacher, **Occasional Thoughts on Universities in the German Sense**, Terrence N. Tice and Edwina Lawler (trans.)
3. Friedrich Schleiermacher, **The Christian Household: A Sermonic Treatise**, Dietrich Seidel and Terrence N. Tice (trans.)
4. Friedrich Schleiermacher, **Christmas Eve**, Terrence N. Tice (trans.)
5. Herbert W. Richardson (ed.), **Friedrich Schleiermacher and the Founding of the University of Berlin: The Study of Religion as a Scientific Discipline**
6. Ruth Drucilla Richardson (ed.), **Schleiermacher in Context: Papers from the 1988 International Symposium on Schleiermacher at Herrnhut, the German Democratic Republic**
7. Ruth Drucilla Richardson, **The Role of Women in the Life and Thought of the Early Schleiermacher (1768-1806): An Historical Overview**
8. Friedrich Schleiermacher, **Reformed But Ever Reforming: Sermons in Relation to the Celebration of the Handing Over of the Augsburg Confession (1830)**, Iain G. Nicol (trans. and introduction)
9. Friedrich Schleiermacher, **On Freedom**, Albert L. Blackwell (trans., annotation, and introduction)
10. Friedrich Schleiermacher, **On the Highest Good**, H. Victor Froese (trans., annotation, and postscript)
11. Sergio Sorrentino (ed.), **Schleiermacher's Philosophy and the Philosophical Tradition**
12. Iain G. Nicol, **Schleiermacher and Feminism: Sources, Evaluations, and Responses**
13. Friedrich Schleiermacher, **Luke: A Critical Study**, Connop Thirlwall (trans., with introduction); Terrence N. Tice (ed.)
14. Friedrich Schleiermacher, **On What Gives Value to Life**, Edwina Lawler and Terrence N. Tice (trans. with introduction and notes)
15. Terrence N. Tice, **Schleiermacher's Sermons: A Chronological Listing and Account**
16. Ruth Drucilla Richardson and Edwina Lawler (eds.), **Understanding Schleiermacher: From Translation to Interpretation:** *A Festschrift in Honor of Terrence Nelson Tice*
17. Timothy R. Clancy, **Translation of Schleiermacher's "General Hermeneutics"**
18. C. Jeffery Kinlaw and Edwina Lawler (eds.), **Reading Schleiermacher: Essays in Honor of Michael Ryan**
19. Craig C. Stein, **Schleiermacher's Construction of the Subject in the Introduction to** *The Christian Faith*: **In Light of M. Foucault's Critique of Modern Knowledge**
20. John S. Park, **Theological Ethics of Friedrich Schleiermacher**
21. Friedrich Schleiermacher, **Letters on the Occasion of the Political Theological Task and The** *Sendschreiben* **(Open Letter) of Jewish Heads of Households**, translated, with an introduction, by Gilya G. Schmidt
22. Friedrich Schleiermacher, **Bouillon zur Ethik/Notes on Ethics (1805/1806)**, translated, with essays and notes, by John Wallhausser / **Notes on the Theory of Virtue (1804/1805)**, translated, with introduction and notes, by Terrence N. Tice. Both works in collaboration with Edwina Lawler. Glossary and analytic indexes by Terrence N. Tice